DATE DUE

OTHER TITLES IN THE GREENHAVEN PRESS LITERARY COMPANION SERIES:

BRITISH AUTHORS

Jane Austen
Joseph Conrad
Charles Dickens
J.R.R. Tolkien

BRITISH LITERATURE

Animal Farm
Beowulf
Brave New World
The Canterbury Tales
Frankenstein
Great Expectations
Hamlet
Heart of Darkness
Jane Eyre
Julius Caesar
Lord of the Flies
Macbeth
Merchant of Venice
Othello
Pride and Prejudice
Romeo and Juliet
Shakespeare: The Comedies
Shakespeare: The Histories
Shakespeare: The Sonnets
Shakespeare: The Tragedies
A Tale of Two Cities
Wuthering Heights

THE GREENHAVEN PRESS
Literary Companion
TO BRITISH LITERATURE

READINGS ON

TESS OF THE D'URBERVILLES

Bonnie Szumski, *Book Editor*

David L. Bender, *Publisher*
Bruno Leone, *Executive Editor*
Bonnie Szumski, *Series Editor*

Greenhaven Press, Inc., San Diego, CA

Every effort has been made to trace the owners of copy-righted material. The articles in this volume may have been edited for content, length, and/or reading level. The titles have been changed to enhance the editorial purpose. Those interested in locating the original source will find the complete citation on the first page of each article.

Library of Congress Cataloging-in-Publication Data

Readings on Tess of the d'Urbervilles /
    Bonnie Szumski, book editor.
        p.   cm. — (Greenhaven Press literary companion
    to British literature)
        Includes bibliographical references and index.
        ISBN 0-7377-0196-X (pbk. : alk. paper). —
    ISBN 0-7377-0197-8 (lib. bdg. : alk. paper)
        1. Hardy, Thomas, 1840–1928. Tess of the d'Urbervilles.
    I. Szumski, Bonnie, 1958–   . II. Series.
    PR4748.R43 2000
    823'.8—dc21   99-16988
                                                                    CIP

Cover photo: Photofest

Copyright © 2000 by Greenhaven Press, Inc.
PO Box 289009
San Diego, CA 92198-9009
Printed in the U.S.A.

*" The business of the poet and
novelist is to show the
sorriness underlying the
grandest things, and the
grandeur underlying the
sorriest things. "*

—*Thomas Hardy*, Autobiography,
April 19, 1885

CONTENTS

Chapter 2: Imagery and Symbols in *Tess*

FOREWORD

*"'Tis the good reader that
makes the good book."*

Ralph Waldo Emerson

The story's bare facts are simple: The captain, an old and scarred seafarer, walks with a peg leg made of whale ivory. He relentlessly drives his crew to hunt the world's oceans for the great white whale that crippled him. After a long search, the ship encounters the whale and a fierce battle ensues. Finally the captain drives his harpoon into the whale, but the harpoon line catches the captain about the neck and drags him to his death.

A simple story, a straightforward plot—yet, since the 1851 publication of Herman Melville's *Moby-Dick*, readers and critics have found many meanings in the struggle between Captain Ahab and the whale. To some, the novel is a cautionary tale that depicts how Ahab's obsession with revenge leads to his insanity and death. Others believe that the whale represents the unknowable secrets of the universe and that Ahab is a tragic hero who dares to challenge fate by attempting to discover this knowledge. Perhaps Melville intended Ahab as a criticism of Americans' tendency to become involved in well-intentioned but irrational causes. Or did Melville model Ahab after himself, letting his fictional character express his anger at what he perceived as a cruel and distant god?

Although literary critics disagree over the meaning of *Moby-Dick*, readers do not need to choose one particular interpretation in order to gain an understanding of Melville's

9

novel. Instead, by examining various analyses, they can gain numerous insights into the issues that lie under the surface of the basic plot. Studying the writings of literary critics can also aid readers in making their own assessments of *Moby-Dick* and other literary works and in developing analytical thinking skills.

The Greenhaven Literary Companion Series was created with these goals in mind. Designed for young adults, this unique anthology series provides an engaging and comprehensive introduction to literary analysis and criticism. The essays included in the Literary Companion Series are chosen for their accessibility to a young adult audience and are expertly edited in consideration of both the reading and comprehension levels of this audience. In addition, each essay is introduced by a concise summation that presents the contributing writer's main themes and insights. Every anthology in the Literary Companion Series contains a varied selection of critical essays that cover a wide time span and express diverse views. Wherever possible, primary sources are represented through excerpts from authors' notebooks, letters, and journals and through contemporary criticism.

Each title in the Literary Companion Series pays careful consideration to the historical context of the particular author or literary work. In-depth biographies and detailed chronologies reveal important aspects of authors' lives and emphasize the historical events and social milieu that influenced their writings. To facilitate further research, every anthology includes primary and secondary source bibliographies of articles and/or books selected for their suitability for young adults. These engaging features make the Greenhaven Literary Companion series ideal for introducing students to literary analysis in the classroom or as a library resource for young adults researching the world's great authors and literature.

Exceptional in its focus on young adults, the Greenhaven Literary Companion Series strives to present literary criticism in a compelling and accessible format. Every title in the series is intended to spark readers' interest in leading American and world authors, to help them broaden their understanding of literature, and to encourage them to formulate their own analyses of the literary works that they read. It is the editors' hope that young adult readers will find these anthologies to be true companions in their study of literature.

INTRODUCTION

Tess of the d'Urbervilles at first seems a tale mired in the Victorian period in which its author, Thomas Hardy, lived. At the age of sixteen, Tess is seduced by Alec d'Urberville and becomes pregnant. Tess endures the subsequent birth and death of the child, but is forever marred by her past. Her husband, Angel Clare, cannot forgive her sin once he is informed of it, and Tess, with only her pride and strength to recommend her, struggles against almost impossible odds. Tess's harsh punishment and hopeless love seem outdated by present-day standards; today, such an early fall would not prevent a woman like Tess from living a normal life and enjoying a full future. Nevertheless, like the story of Hester Prynne in *The Scarlet Letter*, Tess's tale remains intriguing today, not as a rather predictable morality tale but for the way her experience reveals the true nature of every other important figure in the novel.

Tess, who struggles to live a dignified and truthful life despite her early undoing, is a hero as are all who resist hypocrisy, poverty, hard labor, and disingenuous and even evil people. She, of all of the characters in the novel, follows her conscience and remains true to herself.

The two men of the novel, Alec and Angel, both project onto Tess their own image of the woman they believe her to be but do not see the Tess the reader sees—the one who struggles to live within her conscience.

Thus, Tess's character reveals the true natures of the characters that surround her, including her own family, Angel's family, and Alec, simply by the way they approach and respond to Tess. She is the divining rod that reveals their ability to face and accept truth.

In this respect, *Tess* is a very modern psychological tale, involving deeper themes of religion and its relationship to hypocrisy, indifferent nature and humanity's place within it, and the struggle to find a meaningful existence.

In this literary companion, a host of critical essays reveals the novel's complexity and the continuing debate it inspires. Interpretations of Tess herself vary under feminist examination; other essays consider the male characters in new ways. Still others examine Hardy's fascination with fate, religion, and nature. The number of interesting interpretations found in this book proves that *Tess of the d'Urbervilles* continues to engage the reader on many levels.

THOMAS HARDY: A BIOGRAPHY

Thomas Hardy was born on June 2, 1840, to Thomas Hardy Senior, a stonemason, and his wife, Jemima. He was born and grew up in Dorset, England, in an isolated cottage in the rural countryside. Thomas was the eldest of the couple's four children, including Mary, born a year after Thomas. Mary and Thomas became constant companions. The younger children, Henry and Katharine, born in 1851 and 1856, were far separated in age from the elder two, but the four siblings remained close through adulthood.

Jemima Hardy was a great reader and imparted her love of reading to Thomas, who claimed later in his autobiography to be "able to read almost before he could walk." Thomas was also apparently musically gifted, receiving an accordion from his father when he was four and a violin shortly thereafter. His father, who also played the violin, taught his son many of the favorite country tunes of the Dorset area; Thomas became sufficiently accomplished on the violin to accompany his father at local country dances while still a boy of ten to twelve years.

Thomas was a sickly child, often confined to the house because his parents were afraid he would take ill and die. Fortunately, the Hardys valued education, however, and as soon as Thomas was deemed healthy enough, at age eight, he was enrolled at the village school for a year. In 1850 he began to attend a school in the nearby town of Dorchester, a distance of three miles, where he excelled at his studies, including mathematics and Latin.

Hardy continued his schooling beyond what was available to most boys his age, entering a private school run by Isaac Last in 1853. He studied Latin, drawing, and advanced courses in arithmetic, algebra, and geometry. He also took French lessons with an instructor from the school that his sister Mary attended.

In 1856, at the age of sixteen, Hardy was apprenticed to

architect John Hicks, who specialized in church restoration. Before leaving for work each morning, Hardy continued to study Latin and Greek and to debate the translation of passages with friend and poet William Barnes. At the urging of another friend, brilliant scholar and teacher Horace Moule, he also read the controversial *The Origin of Species,* published five years earlier by Charles Darwin. Moule was eight years older than Hardy; the two had a decidedly intellectual relationship in which Moule recommended books to Hardy for subsequent discussion. Hardy also trusted Moule enough to consult him about his future plans. When Hardy was pressed by his father to further his architectural career, Hardy asked Moule whether he should continue the life of a scholar and possibly enter the church, or follow his father's advice and stick with a career in architecture. Moule counseled Hardy to follow his father's advice, and Hardy narrowed his studies to pursue architecture. He left for London for this purpose in April 1862.

Before moving to London, Hardy attended the public hanging of a young woman. Most critics and biographers believe that this event had a marked effect on Hardy, who recreated the event in *Tess of the d'Urbervilles* many years later. Hardy frequently committed events, places, and persons to memory for use much later in his fiction.

In London, Hardy soon found employment with distinguished architect Arthur William Blomfield. Hardy and Blomfield not only shared career interests but were also both interested in art, singing, and acting, and the two became friends as well as employer and employee. Blomfield included Hardy in his office and church choirs.

Hardy took advantage of London's cultural and artistic opportunities, attending the theater and browsing museums and the exhibits at the Crystal Palace. A most influential function that Hardy personally attended was the outdoor lecture of John Stuart Mill in 1865. Mill's thoughts on liberty and free speech struck a chord in Hardy, prompting theological searching. Hardy read more of Charles Darwin, as well as the works of French sociologist August Comte, and his orthodox Christian views began to shift to a more humanitarian, almost existential view of religion. Hardy began to reject church dogma in favor of the theories of philosophers who claimed that, faced with uncertainty about what happens after death, humanity must focus on the earthly life. This new perception would later become a constant theme in his novels.

Hardy's architectural career thrived; he was elected to the

Architectural Association in 1862 and won a prize from the Royal Institute of British Architects for his essay "On the Application of Coloured Bricks and Terra Cotta to Modern Architecture." With the publication of his essay, Hardy briefly considered a career as a writer of architectural reviews, but never pursued it.

Despite his early success, Hardy began to find architecture less appealing than writing, which he dabbled in with some success. In 1864 he submitted for publication a satirical essay called "How I Built Myself a House" to the editor of *Chamber's Journal*, who published it anonymously. He also devoted himself exclusively to the reading and writing of poetry.

Increasingly dissatisfied with architecture and feeling ill, Hardy decided to take a country vacation at the urging of his employer. Coinciding with Blomfield's suggestion was a plea from Hardy's old employer, John Hicks, for Hardy's recommendation of an architectural assistant. Hardy decided to return home and work with Hicks in 1867.

Hardy continued to pursue poetry, producing many poems but publishing none. Eventually, he decided writing poetry was "a waste of labour" and began to try his hand at novel writing. The result was *The Poor Man and the Lady*. Hardy submitted the manuscript to several publishers, all of whom rejected it for publication. In the course of his pursuit, however, Hardy made a friend of publisher Alexander Macmillan, who suggested Hardy write reviews. Hardy, deciding that if his goal was simply earning a living he would do better to go back to architecture, rejected this idea to continue writing novels. Cannibalizing his first novel, Hardy wrote *Desperate Remedies*, altering scenes to make it more marketable to publishers. Sending it off, he left for Cornwall to work on the restoration of a church under John Hicks.

At Cornwall, Hardy met his future wife, Emma Lavinia Gifford, whose gregarious nature he immediately found appealing. Emma and Hardy soon become fast companions, and she helped him revise *Desperate Remedies*, which was published in 1871. Hardy continued to be productive as an author during this period, completing *Under the Greenwood Tree* in 1872 and *A Pair of Blue Eyes* in 1873. Hardy agreed to serialize *A Pair of Blue Eyes* for *Tinsley's Magazine*. Meanwhile, Leslie Stephen, editor of the distinguished literary magazine *Cornhill*, asked Hardy to contribute an original work in serialized form. Hardy, already at work on another novel, which he tentatively titled *Far from the Madding*

Crowd, offered it to Stephen.

In 1873, while Hardy was touring a sheep farm as background for some of the scenes in *Far from the Madding Crowd,* he learned that friend and inspiration Henry Moule had committed suicide. Moule had been prone to bouts of severe depression, but his suicide came as a blow to Hardy nonetheless. Many biographers believe that the character of the tortured scholar found in many of Hardy's works is modeled after Moule.

Hardy married Emma on September 17, 1874. After a honeymoon in Normandy and Paris, the couple settled in London. By this time, Hardy had gained a well-known reputation with the great success of *Far from the Madding Crowd.* He began work on *The Hand of Ethelberta,* a satirical comedy, which was published in 1876. The work describes upperclass society through the eyes of servants.

The Hardys let a house in Blackmoor Vale in England, a relatively remote location that allowed Hardy to indulge in reading current writers and philosophers and to complete work on *The Return of the Native,* which was published both in England and the United States in 1878 in serial form before being published as a book.

Sales of *The Return of the Native* were poor, so Hardy turned to writing and selling short stories to keep up his income. He also began to research his next novel, *The Trumpet Major,* about the defeat of Napoleon. Hardy was able to obtain an advance contract for the serialization of *The Trumpet Major* in the literary magazine *Good Words.* He completed the novel early in 1880, though, again, it did not sell as well as *Far from the Madding Crowd.*

Immediately after finishing *The Trumpet Major,* Hardy began writing *A Laodicean* and was successful in getting Harper and Brothers to serialize the work in *Harper's New Monthly Magazine* for higher pay than he had received to date.

After a vacation to visit his parents and sister, however, Hardy became seriously ill. Although his doctors recommended surgery, Hardy refused the operation, fearing a hemorrhage. (Knowing the crudeness of medicine during this time, Hardy's choice probably saved his life!) Hardy could not work, was not secure financially, and had promised Harper's the installments of *A Laodicean* beginning in December 1880. By April, Hardy's health had improved enough that he could walk outside, and he began to feel well enough to work. He completed *A Laodicean*, which was also published in book form by Harper's, but the novel sold poorly and was quickly remaindered. During this time, Hardy and Emma sought and found a place to build a home in Dorset, deciding to live permanently in the country with sojourns to London for a few months of the year.

Before building their dream house, the Hardys rented a house in a small market town called Wimborne Minster, where Hardy continued to write short stories, including *Two on a Tower*, a serial to be published in 1882 in the *Atlantic Monthly*. In October 1881, Hardy was appointed representative of the Society for the Protection of Ancient Buildings, a consultant-advisory post on building projects in the small town.

At the end of 1881, Hardy was involved in a dispute with a playwright who, unknowingly, stole the plot of *Far from the Madding Crowd* and adapted it for the stage. Under Hardy's direction, the playwright rewrote the script, retitling it with the original title. The new play had a fairly successful run at the Globe Theater.

Early in 1883 Hardy published an essay in *Longman's Magazine* about the local peasantry and changes in the countryside. This essay is seen as pivotal in Hardy's career, in that it marked a sympathetic attitude toward the peasants as well as an awareness of a time that was quickly passing, ideas that would become recurrent themes in his later novels.

Hardy began work on his house, called Max Gate, in earnest in 1883. The time and effort he dedicated to supervising the project delayed work on his next novel, *The Mayor of Casterbridge*, but he completed the book in early 1884 and his home shortly thereafter in 1885. The new novel was serialized in *Graphic* and *Harper's Weekly* in 1886.

Hardy kept up a continuous writing schedule, beginning and completing *The Woodlanders* in 1886. Of all his novels, Hardy liked *The Woodlanders* best. Once the novel was published in 1887, the Hardys left on a tour of Italy, visiting the ruins of ancient Rome, the Vatican, the Sistine Chapel, and other sites. Upon his return to Max Gate, he continued to write short stories.

From March through July 1888, Hardy spent time in London researching his next novel, *The Dynasts*, which covered the Napoleonic Wars. While still in London, he continued to write short stories and visit friends. He also began to plan *Tess of the d'Urbervilles*. Hardy, depressed by negative reviews of his previous books and criticism of his bleak outlook on life, nevertheless claimed in a letter that he was not able to exclude "the tragical conditions of life." Such thoughts must have occupied him throughout the writing of *Tess* and her "tragical conditions." When he sent off the first chapters for serial publication, his editor immediately wanted Hardy to rewrite the seduction scenes. This proved to be a problem with Hardy's work throughout his career; a serialization in a family-oriented publication was almost always a precursor to publication, and serial publishers usually served a different, more sensitive audience. Hardy saw such editing as censorship, once claiming, "What this practically amounts to is that the patrons of literature . . . acting under the censorship of prudery, rigorously exclude from the pages they regulate subjects that have been made, by general approval of the best judges, the bases of the finest imaginative compositions since literature rose to the dignity of an art."

Instead of cutting *Tess*, Hardy canceled the contract with the publisher. In order to get out of the contract, Hardy agreed to write a series of short stories entitled *A Group of Noble Dames*. The publisher of the *Graphic* accepted *Tess*, saying he would publish it beginning in July 1891.

During this period, Hardy wrote and published an essay on writing called "Candor in English Fiction." In it, Hardy preempts the reaction he will get to *Tess*, maintaining that fiction should not be "shackled by conventions concerning budding womanhood. . . . The position of man and woman in nature, and the position of belief in the minds of man and woman—things which everybody is thinking but nobody is saying should be taken up and treated frankly."

Before *Tess* was published, Hardy continued to write short stories, including sketches of local Wessex individuals that would eventually be serialized in *Harper's*. *Tess* became a runaway best-seller; though his subtitle, "A Pure Woman," was criticized, the controversy worked in his favor and increased sales. In an interview following the novel's success, Hardy expressed his continued frustration with his prudish Victorian readers: "If this sort of thing continues no more novel-writing for me. A man must be a fool to deliberately stand up and be shot at."

The Pursuit of the Well-Beloved was published almost concurrently with *Tess*, and Hardy immediately began work on *Jude the Obscure*. During this period J.M. Barrie, author of *Peter Pan*, told Hardy that he should adapt his short story "The

Three Strangers" for the stage. Hardy followed the advice, and the play was produced in London.

There followed a busy year, with *Jude* bumped as Hardy designed a house for his brother called Talbothay's, continued to travel, and proofread a collection of his stories, *Life's Little Ironies.* He also began a collaborative writing and personal relationship with Florence Henniker, with whom he worked on a couple of short stories. His relationship with Henniker might have worsened his relationship with Emma, who began to exhibit eccentric behavior among mutual friends.

Hardy finally resolved to finish *Jude,* which was published in 1895 to harsh reviews. Critics particularly objected to the common-law marriage between Jude and Sue Bridehead, and the overall theme of the novel was rejected. A few critics did appreciate the novel; reviewer William Archer named it book of the year in the *Daily Chronicle* paper.

After *Jude*'s publication, Hardy began work on a stage version of *Tess,* which was produced in March 1897 in New York and later in London.

The Hardys next went on a sightseeing tour of the English countryside in the summer of 1896. Hardy, depressed by critical reviews of *Jude* and his difficult marriage, decided to give up writing fiction for poetry. He resolved to write three more stories but devote his career to poetry.

Toward the end of the century, Hardy took up bicycling with fervor, sometimes cycling forty to fifty miles a day, often with Emma. He continued work on his next book, *The Dynasts,* and wrote poetry. In 1898, Hardy published a collection of his poems and drawings entitled *Wessex Poems.* In 1901 a second volume of Hardy's poetry, *Poems of the Past and Present,* was also published.

During the six-year period from 1903 to 1909, Hardy struggled to complete *The Dynasts.* After refusing a knighthood for his lifelong literary accomplishments, Hardy accepted the Order of Merit in 1910.

During this period, a reader, Florence Emily Dugdale, wrote to Hardy, asking to meet him. Dugdale held increasingly agnostic views, and had become enamored of Hardy's work, especially his theological views. Hardy, Emma, and Florence became friends, and Florence often performed secretarial work—copying manuscripts—for Hardy.

A frequent visitor to Max Gate, Florence also became all too familiar with Emma's strange bouts of vindictiveness toward Hardy. At one point, Emma read a newspaper description of a criminal case in which a husband poisoned his wife and told Florence she wouldn't be surprised if Hardy did that to her one day. Emma often had cruel fantasies about Hardy in her later life, and would tell friends and Hardy that her father was right in considering Hardy an uncultured peasant. Florence was disturbed by Emma's behavior and felt Hardy should have condemned it.

On his seventy-second birthday, in 1912, Hardy received the gold medal of the Royal Society of Literature. Henry Newbolt and W.B. Yeats traveled by train to Max Gate to present Hardy with the award, but, to their surprise, no one met them at the station that Sunday: Hardy mistakenly believed their arrival was planned for the following Saturday. The awkwardness continued, as Newbolt recorded what transpired that evening at dinner. The Hardys sat at opposite ends of a long table. Hardy asked Newbolt, sitting at one end of the table, many questions about architecture; Emma, seated with Yeats at the other end, seemed oddly attentive to her two cats, who sat perched on either side of her dinner plate.

That year, Emma had a sudden attack of illness, wrongly diagnosed as indigestion, and died suddenly. An autopsy revealed that Emma had died of impacted gallstones that had perforated her intestine. Although Emma had been increasingly cruel and mean-spirited toward Hardy during her final years, Hardy wrote several love poems in her memory and refused to speak ill of her.

In 1913 Hardy traveled to many of the places he and Emma had enjoyed and made an attempt to visit Emma's birthplace, much to Florence Dugdale's irritation, who believed that Hardy should be rather relieved to have been rid of Emma. Continuing to write, Hardy completed his last volume of short stories, *A Changed Man*, published in 1913.

In 1914, Hardy proposed to and married Florence, hoping for a little affection in his later years. During the same year, a volume of Hardy's poetry, *Satires of Circumstance*, was also published. He and Florence were happy together, although they increasingly spent more time isolated at Max Gate, rather then spending several months in London every year. In 1917, Hardy's fifth volume of poems, *Moments of Vision*, was published, and he and Florence began work on a third-person autobiography attributed to Florence.

In 1920, Hardy received an honorary doctorate from Oxford University. A warm welcome from Oxford students and the award itself greatly pleased Hardy, who was entertained by a student production of *The Dynasts.*

In 1922, a film version of *The Mayor of Casterbridge* was shot in Dorchester; Hardy enjoying visiting the set and witnessing the filming. In the same year, another book of poetry, *Late Lyrics and Earlier*, was published.

In 1924, Hardy wrote his own stage adaptation of *Tess,* which was performed in Dorchester and London, and in 1925, Hardy's seventh volume of poems, *Human Shows Far Phantasies Songs and Trifles*, was published.

Increasingly feeble and homebound, Hardy died in 1928 while revising his final book of poems, *Winter Words*, which was published posthumously. His ashes are buried at Poets' Corner in Westminster Abbey. At the request of his family, however, his heart was removed and buried at Stinsford Church in Dorset, where his parents, grandparents, and first wife are buried.

After his death, Florence burned many of his personal papers, letters, and clothing. She also supervised the publication of the two-volume autobiography that bears her name, *The Early Life of Thomas Hardy* and *The Later Years of Thomas Hardy.* Florence died of cancer in 1937.

CHARACTERS AND PLOT

Angel Clare: The son of a pastor, Angel eschews his father's view of God, using his education to study the great secular philosophers. Angel's father, who believes education should only be used to prepare for the clergy, refuses to continue Angel's schooling. Angel decides to become a farmer and meets Tess at a dairy farm. Angel idealizes Tess, associating her with all that is good and natural. It is this idealization that makes it impossible for him to forgive her past. After spending time in Brazil and becoming ill, however, Angel has a change of heart and realizes his unfairness toward Tess. Unfortunately, by the time he finds Tess again, it is too late.

Cuthbert Clare: A theological scholar and a prejudiced prude. He is seen as close-minded and his type of scholarly Christianity is obviously scorned by Hardy.

Felix Clare: Also a cleric like his father, Felix shares Cuthbert's narrow-minded views.

Mr. and Mrs. Clare: Angel's parent live the life of self-sacrificing evangelical Christians. Although they help the people in the community, their beliefs are somewhat parochial. They wish Angel to marry Mercy Chant, and are somewhat disappointed, though supportive, of Angel's choice of Tess. The narrator makes the point that the Clares would have helped and welcomed Tess if she had had the nerve to approach them.

Richard Crick: Owner of the dairy farm at which Tess works.

Alec d'Urberville: Alec is a self-centered, shallow rake who seduces the peasant women of his choosing. He cons Tess into taking the position of taking care of his mother's fowls, but says nothing to his mother about who she is. Because Tess is proud and leaves once she figures out that Alec has no intention of marrying her, she holds a fascination for Alec. After his mother's death, Alec becomes an itinerant preacher, a role he sheds as soon as he sees Tess again and realizes how deeply he wants her. He finally convinces Tess to come back to him after wearing her down, and is shot by Tess when Angel returns.

Joan Durbeyfield: Tess's mother; a cheerful but naive woman who is the mother of many children whom she cannot support. She makes Tess go to the d'Urbervilles, naively believing that Alec will fall in love with Tess and marry her. She is surprised that this does not happen. She also advises Tess against telling Angel of her past and is disappointed when Tess returns home after having ignored her advice.

John Durbeyfield: A nice but extremely lazy alcoholic, John observes his family's poverty and misery but does not lift a hand to help them out of it. Once he hears that he is descended from the great d'Urbervilles this attitude is enhanced and he falls further into a life of sloth. John does nothing to oppose his wife's advice that Tess "claim kin" with the d'Urbervilles, and is disappointed and ashamed by Tess's seduction and pregnancy.

Tess Durbeyfield: The heroine, she is the daughter of Joan and John Durbeyfield. Tess is seduced by Alec d'Urberville when she is sixteen, becomes pregnant, and gives birth to a baby who dies in infancy. This seduction ruins her life and marriage to Angel Clare, her true love. She murders Alec and is hanged.

Izz Huett: One of the dairymaids at Crick's dairy farm. Izz loves Angel Clare from afar. When Angel asks Izz to accompany him to Brazil, she gladly accepts, but when Clare asks Izz if she loves him more than Tess, Izz admits that she cannot love him more, and Angel decides not to take her with him.

Marian: One of the dairymaids at Crick's dairy farm, Marian is also in love with Angel Clare. After Tess and Angel are married, Marian falls into a hard-drinking, hard-living life. It is Marian who helps find Tess a job at Flintcomb-Ash, and who tries to protect Tess from the harder labor.

Plot Summary

The structure of *Tess of the d'Urbervilles* is a very important aspect of the book: The novel is divided into seven named "phases," each with significant import, both in the title of the section and in the climactic plot events that divide each section. Although this device probably reflects the novel's original serialization in magazine issues, Hardy makes the divisions significant rather than saleable but meaningless, as narrative breaks sometimes are in the novels of Charles Dickens.

In "Phase the First: The Maiden," one of the most significant facts of the novel reveals itself. Tess's father, John (Jack) Durbeyfield, an unsuccessful peddler by trade, finds out from the local parson that he has royal roots. The parson informs him that he is descended from an "ancient and knightly family." Though the parson says that the same is true for many of the peasant families in the village of Marlott, Durbeyfield uses this knowledge to indulge his already lazy leanings. He decides to use the family's scant funds to ride home in a carriage, as is fitting for his royal status.

As he rides in the carriage, the reader meets sixteen-year-old Tess, who, along with several other young girls, is engaged in a May Day dance. Tess is described as a beautiful, yet still innocent, young woman. When the others girls spy Tess's father in the carriage, obviously inebriated, Tess defends her father, saying he is just tired. As the girls return to the dance, another important character is introduced, Angel Clare. Clare, on a long trek with his two brothers, stops to dance with the girls, but not Tess. As Angel continues on his journey, he gazes back at Tess, who also gazes at him, both regretfully.

When Tess arrives home, she greets her mother, Joan, who is singing, rocking a baby, and working on the Monday wash. The family's poor dwelling and her mother's cheerful nature are revealed. As soon as Tess is home, her mother leaves to fetch her father at the local tavern, Rolliver's. She is concerned because John must get up early in the morning to deliver the family's beehives into town. The narrator reveals that Tess's family is a large one: She is the oldest child; Eliza-Louisa is twelve; Abraham is nine; the ages of two girls, Hope and Modesty, are unstated; an unnamed boy is three; and the baby. All share the family's small dwelling.

At Rolliver's, Tess's mother hatches a plot with her husband that will prove to be crucial: She has heard of a d'Urberville relative in nearby Tantridge, and wants Tess to go and "claim kin." Mrs. Durbeyfield is hoping that Tess will impress the rich relations and be able to get something from the connection.

Back at home, Tess sends Abraham to fetch their parents. When he does not return Tess herself goes, and the reader sees the interior of Rolliver's, an illegal tavern whose customers must pretend that the owners are just having friends over whenever a new person arrives. Tess manages to convince her parents to leave.

It is late as the family walks home; by the time they are in bed it is 11:00. At 2:00, Joan wakes Tess to tell her she must take the hives, as her father probably cannot be roused. Tess takes Abraham, saddles up the cart and horse, and leaves for town. Tess and Abraham talk about discovering a wealthy lineage and Tess's idea that the stars are worlds like their own, but some "blighted" and some "sound." Tess informs Abraham that they live on a "blighted" world.

As the wagon clip-clops along, Tess falls asleep. She awakens to find that a fast-paced postal cart has run into their cart. In the crash, their horse's chest is pierced by the shaft of the mail cart, and the horse bleeds to death as Tess watches.

Tess resolves to claim kin, as her mother wishes, because she blames herself for the death of the horse, the family's source of income. When she arrives in Tantridge, she meets Alec d'Urberville. The reader understands that the family has merely assumed the d'Urberville name, and are not, unlike Tess, descended from the true line. Alec shows Tess around the estate, flirting with her. He feeds her strawberries and decorates her basket, bosom, and hair with flowers.

After she returns home, Tess's mother informs her that the old lady, Alec's mother, has summoned her to be a handler of her exotic fowl. Tess is wary, as she never met the woman, but is overcome by guilt and decides to try her hand at the job. A cart arrives for Tess; as she is loading her things, Alec drives up in his horse and cart and urges her into it. They speed off and Tess asks Alec to slow down. Alec threatens to go even faster unless she grasps his waist and kisses him. Tess cleverly loses her bonnet, Alec stops the cart, and Tess refuses to get in the cart again. At the estate Tess learns where she will live and work, and that she must whistle to the birds, which Alec teaches her to do.

After some time at the d'Urbervilles, Tess attends a local fair with the other peasants of the area. As the fair and dance wears on, Tess can see that the revelers show no sign of leaving, and that some of them are drunk. This makes her uncomfortable, but she feels it is too late to walk home by herself. Alec drops by and she refuses his offer of a ride. She waits and finally sets out for home with the others, but when she is threatened by a jealous girl and Alec again shows up to rescue her, she mounts his horse behind him.

Alec rambles along, claiming he is lost. He makes a bed for Tess in the brush, and tells her he will try to find the way back and come back and get her. When Alec arrives back at Tess's resting place, he finds her asleep. Although Hardy is not explicit, it is clear that Alex seduces Tess that night.

PHASE THE SECOND: MAIDEN NO MORE

The section opens with Tess pulling her belongings up a hill, clearly leaving Tantridge and the d'Urberville residence. Alec comes after her, chastises her for leaving secretly, and propels her into a cart, heading for a junction at which she will take a cart back home. From their conversation, it is clear that Tess has had an emotional and physical relationship with Alec that she regrets and that she blames him for taking advantage of her. Alec seems rather flippant about the affair; he offers to help Tess financially, but she refuses.

Upon arriving home, Tess's mother tells her she should have gotten Alec to marry her, and Tess breaks down, telling her mother the story of her seduction, and asking her mother why she hadn't prepared her better to avoid it.

Tess is next seen bundling hay off a reaping machine. As she takes her lunch, her sister brings her a baby, which she feeds. The narrator explains that the baby is the product of her relationship with Alec.

The baby becomes gravely ill, and Tess begs her parents to send for a pastor to perform the last rites, but her father refuses, saying that Tess has embarrassed the family and betrayed their aristocratic roots. In desperation, Tess baptizes the baby herself, gathering her siblings around her to pray.

The baby dies. Tess, distraught over whether the baby will go to hell, accosts the vicar, asking if the baby will be saved and whether he can have a Christian burial. The vicar, mercifully, tells Tess that the baby will be saved.

Tess decides that she can no longer live in her family's home nor escape the identity of a fallen woman. She decides to leave.

PHASE THE THIRD: THE RALLY

Tess has found work at a dairy farm and, as the section opens, she is on her way there on foot. She accepts a ride from a farmer, and wishes to herself that her father had never found out about his ancestral beginnings, bringing her into contact with Alec and her tragic life.

The dairy is idyllic, the people there generous and kind, and Tess meets the other dairymaids, primarily Marian, Retty Priddle, and Izz Huett, with whom she becomes friends. The dairy is owned by Richard Crick, who employs nearly one hundred men and women.

While milking, Tess recognizes twenty-six-year-old Angel Clare, the young man who did not dance with her in phase one. Tess learns later that he is there to learn the art of dairy farming, as he eventually wants to become a farmer.

As the days wear on, Angel and Tess become more

friendly, and Tess and he tacitly agree to wake earlier than the others to enjoy an hour of conversation before the work of the dairy starts.

One afternoon, before retiring for their nap, Retty, Marian, and Izz are looking out the window at Angel, all of them clearly in love with him. When Tess realizes that they are all infatuated, she feels guilty for also wanting him, realizing that she, compared with them, is unworthy of Angel.

One day the girls decide to go to church, but, when they reach the river, they find the water too high to cross. Angel carries all of them across, saves Tess for last, and tells her that he cares for her. Later, while milking the cows, Angel embraces Tess and tells her that he is in love with her.

PHASE THE FOURTH: THE CONSEQUENCE

Angel decides to travel home to his family to tell them of his plans to marry Tess. On his way home, he meets Mercy Chant, the chaste, devout young woman whom his parents wanted him to marry. It is clear from their conversation that Mercy is indeed very devout.

The reader is introduced to Angel's entire family: his mother, father, and brothers, Felix, a curate, and Cuthbert, also a reverend but a scholar.

Mr. and Mrs. Clare are presented as self-sacrificing Christians who will not even partake of the blood sausage and mead that Clare has brought for the family to share. They decide they will donate it to their parishioners.

Angel's parents try to discuss his potential marriage to Mercy Chant, but Angel claims that he wants to marry a farm girl—for practical reasons. A farmer's wife needs to be strong, and familiar with animals and crops. He also assures his parents of Tess's innocence, virginity, and faith, revealing both his ignorance of Tess and the importance of these qualities to himself and his family.

In another bit of foreshadowing, old Mr. Clare tells his son of his encounter with Alec d'Urberville, and how d'Urberville insulted him.

Rushing back to the dairy, Clare asks Tess to marry him. Tess, amazed and frightened, says no. For a time Tess alternately refuses Angel's proposals and contemplates possibly marrying him. He continues to press her. At supper one afternoon, one of the dairymen tells a story of a man who marries a woman with an income who will lose it after marrying. The woman does not tell the man that she will have no income, and, after marrying her, the man leaves her. Opinions are given round the room whether the woman should have told the man before or after, echoing Tess's dilemma.

As Angel and Tess are taking the milk into town for Crick, they muse upon the world, and Angel again presses his suit. Tess tells him she cannot marry him because she knows he hates aristocratic families, and she is a member of one. Angel is relieved to hear this, tells her he is glad she has aristocratic roots, and the two finally resolve to marry.

Tess then writes to her mother, asking her if she should tell Angel of her past. Her mother writes back that she must not tell her fiancé. Tess ignores the advice, and resolves to tell him in a letter, to slip it under his door, and to let him decide whether or not he still wants to marry her.

The next morning, there is no trace of changed feeling in Angel, and Tess feels a great relief. She thinks this means that Angel has decided to forgive her and not mention it again. Unfortunately, days later, Tess looks under the door and notices that the letter remains caught under the carpet. She takes it back, and does not give it to Clare.

Two portents follow the wedding. Tess believes she has seen their wedding carriage before, and Angel says that she is probably remembering the d'Urberville curse, that a true member of the d'Urbervilles sees a coach when something bad is about to occur. Tess claims ignorance of the curse. In addition, as they are leaving the dairy farm, a cock crows three times.

Clare has arranged to spend the night at an ancestral d'Urberville castle. The place is gloomy, and Tess feels uncomfortable. They are awaiting Jonathan, from the dairy, with their luggage, but he is late. When Jonathan arrives, he tells them that Tess's fellow dairymaids seem to have gone crazy after they left. Retty Priddle has tried to drown herself. Marian is found dead drunk and Izz is extremely depressed. Tess knows it is because they are heartsick over Angel and feels guilty that she did not encourage Angel to marry one of them.

After Jonathan leaves, Angel reminds Tess of their promise to tell each other of their pasts. Angel goes first, recounting an affair with an older woman. Tess rejoices, because her sin is no worse than his, and exclaims her happiness at this, saying, "tis just the same."

PHASE THE FIFTH: THE WOMAN PAYS

Tess learns that Angel's sin and her own are not the same. On hearing of Tess's seduction, baby's birth and death, and subsequent life, Angel becomes distressed and cannot forgive Tess. They stay in the rented house for a couple of days while Angel looks into a nearby sawmill. Also during their stay, Angel sleepwalks while carrying Tess and places her in a coffin. Angel and Tess set out together, she going on to her parents and he to unknown parts. Angel gives Tess some money and instructs her to contact his parents if she needs more. He also tells her not to try to contact him, that if he can manage to forgive her, he will find her. He also tells her that she can write to him, but only if she is in trouble and needs help. He vaguely tells her that he will keep in touch with her through her parents, and that his parents will always know of his whereabouts.

When Tess arrives home, she tells her mother what has transpired. She gives her mother money, and, when she finds that her father doubts that she is married, she resolves to leave Marlott so as not to be the object of gossip.

Angel, meanwhile, visits his parents and, when questioned about the whereabouts of his wife, says that she is with her parents, as he has decided to travel to Brazil to find a farm and will send for her later.

Angel returns to the house he and Tess rented to pay a bill and meets Izz Huett. Clare suddenly asks her if she loves him and if she will go to Brazil with him. Izz is excited by the prospect but reveals to Clare that she loves him no more than Tess, who would have laid down her life for him. Clare changes his mind, to Izz's obvious regret.

Tess, meanwhile, receives money from Clare's bankers, only to give most of it to her parents, who need a new roof. Tess now needs to find work, and Marian, from the dairy, contacts her about farmwork. Tess makes her way to the farm, and, because she elicits attention from men when she travels alone, cuts her hair and eyebrows to make herself less attractive.

She travels at night to avoid encountering men. On the road late at night, she makes a nest of leaves for a bed, but odd noises awaken her and she finds pheasants that have been shot earlier in the day dying and dropping from the branches around her. Tess breaks the necks of these birds to put them out of their misery.

Tess finally reaches the farm and finds Marian, who is surprised to find Tess in such destitute circumstances though she is married. Tess defends Angel but makes Marian promise that she will not mention her married state to anyone on the farm. Marian and Tess perform the arduous work of digging turnips. When it gets too cold for the work, the employer finds them work in the barn, bundling straw for thatching. When they reach the barn, they discover Izz, who has also come to join them.

Unfortunately, Tess learns that one of the men whom she rebuffed while traveling is the overseer on the farm. The man pays her back by being particularly surly to her.

Tess resolves to go see Angel's parents, concerned by Marian's description of the strange encounter between Angel and Izz before his departure. She arrives on Sunday, and his parents are at church. Tess takes off her rough work boots at the gate, and decides to wait until after the service to go to their home. On the way back from the church, Tess follows behind Angel's brothers and Mercy Chant. The three stop at the gate, and Mercy notices the boots. She picks them up to give them to charity, chastising their unknown owner for throwing them away. After Tess hears this, she resolves not to enter the house.

On her way home, Tess hears an itinerant preacher from afar, recounting how he had led a life of sin and was transformed by Christ. Tess realizes the preacher is Alec d'Urberville.

PHASE THE SIXTH: THE CONVERT

Alec sees Tess in the crowd and tells her that his mother has died, and that her death has made him remorseful over his past, including his bad treatment of Tess. He wants to make it up to her, though Tess insists that he should just leave her alone. She tells him about the baby.

Alec insists that Tess's very presence is a temptation to him, and makes her swear on an old stone pillar, which he claims is sacred, that she will not tempt him. This makes Tess very nervous, as the last thing she wants is to tempt Alec, but she makes the promise. Later she finds that the stone is not sacred, but a place of torture.

Tess continues to perform hard labor on the farm and Alec continues to pursue her. He asks for her hand in marriage; she refuses, telling Alec that she is already married.

As her labor at the farm becomes more and more difficult, and Alec continues to pursue her, Tess writes a letter to Angel begging him to return. She is tempted by Alec's proposal, even though he repels her.

Alec begins to shed his newfound Christianity, especially after Tess and he engage in a theological discussion in which Tess speaks of her lack of belief in the supernatural. Alec then decides to abandon Christianity altogether and to renew with new fervor his pursuit of Tess, insisting that he is her true husband.

In a scene on the farm, Tess feeds a thresher for hours and hours until she is exhausted. The overseer, having been bribed by Alec, allows Tess to rest. Alec again puts forth his suit, saying that he will help her brothers and sisters. Tess barely resists. She goes back to her lodging that night to write another appeal to Angel to come home before she is tempted to go with Alec.

The letter arrives at Angel's parents, who forward it.

The narrator gives us a glimpse of a much-battered Angel in South America. Angel has been deathly ill and has seen much hardship. During his travels, he befriends another man and tells him about Tess. The other man tells Angel that Tess's sin should be forgiven. Angel begins to ponder the man's words and decides that he is wrong to have turned against Tess.

While Tess is still at the farm, 'Liza-Lu visits, telling Tess that their mother is deathly ill and Tess must come at once. Tess leaves on foot immediately to nurse her mother. At home she sits with her mother or tries to revive the family's plot of land. Alec follows her here, renewing his suit. At this time, Tess learns that her mother has recovered, but that her father has suddenly died. She also discovers that when her father dies, the cottage that they lived in is no longer theirs—the family is allowed to live there only as long as her father lives. Tess prepares to move the family to a new location where she can find work.

On the last night before they must leave, Alec approaches the window from which Tess stares out. Tess claims to have heard a coach, and Alec tells her the full version of the curse of the d'Urbervilles. The curse has been placed on the family because of a murder; now, whenever a family member is about to experience tragedy, a coach is heard.

Again, Alec offers his assistance, which Tess again refuses. She writes Angel a long, bitter letter, saying that she will try to forget him.

The next day, Tess hires a cart to take the family to Kingsbere, the ancestral homeland of the d'Urbervilles. They cannot find a place to stay, and Tess and her mother make up a bed near the d'Urberville grave vault. Tess decides to tour the vault, wherein Alec, pretending he is a corpse, accosts her again.

Meanwhile, Izz and Marian also decide to write Angel a letter, telling him that he should come home at once. Izz and Marian are afraid that Tess, worn down, will give in to Alec.

PHASE THE SEVENTH: FULFILLMENT

Angel arrives at his parents' house, wasted in body and soul. He reads both Tess's last letter and the letter of warning from Izz and Marian. He decides to disregard Tess's letter and to go to her mother's to find her. He finds her mother, in Kingsbere, and her mother tells him where Tess has gone, but not where she lives.

He goes to Sandbourne, at first asking for a Mrs. Clare with no success, then asks the mailman for a Mrs. Durbeyfield. The postman answers that he knows only a Mrs. d'Urberville. Clare jumps at this, somewhat glad that Tess has decided to use the ancient version of her name.

He arrives at Tess's apartments, and asks the maid to see her, though the maid says it is a bit early. Tess comes to the door and announces that Alec "has won me back to him." She also says that she hates him, because he had promised her Angel would not come back, but he has.

Clare turns to leave. Meanwhile, the landlady heads up the stairs to spy on the d'Urbervilles; he hears Tess berating Alec for telling her that Angel would not come home. The landlady descends the stairs to eat her own breakfast and sees Tess leave. While the landlady eats, she notices a stain spreading across the ceiling, and discovers that the stain is blood, and that Tess has shot Alec in bed.

Tess finds Angel on the road and tells him that she has murdered Alec so that Alec can no longer stand between them. Angel then decides to flee with Tess, buying provisions at a local inn. The two find an abandoned mansion that is entered only in the morning and evening by an elderly caretaker who comes to open and shut the windows.

After the caretaker has shut the windows, Angel and then Tess enter the mansion and spend the night. Avoiding the caretaker, Tess manages to convince Angel to stay in the mansion another night. Unfortunately, they are seen by the caretaker, who peers in the keyhole early in the morning. The caretaker reports the news to the townspeople.

Tess and Angel awaken, sensing something is wrong, and decide to leave. They come upon Stonehenge, where Tess falls asleep. As dawn approaches, Angel realizes that they are surrounded by approaching men. He begs them to let Tess sleep, and so they do. When she awakens, she announces "I am ready."

In the next chapter, Angel and 'Liza-Lu, climbing into the hills, watch as Tess is hanged. They then climb back out of the hills, holding hands.

CHAPTER 1

Themes in *Tess of the d'Urbervilles*

Aristocracy in *Tess*

D.H. Lawrence

D.H. Lawrence is a well-known English writer (1885–1930) whose novels include *Lady Chatterley's Lover* and *Sons and Lovers*. In the following article, Lawrence describes Tess's natural aristocracy and how the two men in her life, Alec and Angel, fail her.

Tess sets out, not as any positive thing, containing all purpose, but as the acquiescent complement to the male. The female in her has become inert. Then Alec d'Urberville comes along, and possesses her. From the man who takes her Tess expects her own consummation, the singling out of herself, the addition of the male complement. She is of an old line, and has the aristocratic quality of respect for the other being. She does not see the other person as an extension of herself, existing in a universe of which she is the centre and pivot. She knows that other people are outside her. Therein she is an aristocrat. And out of this attitude to the other person came her passivity. It is not the same as the passive quality in the other little heroines, such as the girl in [Hardy's novel] *The Woodlanders*, who is passive because she is small.

Tess is passive out of self-acceptance, a true aristocratic quality, amounting almost to self-indifference. She knows she is herself incontrovertible, and she knows that other people are not herself. This is a very rare quality, even in a woman. And in a civilization so unequal, it is almost a weakness.

Tess never tries to alter or to change anybody, neither to alter nor to change nor to divert. What another person decides, that is his decision. She respects utterly the other's right to be. She is herself always.

But the others do not respect her right to be. Alec d'Urberville sees her as the embodied fulfilment of his own desire: something, that is, belonging to him. She cannot, in his conception, exist apart from him nor have any being apart from his being. For she is the embodiment of his desire.

Excerpted from "A Study of Thomas Hardy," from *Phoenix: The Posthumous Papers of D.H. Lawrence*, by D.H. Lawrence, edited by Edward McDonald. Copyright 1936 by Frieda Lawrence, renewed © 1964 by the Estate of the late Frieda Lawrence Ravagli. Used by permission of Viking Penguin, a division of Penguin Putnam Inc.

This is very natural and common in men, this attitude to the world. But in Alec d'Urberville it applies only to the woman of his desire. He cares only for her. Such a man adheres to the female like a parasite. It is a male quality to resolve a purpose to its fulfilment. It is the male quality, to seek the motive power in the female, and to convey this to a fulfilment; to receive some impulse into his senses, and to transmit it into expression. Alec d'Urberville does not do this. He is male enough, in his way; but only physically male. He is constitutionally an enemy of the principle of self-subordination, which principle is inherent in every man. It is this principle which makes a man, a true male, see his job through, at no matter what cost. A man is strictly only himself when he is fulfilling some purpose he has conceived: so that the principle is not of self-subordination, but of continuity, of development. Only when insisted on, as in Christianity, does it become self-sacrifice. And this resistance to self-sacrifice on Alec d'Urberville's part does not make him an Individualist, an egoist, but rather a non-individual, an incomplete, almost a fragmentary thing.

There seems to be in d'Urberville an inherent antagonism to any progression in himself. Yet he seeks with all his power for the source of stimulus in woman. He takes the deep impulse from the female. In this he is exceptional. No ordinary man could really have betrayed Tess. Even if she had had an illegitimate child to another man, to Angel Clare, for example, it would not have shattered her as did her connexion with Alec d'Urberville. For Alec d'Urberville could reach some of the real sources of the female in a woman, and draw from them. And, as a woman instinctively knows, such men are rare. Therefore they have a power over a woman. They draw from the depth of her being.

And what they draw, they betray. With a natural male, what he draws from the source of the female, the impulse he receives from the source he transmits through his own being into utterance, motion, action, expression. But [Alec d'Urberville,] what [he] received [he] knew only as gratification in the senses; some perverse will prevented [him] from submitting to it, from becoming instrumental to it.

Which was why Tess was shattered by Alec d'Urberville, and why she murdered him in the end. The murder is badly done, altogether the book is botched, owing to the way of

TWO WRITERS DISCUSS *TESS*

In the following excerpt, Robert Louis Stevenson exchanges a letter with Henry James about their opinion of Tess of the d'Urbervilles.

STEVENSON: Hurry up with another book of stories. I am now reduced to two of my contemporaries, you and [*Peter Pan* author James] Barrie. . . . As for Hardy—you remember the old gag?—Are you wownded, my lord?—Wownded, Ardy.—Mortually, my lord?—Mortually, Ardy.—Well, I was mortually wownded by Tess of the Durberfields. I do not know that I am exaggerative in criticism; but I will say that Tess is one of the worst, weakest, least sane, most *voulu* [forced] books I have yet read. Bar the style, it seems to be about as bad as [the novels of G.W.M.] Reynolds—I maintain it—Reynolds: or to be more plain, to have no earthly connection with human life or human nature; and to be merely the ungracious portrait of a weakish man under a vow to appear clever, as a ricketty schoolchild setting up to be naughty and not knowing how. I should tell you in fairness I could never finish it; there may be the treasures of the Indies further on; but so far as I read, James, it was (in one word) damnable. *Not alive, not true,* was my continual comment as I read; and at last—*not even honest!* was the verdict with which I spewed it from my mouth. I write in anger? I almost think I do; I was betrayed in a friend's house—and I was pained to hear that other friends delighted in that barmicide feast. I cannot read a page of Hardy for many a long day, my confidence [in him] is gone. So that you and Barrie and [Rudyard] Kipling are now my Muses Three.

JAMES: I grant you Hardy with all my heart and even with a certain quantity of my boot-toe. I am meek and ashamed where the public clatter is deafening—so I bowed my head and let "Tess of the D's" pass. But oh yes, dear Louis, she is vile. The pretence of "sexuality" is only equalled by the absence of it, and the abomination of the language by the author's reputation for style. There are indeed some pretty smells and sights and sounds. But you have better ones in Polynesia.

Dan H. Laurence, "Henry James and Stevenson Discuss 'Vile Tess,'" *Colby Library Quarterly*, May 1953.

thinking in the author, owing to the weak yet obstinate theory of being. Nevertheless, the murder is true, the whole book is true, in its conception.

Angel Clare has the very opposite qualities to those of Alec d'Urberville. To the latter, the female in himself is the only part of himself he will acknowledge; the body, the senses, that which he shares with the female, which the female shares with him. To Angel Clare, the female in himself is detestable, the body, the senses, that which he will share with a woman, is held degraded. What he wants really is to receive the female impulse other than through the body. But his thinking has made him criticize Christianity, his deeper instinct has forbidden him to deny his body any further, a deadlock in his own being, which denies him any purpose, so that he must take to hand, labour out of sheer impotence to resolve himself, drives him unwillingly to woman. But he must see her only as the Female Principle, he cannot bear to see her as the Woman in the Body. Her he thinks degraded. To marry her, to have a physical marriage with her, he must overcome all his ascetic revulsion, he must, in his own mind, put off his own divinity, his pure maleness, his singleness, his pure completeness, and descend to the heated welter of the flesh. It is objectionable to him. Yet his body, his life, is too strong for him.

Who is he, that he shall be pure male, and deny the existence of the female? This is the question the Creator asks of him. Is then the male the exclusive whole of life?—is he even the higher or supreme part of life? Angel Clare thinks so: as Christ thought.

Yet it is not so, as even Angel Clare must find out. Life, that is Two-in-One, Male and Female. Nor is either part greater than the other.

It is not Angel Clare's fault that he cannot come to Tess when he finds that she has, in his words, been defiled. It is the result of generations of ultra-Christian training, which had left in him an inherent aversion to the female, and to all in himself which pertained to the female. What he, in his Christian sense, conceived of as Woman, was only the servant and attendant and administering spirit to the male. He had no idea that there was such a thing as positive Woman, as the Female, another great living Principle counterbalancing his own male principle. He conceived of the world as consisting of the One, the Male Principle.

Which conception was already gendered in [Renaissance artist Sandro] Botticelli, whence the melancholy of the Virgin. Which conception reached its fullest in [painter Joseph]

Turner's pictures, which were utterly bodiless; and also in the great scientists or thinkers of the last generation, even [naturalist Charles] Darwin and [philosopher Herbert] Spencer and [biologist Thomas] Huxley. For these last conceived of evolution, of one spirit or principle starting at the far end of time, and lonelily traversing Time. But there is not one principle, there are two, travelling always to meet, each step of each one lessening the distance between the two of them. And Space, which so frightened Herbert Spencer, is as a Bride to us. And the cry of Man does not ring out into the Void. It rings out to Woman, whom we know not.

This Tess knew, unconsciously. An aristocrat she was, developed through generations to the belief in her own self-establishment. She could help, but she could not be helped. She could give, but she could not receive. She could attend to the wants of the other person, but no other person, save another aristocrat—and there is scarcely such a thing as another aristocrat—could attend to her wants, her deepest wants.

So it is the aristocrat alone who has any real and vital sense of "the neighbour," of the other person; who has the habit of submerging himself, putting himself entirely away before the other person: because he expects to receive nothing from the other person. So that now he has lost much of his initiative force, and exists almost isolated, detached, and without the surging ego of the ordinary man, because he has controlled his nature according to the other man, to exclude him.

And Tess, despising herself in the flesh, despising the deep Female she was, because Alec d'Urberville had betrayed her very source, loved Angel Clare, who also despised and hated the flesh. She did not hate d'Urberville. What a man did, he did, and if he did it to her, it was her look-out. She did not conceive of him as having any human duty towards her.

The same with Angel Clare as with Alec d'Urberville. She was very grateful to him for saving her from her despair of contamination, and from her bewildered isolation. But when he accused her, she could not plead or answer. For she had no right to his goodness. She stood alone.

The female was strong in her. She was herself. But she was out of place, utterly out of her element and her times. Hence her utter bewilderment. This is the reason why she was so overcome. She was outwearied from the start in her spirit. For it is only by receiving from all our fellows that we are kept fresh and vital. Tess was herself, female, intrinsically a woman. The female in her was indomitable, unchangeable, she was utterly constant to herself. But she was, by long breeding, intact from mankind. Though Alec d'Urberville was of no kin to her, yet, in the book, he has always a quality of kinship. It was as if only a kinsman, an aristocrat, could approach her. And this to her undoing. Angel Clare would never have reached her. She would have abandoned herself to him, but he would never have reached her. It needed a physical aristocrat. She would have lived with her husband, Clare, in a state of abandon to him, like a coma. Alec d'Urberville forced her to realize him, and to realize herself. He came close to her, as Clare could never have done. So she murdered him. For she was herself.

And just as the aristocratic principle had isolated Tess, it had isolated Alec d'Urberville. For though Hardy consciously made the young betrayer a plebeian and an imposter, unconsciously, with the supreme justice of the artist, he made him a true aristocrat. He did not give him the tiredness, the touch of exhaustion necessary, in Hardy's mind, to an aristocrat. But he gave him the intrinsic qualities.

With the men as with the women of old descent: they have nothing to do with mankind in general, they are exceedingly personal. For many generations they have been accustomed to regard their own desires as their own supreme laws. They have not been bound by the conventional morality: this they have transcended, being a code unto themselves. The other person has been always present to their imagination, in the spectacular sense. He has always existed to them. But he has always existed as something other than themselves. . . .

It may be, also, that in the aristocrat a certain weariness makes him purposeless, vicious, like a form of death. But that is not necessary. One feels that in Alec d'Urberville, there is good stuff gone wrong. Just as in Angel Clare, there is good stuff gone wrong in the other direction.

There can never be one extreme of wrong, without the other extreme. If there had never been the extravagant Puritan idea, that the Female Principle was to be denied, cast out by man from his soul, that only the Male Principle, of Abstraction, of Good, of Public Good, of the Community, embodied in "Thou shalt love thy neighbour as thyself," really existed, there would never have been produced the extreme Cavalier type, which says that only the Female Principle endures in man, that all the Abstraction, the Good, the Public Elevation, the Community, was a grovelling cowardice, and that man lived by enjoyment, through his senses, enjoyment which ended in his senses. Or perhaps better, if the extreme Cavalier type had never been produced, we should not have had the Puritan, the extreme correction.

The one extreme produces the other. It is inevitable for Angel Clare and for Alec d'Urberville mutually to destroy the woman they both loved. Each does her the extreme of wrong, so she is destroyed.

The book is handled with very uncertain skill, botched and bungled. But it contains the elements of the greatest tragedy: Alec d'Urberville, who has killed the male in himself. . . ; Angel Clare, who has killed the female in himself. . . ; and Tess, the Woman, the Life, destroyed by a mechanical fate, in the communal law.

There is no reconciliation. Tess, Angel Clare, Alec d'Urberville, they are all as good as dead. For Angel Clare, though still apparently alive, is in reality no more than a mouth, a piece of paper. . . .

There is no reconciliation, only death. And so Hardy really states his case, which is not his consciously stated metaphysic, by any means, but a statement how man has gone wrong and brought death on himself: how man has violated the Law, how he has supererogated himself, gone so far in his male conceit as to supersede the Creator, and win death as a reward. Indeed, the works of supererogation of our male assiduity help us to a better salvation.

Christianity in *Tess*

Lance St. John Butler

Lance St. John Butler is a lecturer in English studies at the University of Stirling, England. In this selection, Butler traces the theme of Christianity throughout *Tess*, concluding that Hardy intends Tess to reflect his own skepticism toward Christianity.

While *Tess* is about love, nature and the cosmos, it is also, without any disruption of its unity, about nineteenth-century beliefs concerning religion and morality. It is the novel in which Hardy integrates all these elements most thoroughly; as a result it is not easy to separate the different strands of the novel's symbolism. However, it is possible to go some way towards this by telling the story of *Tess* from various points of view: it can be seen as a love story, a pastoral romance, an allegory of man's progress through the world, and a study of late-nineteenth-century agnosticism in its impact on a Christian or supposedly Christian society. . . .

TESS AS AN ALLEGORY

Tess Durbeyfield, a maiden, sees but fails to dance with Angel Clare, a personification of grace, at a traditional village occasion into which he has descended. She is dressed in white and carries a white wand and white flowers. Alone among the maidens, she is marked by a red ribbon in her hair. A little later, when she is driving at night, her father's horse is killed in a collision and the maiden is ominously stained with its blood. The collision is no fault of hers but she feels guilt at having thus damaged her family's livelihood.

To make amends for her supposed fault, Tess agrees to save the family fortunes by, in effect, begging from rich relatives. These "relatives," assumed to be such because their name (d'Urberville) is the uncorrupted version of Tess's own, are in fact spurious. One of them, Alec d'Urberville, represents the snares into which human innocence can

Excerpted from *Thomas Hardy*, by Lance St. John Butler. Copyright © Cambridge University Press, 1978. Reprinted with the permission of Cambridge University Press. (Footnotes in the original have been omitted in this reprint.)

walk. His real surname, Stoke, and his aura of cigar smoke mark him with faintly devilish qualities. He tempts Tess by offering her strawberries, much as Satan offers Eve an apple, and by loading her with roses, on the thorns of which she significantly pricks her chin. Eventually she succumbs to him and they make love. The maiden is a maiden no more: she has learnt the lesson that "the serpent hisses where the sweet birds sing." She is pregnant: she sees her future life as "a long and stony highway" along which she must tread. In spite of all this, and in spite of everything we discover about her she is, perhaps surprisingly, described as "an almost standard woman." Is this, then, the story of Everywoman's pilgrimage?

Tess christens her child Sorrow. Sorrow is the result of man's involvement with the world, the natural child, at any rate, of woman's involvement with man, perhaps the fruit of original sin. Sorrow, the baby, dies. Tess's sorrow seems likely to die with it, but, unlike the baby, the mother's trials are capable of resurrection. However, she rallies after the baby's death and moves away to a place where she is unknown. Nature appears to heal her at the dairy she goes to, but the seed of new sorrow is sown, because there at Talbothays, complete with harp, is Angel Clare again, ready to sing and talk his way into her heart and soul. Angel and Tess, twice specifically linked to Adam and Eve, fall in love and find themselves, indeed, in the same position that Adam and Eve occupy once they have been banished from Eden: it is a mishap to be alive, they agree, but at least there is their love for each other. The garden at Talbothays dairy comes to represent the lost Eden to them.

Just as [author John] Bunyan's Christian is a pilgrim [in his religious allegory *The Pilgrim's Progress*], so Tess several times sees herself as being on a pilgrimage through life. She feels that her life is in some way a penance, an expiation for the sin of being born. But, unlike Christian, Tess is no mere symbol, no abstraction. She is Everywoman in flesh and blood, passionate, physical, luxuriant.

Tess and Angel marry on New Year's Day. On their wedding night, Angel, as Adam or Everyman, confesses a past sin. Tess confesses her sin in return. We are clearly told that in nature she has committed no sin at all, that her behaviour—seen objectively—has been quite natural; but man exists under a different dispensation from the animals: man is cursed with consciousness, guilt, self-accusations and social flagellations. As Tess tells the story of her affair with the tempter Alec, the coal in the fireplace glows red and puts Hardy in mind of a "Last Judgement luridness." Angel judges. His judgement is that Tess is guilty, as she agrees; and he punishes her as God is said to punish the damned by removing his divine presence from her. He wants to love her, as we see when he sleepwalks with her in his arms before they separate, but he is blind at that time and cannot rise above the self-destructive urges of mankind, since, like Christ, he is God *and* man. Tess walks penitentially barefoot beside him as she leads him back to his solitary bed, still asleep.

Left without angelic grace or protection, Tess stoically suffers hardship and loneliness, hoping against hope that she will be forgiven or that she will die. She attempts to call upon Angel's father, theologically a stern patriarch, in fact kind to sinners, but her cry never reaches him. Numberless social and personal inhibitions keep her from intruding upon this God-the-father figure: indeed, when she arrives at his village she cannot see him at first because he is in church. Her long, hard journey to visit this source of help and comfort is in vain.

While Angel, by experiencing and witnessing suffering in a distant land, is learning that it is at times better to be human than to be divine, the tempter returns to Tess. Everywoman, Eve, is beset by the same difficulties, offered the same choice, lured into the same sin as she always is. The snake is always there. Alec d'Urberville is momentarily possessed by a spirit of evangelical Christianity, but nature prevails and his powerful desire for Tess blows away his new religious resolutions like mist. But if natural forces prevail over ideology, so do the social and psychological forces that man has himself chosen. On the one hand Mrs. Durbeyfield can say of Tess's pregnancy that "'Tis nater, after all, and what do please God!" and on the other hand, society's view of Tess's relationship with Alec and, above all, the traumatic psychological effect it has on Tess herself, indicate that mankind is at variance with "nater."

The angel returns having learnt the lesson of humanity, but too late. Tess has already yielded again to the tempter. In despair she destroys her destroyer in a way that will inevitably destroy herself. After a brief experience of fulfilled human love (the only paradise available: Angel explains at this point that there is no life after death) Tess is offered as a sacrifice, on Stonehenge, to the twin gods of nature (the sacrifices at Stonehenge were to honour the sun) and man's blighted social and psychological arrangements (the policemen who take her to her death). Angel, now to be presumed quite free of all commitment to religious or social dogmas, leaves the scene with 'Liza Lu, Tess's sister, like Adam with another Eve leaving Eden, hand in hand, bowed but stoical.

TESS AS A STUDY OF NINETEENTH-CENTURY BELIEF

It is not necessary to recapitulate the entire plot again to illustrate how much of it turns on questions of religious beliefs. What follows is not really a fair summary of the novel, but makes the point the more clearly for omitting irrelevant sections.

A parson who perhaps has not quite enough to do informs John Durbeyfield of his illustrious ancestry. Angel Clare meets Tess Durbeyfield when on a walking tour with his ardently Christian brothers. Angel dances, though not with her, when he should be hastening on to the village where the three are to read another chapter of *The Counterblast to Agnosticism* before going to bed. Tess goes to "claim kin" with a supposed d'Urberville cousin who proves to be a libertine and a cynic. He seduces her. She is a Wessex heathen with some vivid scraps of Old Testament theology stuck on to her paganism. As a heathen daughter of nature she yields to d'Urberville: as a nominal Christian she develops an oppressive sense of guilt and a strong conviction that she deserves punishment.

Tess is in agonies lest the baby she has by d'Urberville, Sorrow, should be denied heaven because it has not been properly baptized. The parson whom she consults on this point is a man who has undergone "ten years of endeavour to graft technical belief on actual scepticism." He is inclined to tell her that Sorrow, having only been baptized by Tess herself, cannot join the blessed, but he wants to be kind to her: "The man and the ecclesiastic fought within him, and the victory fell to the man." He tells her (truthfully, some will say) that all baptisms will be "just the same" in their results.

Meanwhile Angel Clare realizes that he is unable to accept the Christian doctrines of his father (a vicar) and his now ordained brothers. Similarly he is unable to show any interest in Mercy Chant, a young lady of intense Christianity marked out for him by his parents. Mercy Chant is described as an "emanation" of the walls of his father's church. Angel becomes something of a pagan at Talbothays while Tess, under his influence, becomes something of an agnostic. He has already abandoned thoughts of Cambridge and the Church and is studying to become a farmer. The revelation of Tess's "past" does not shock Angel in a religious sense so much as in a personal and conventional one, although, of course, his personal feelings and his social conventions are partly grounded in centuries of Christianity.

And Angel's father, who is responsible for Alec d'Urberville's temporary conversion, gives us a brief insight into one of the less attractive sides of Christian belief. His personal charity does not altogether compensate for the rigour of his sectarian opinions. Tess's sense of guilt clearly stems from her childhood conception of an avenging deity whose lesson for man is that his "damnation slumbereth not." D'Urberville turns out to be Tess's "damnation," although not in quite the sense intended in that text. His evangelical enthusiasm is short-lived, and the man in him overcomes the ecclesiastic. This scheme—nature asserting her rights against religion and morality—is one of the motifs of the novel: Tess, for all her scruples, twice becomes d'Urberville's lover, impelled at least in part by nature's reckless urges; Angel chooses farming instead of the Church and, eventually, chooses Tess in preference to the letter of the law; Izz Huett knows that it will be sinful to live with Clare in Brazil, but she agrees to go; Angel's mother is unaffectedly delighted when he returns from Brazil—and Hardy specifically comments on the natural strength of her maternal feelings and their capacity to outweigh any scruples she may have as to the state of Angel's beliefs; as we have seen, "the man" overcomes "the ecclesiastic" in the case of the parson consulted about Sorrow's baptism and in the case of Alec himself. There are stronger forces in man than those created by faith, especially waning faith.

All this is a picture of some of the currents of belief and disbelief that coexisted in Britain towards the end of the nineteenth century. By implication Hardy introduces into the story the volume *Essays and Reviews* of 1860 in which many of the Church's more traditional and dogmatic teachings were questioned; further, he refers to [economist

Thomas] Malthus, whom we may take as an instance of objective investigation, and to [French writer] Voltaire and [biologist Thomas] Huxley, whose clear-minded objectivity, in two different centuries, brought them into conflict with orthodox religious teaching. At one level, then, Tess's story comes to us as the struggle of Hardy's contemporaries to reconcile reality as they saw it (including natural forces and social conventions) with their belief in an approximately Christian supernatural scheme. At moments we can almost feel Hardy breaking through the surface of his story and attempting to address us directly on this subject of belief. For example, we are carried along with Tess in her assumption that Alec d'Urberville's brief bout of Christianity is wrongheaded, and Hardy seems to he challenging us when he reveals that her simple scepticism destroys Alec's faith: she doesn't "believe in anything supernatural" and her "drops of logic" fall into "the sea of his enthusiasm" with devastating effect. It is Hardy, we notice, who chooses the words "logic" and "enthusiasm." And at times Hardy's presence as commentator is even more apparent. Early in the novel, for instance, a paragraph describing the shiftless muddle of the Durbeyfield household concludes with the sentence

> Some people would like to know whence the poet whose philosophy is in these days deemed as profound and trustworthy as his song is breezy and pure, gets his authority for speaking of "Nature's holy plan."

The voice here can only be Hardy's own, talking directly to his Wordsworthian [in the style of poet William Wordsworth] contemporaries. . . .

Whatever the reasons, it is certainly the case that Christianity looms larger in *Tess* than in any previous Hardy novel. . . . Angel Clare moves from conventional Christianity to a sceptical agnosticism; so does Tess herself. . . . The move *towards* Christianity is left to the villain, Alec. Hardy is mainly interested in examining the loss of faith and its effect on the development of the person concerned. One of the more original results of this loss of faith is that Hardy's main characters, in the absence of God, start themselves to take on some of the attributes of God and of Christ.

The Clare family first brings Christianity into *Tess*; from one point of view it is a novel about Angel's progressive loss of faith. But most of the comments on Christianity come to us directly from Hardy himself. It is his idea to paint "THY,

DAMNATION, SLUMBERETH, NOT" on the stile in front of Tess (it comes as a slight shock to us to discover that this text is taken not from the Old Testament but from the New); then it is Hardy, in pursuit of his thorough association of Tess with nature, who writes this of her evening walks during her pregnancy:

> Her flexuous and stealthy figure became an integral part of the scene. At times her whimsical fancy would intensify natural processes around her till they seemed a part of her own story. . . . A wet day was the expression of irremediable grief at her weakness in the mind of some vague ethical being whom she could not class definitely as the God of her childhood, and could not comprehend as any other.

> But this encompassment of her own characterization, based on shreds of convention, peopled by phantoms and voices antipathetic to her, was a sorry and mistaken creation of Tess's fancy—a cloud of moral hobgoblins by which she was terrified without reason. It was they that were out of harmony with the actual world, not she.

Here Christianity is not directly referred to, but the sorry muddle of Tess's mind is certainly intended to reflect the "Christian" and social teaching that she has had. She is "terrified" by "moral hobgoblins" because she has committed fornication, and this is a sin about which a Christian should feel guilty: under the guise of talking about Tess's unnatural conscience Hardy is presenting the unnatural conscience prescribed by Christianity.

This is made obvious when we read the description of what Tess imagines will happen to Sorrow if he is not baptized:

> She thought of the child consigned to the nethermost corner of hell . . . saw the arch-fiend tossing it with his three-pronged fork . . . to which picture she added many other quaint and curious details of torment sometimes taught the young in this Christian country.

TESS AS HARDY

Here Hardy is quite definitely intruding on us: the irony of "this Christian country" is all his own. When, a few paragraphs later, we find Tess baptizing the child "SORROW . . . in the name of the Father, and of the Son, and of the Holy Ghost" we can hardly avoid misreading the ritual words so that they mean that Father, Son and Holy Ghost are the origins of Sorrow's sorrow.

Hardy's own intrusions continue through the novel; but after a time Tess herself reaches a point where her natural paganism and her experience of suffering combine with Angel Clare's sceptical teaching to bring her to an intellectual point of view almost identical to Hardy's own. Even before going to Talbothays she interrupts her own chanting of the *Benedicite* ("Bless ye the Lord") with the comment "But perhaps I don't quite know the Lord as yet." This tendency of Tess's to adopt Hardy's own views, as expressed in his intrusion and asides, culminates in her destruction of Alec d'Urberville's temporary religious enthusiasm where, interestingly, Tess claims to have a religion and to believe in "the *spirit* of the Sermon on the Mount" although she doesn't believe in "anything supernatural."

ANGEL

Angel Clare, meanwhile, the part-author of these views of Tess's, also expresses Hardy's views as we know them from . . . his other novels and his poems. Angel explains to his father that he cannot conscientiously take Holy Orders:

> I love my church as one loves a parent . . . but I cannot honestly be ordained her minister . . . while she refuses to liberate her mind from an untenable redemptive theolatry.

At first reading, this may sound as if Angel is a fully believing Christian who has a scruple about some small technical detail called "redemptive theolatry." An analysis of what this term actually means, however, and a consideration of the conversation with his father that follows, in which Angel gives a few more of his opinions, show that he does not believe in the Resurrection, the divine nature of Christ, or even that Christ's mission on earth had supernatural significance. By most definitions Angel is not a Christian at all, and the position that he shares with Tess represents at least a stage in the development of Hardy's own thinking. We will find this same trio of hero-heroine-author ranged critically against normal Christian doctrine in [Hardy's 1895 novel] *Jude*. In *Tess* the three are brought together in at least one place: when Angel returns home to Emminster Vicarage after his first sojourn at Talbothays he is full of Tess's heathen spirit; he finds his family's Christianity to be "like the dreams of people on another planet," and, in what are unmistakably the tones of Thomas Hardy, he is described thus:

> Latterly [i.e. at Talbothays] he had seen only Life, felt only the
> great passionate pulse of existence, unwarped, uncontorted,
> untrammelled by those creeds which futilely attempt to
> check what wisdom would be content to regulate.

In this striking summary of Angel's state of mind, hero,
heroine and author are united. Tess's pagan involvement in
nature at Talbothays is the "great passionate pulse of existence" that Clare has come up against: he has been altered
by it and has accepted its wisdom, and Hardy clearly approves of this development in his hero's views, as the second
part of the sentence makes clear. It is interesting to see
Hardy here entering the lists behind the figure of his own
character: at first it seems as if the sentiments conveyed are
only Angel's, but their breadth, their switch into the present
tense and their self-assured quality derive from some other
mind, a mind that is not involved in a taxing emotional situation such as that of Angel when visiting his father's house.
From Hardy's mind, in fact.

To sum up this matter of the personal intellectual development of Hardy's heroes and heroines, we can say that they
move, through the hard school of life, towards something
like Hardy's own position. If it is objected that Hardy has no
fixed philosophy, and therefore no "position," I think the objection can be met. It may be true that Hardy did not have a
consistent philosophy, but it is equally true that in novel after novel and poem after poem he passes opinions on a
number of topics which are forthright and usually echo one
another accurately. Towards these opinions, Angel, Tess,
Jude and Sue [characters from *Jude the Obscure*] painfully
move.

Besides this matter of personal development away from
Christian views, there is the curious question of Hardy's tendency to replace God and the divine Christ by man. This appears quite markedly in *Jude*, but there are traces of it in *Tess*
which I shall try to follow.

Tess herself briefly acquires divine status in the eyes of
her young brothers and sisters when she baptizes Sorrow:

> The children gazed up at her with more and more reverence.
> . . . She did not look like Sissy to them now, but as a being
> large, towering, and awful—a divine personage with whom
> they had nothing in common.

In the eyes of Angel, in the early mornings at the dairy, Tess
seems a very "divinity," Artemis or Demeter, and he thinks,

in the "luminous gloom" of the dawn, of the "Resurrection hour," little knowing that "the Magdalen might be at his side." This addition of an ironic Christian touch to the basic identification of Tess with the divine is several times developed in the novel. Tess's feeling of being unworthy of Angel is described as a "thorny crown"; her patience under Angel's neglect of her leads Hardy to quote St Paul's famous description of charity and to conclude that "she might just now have been Apostolic Charity herself"; Angel's mother is influenced by his enthusiasm for Tess to the point that "she had almost fancied that a good thing could come out of Nazareth—a charming woman out of Talbothays dairy"; when Tess walks to Emminster, Mercy Chant finds her boots in a hedge and attributes them to "some imposter who wished to come into the town barefoot, and so excite our sympathies," a vague reference that just associates Tess with Christ and Mercy with the Pharisees; when Tess overhears Alec d'Urberville's sermon at Evershead, his text concerns the doctrine that Christ is "set forth, crucified" among Christians: the Christ set forth in Wessex is Tess herself; finally, at a more mundane level, when the care of her brothers and sisters falls on Tess's shoulders, she muses:

> If only she could believe [in Providence] . . . how confidently she would leave them to Providence and their future kingdom! But, in default of that, it behoved her to do something; to be their Providence.

Thus Hardy keeps on jarring us, opening new vistas of possible metaphor, making us think about the supernatural and about Christianity as he likens his heroine to God, to goddesses, to the Magdalen and to Christ. Just as frequent, however, is the association of Angel with God, especially in Tess's eyes. His name, of course, points to the divine, and Hardy is at some pains to show us what a perfect being he becomes for Tess. Even before their marriage he can do no wrong, and afterwards she feels that she has "delivered her whole being up to him." At times her worship of him seems ominous to Tess herself:

> She tried to pray to God, but it was her husband who really had her supplication. Her idolatry of this man was such that she herself almost feared it to be ill-omened.

And, indeed, her idolatry wrecks her judgement, so that when the divine Angel metes out to her suffering and punishment she welcomes it, with the masochism of the martyr, as just: "I agree to the conditions, Angel; because you know best what my punishment ought to be." Her long letter to Angel that concludes chapter 48 reads very like a human address to divine ears, a *De profundis:* "The punishment you have measured out to me is deserved . . . only [be] a little kind to me . . . I live entirely for you . . . it has been so much my religion ever since we were married to be faithful to you . . ." and the letter ends with an appeal to Angel to come to her and to save her from what threatens her—the onslaughts of the devil, Alec. Tess's "reckless acquiescence" in all that Angel has commanded also accords him divine status:

> she had adhered with literal exactness to orders which he had given and forgotten . . . [she] admitted his judgement to be in every respect the true one, and bent her head dumbly thereto.

Angel, struck with remorse, remembers her in his turn: "How her eyes had lingered upon him; how she had hung upon his words as if they were a god's!" When he returns from his Brazilian ordeal, Angel looks like "Crivelli's dead *Christus.*"

At Stonehenge, Angel, asked by Tess whether there is a life after death, remains silent. . . . The silence implies that Angel feels there to be no life after death, the "greater" is Christ, tempted by Pilate to make rash claims. Here we have an example of the breadth of reference Hardy gains by using Christian parallels, an example that perhaps sums up Hardy's purposes in this connexion. Christ was the supremely suffering man, the archetype of all suffering men and women. Christ was pure and faithful; his reward at the hands of the world, and at the hands of his Father, was ignominy and death. Such are the rewards of men and women at the hands of the world and at the hands of an indifferent fate. For all his greatness, Christ's suffering is in the end irrelevant if there is no life after death. Like Christ, Tess suffers here for no reward hereafter.

A Critique of Education and Urban Attitudes

Bruce Hugman

In the following selection, Bruce Hugman points out that the characters who are educated or are related to an urban setting are satirized in *Tess*. These characters are seen as corrupt and insensitive in comparison to the rural and not formally educated Tess. Hugman cites the example of Angel, who, only after removing himself from all urban and intellectual influences, can come to understand Tess. Bruce Hugman is the author of *Hardy:* Tess of the d'Urbervilles, from which this article is taken.

Hardy makes it clear that conventional moral judgments are less when rigidly applied without regard for particular circumstances. He also records much comment on general, social and educational matters. These provide us with a clearer picture of some of the adverse influences which he sees shaping men's lives. They also help to give us glimpses of what may be a more honest and wholesome way of life.

Hardy refers with irony to various aspects of the educational system. Tess had been to the village school and had acquired

> . . . trained National teachings and Standard knowledge under an infinitely Revised Code.

There is a perceptible sneer in the insistence on the capital letters: "National," "Standard," "Revised Code." The bland bureaucracy of educational administration is mocked. It is this "Standard" knowledge which had developed in people the ". . . habit of taking long views . . ." which had ". . . reduced emotions to a monotonous average." And we see how ill this carefully formulated education had prepared Tess for life.

As Angel Clare finds his true education at Talbothays, through his involvement with real and not philosophical or theoretical situations, so Tess finds hers through the sorrows and joys of life.

Most of us will recall our reluctance as children to believe in the wisdom and advice of our elders. Experience (and often painful experience) proves to be the surest teacher. Hardy maintains the importance of this in opposition to the useless platitudes of the classroom. It presents a sad paradox:

> "By experience," says Roger Ascham, "we find out a short way by long wandering." Not seldom that long wandering unfits us for further travel, and of what use is our experience then? Tess Durbeyfield's experience was of this incapacitating kind. At least she had learned what to do; but who would now accept her doing?

> If before going to the d'Urbervilles she had vigorously moved under the guidance of sundry gnomic texts and phrases known to her and to the world in general, no doubt she would never have been imposed on. But it had not been in Tess's power, nor is it in anybody's power—to feel the whole truth of golden opinions while it is still possible to profit by them. She—and how many more—might have said to God with St. Augustine: "Thou hast counselled a better course than Thou hast permitted."

Her seduction by Alec

> ... but for the world's opinion ... would have been simply a liberal education.

The qualification "but for the world's opinion" is at once trivial and incapacitating. Trivial, because at first it seems so obviously irrelevant to the matter; but incapacitating because we know from sad experience how despotic are the irrational opinions of the world.

The elder Clare brothers are the objects of Hardy's irony. They were

> ... well educated, hall-marked young men, correct to their remotest fibre, such unimpeachable models as are turned out yearly by the lathe of a systematic tuition.

They were incapable of original thought, and consequently slavish followers of the prevailing fashions:

> They were both somewhat short-sighted, and when it was the custom to wear a single eyeglass and string they wore a single eyeglass and string; when it was the custom to wear a double glass they wore a double glass; when it was the custom to wear spectacles they wore spectacles straightway, all without reference to the particular variety of defect in their own vision.

And so also is it with their opinions about poets and artists. They are shown to be pathetic and somewhat ridiculous in these attitudes.

They were also worshippers of words rather than deeds, and neither could see beyond his narrow vocational channel:

> Perhaps, as with many men, their opportunities of observation were not so good as their opportunities of expression. Neither had an adequate conception of the complicated forces at work outside the smooth and gentle current in which they and their associates floated. Neither saw the difference between local truth and universal truth; that what the inner world said in their clerical and academic hearing was quite a different thing from what the outer world was thinking.

ANGEL'S RURAL LEANINGS

Angel's involvement in the "outer world" has a salutary effect upon him. He began to discard the academic view, and to suit his behaviour to the simple needs of his surroundings. He became freed even from a certain muscular constraint instilled by society, and he began to value human beings for what they proved themselves to be, rather than for what society said they were. His brothers noticed this "growing social ineptness."

It is significant that this process of "naturalisation" began as soon as he and his father had decided that he was not going to Cambridge. He abandons the limited vision imposed by a vocational purpose and well-trodden road:

> He spent years and years in desultory studies, undertakings and meditations; he began to evince considerable indifference to social forms and observances. The material distinctions of rank and wealth he increasingly despised.

These new liberal views are ironically labelled "austerities" by Hardy. They are, of course, quite the reverse. His conditioned self is the austere one, because it would deny his mind these natural and reasonable convictions, and his body its natural freedom:

> As a balance to these austerities, when he went to live in London . . . he was carried off his head, and nearly entrapped by a woman, much older than himself. . . .

This was rather a concomitant of his yet roughly formulated liberalism, and a reaction against the true austerities of his childhood home. Hardy states several times that human energies cannot be completely or justly suppressed.

Successive layers of Clare's acquired education and conventional attitudes are removed as his experience brings him closer to the reality of personal relationships.

Educational and social influences are not seen to be evil, but unnecessary and unhelpful in the discovery of life.

Hardy's view of the urban, educated world is not a flattering one. He is a countryman who has little sympathy for the "advanced" ideas of town-dwellers. Like the acquired attitudes of Clare, the attitudes of urban life seem to be out of harmony with the natural world.

MACHINERY AND NATURE

The milk-train and the steam threshing machine are two obvious (and symbolic) examples of this. They are certainly visually and aesthetically out of harmony with the farming world, although they are of great importance to it:

> ... the feeble light, which came from the smoky lamp of a little railway station: a poor enough terrestrial star, yet in one sense of more importance to Talbothays Dairy and mankind than the celestial ones to which it stood in such humiliating contrast.

The portrait of the "engineer" who travels with his steam engine, is full of gentle satire, and conjures up an enchanting picture of a reluctant being from the nether regions, arrogantly conscious of the mysteries of his craft:

> By the engine stood a dark motionless being, a sooty and grimy embodiment of tallness, in a sort of trance, with a heap of coals by his side: it was the engineman. The isolation of his manner and colour lent him the appearance of a creature from Tophet, who had strayed into the pellucid smokelessness of this region of yellow grain and pale soil, with which he had nothing in common, to amaze and discompose its aborigines. . . . He spoke in a strange northern accent; his thoughts being turned inwards upon himself, his eye on his iron charge, hardly perceiving the scenes around him, and caring for them not at all; holding only strictly necessary intercourse with the natives, as if some ancient doom compelled him to wander here against his will in the service of his Plutonic master.

This mysterious being and his machine are the "primum mobile" of the small agricultural world for one day: apart from that contact they might be on different planets. For that one day the machine exercises a fierce tyranny over the farm people: to satisfy its demands they are pushed to the limits of endurance.

For various reasons many rural families found that they were forced to leave their villages and to move to the towns. This depopulation of the country resulted primarily from the avaricious self-interest of farmers who required cottages for their workers and their farms. The families moved reluctantly and their going impoverished the villages:

> These families, who had formed the backbone of the village life in the past, who were the depositories of the village traditions, had to seek refuge in the large centres; the process, humorously designated by the statisticians as "the tendency of the rural population towards the large towns," being really the tendency of water to flow uphill when forced by machinery.

Here is another ironic reference to the administrative bureaucracy, which, while totally out of touch with the facts and needs of a situation, has a neat label for it. Sadly, but inevitably, these officials, like Angel Clare in other circumstances, were ". . . in the habit of neglecting the particulars of an outward scene for the general impression." The "rural population" is for them a single unit, with "tendencies," instead of a multitude of infinitely varying individuals, forced, against their wishes, for one reason or another, into one course of action. Linguistically there is very little difference, but in terms of humanity there is a world of difference.

Tess's limited experience leads her to fear

> . . . towns, large houses, people of means and social sophistication, and manners other than rural. From that direction gentility Black Care had come.

Hardy gives us no reason to suppose that he believes this to be a completely false inference.

The town of Sandbourne seems to Angel Clare a slightly tawdry creation of fantasy.

> This fashionable watering place, with its eastern and its western stations, its piers, its groves of pines, its promenades, and its covered gardens, was, to Angel Clare, like a fairy palace suddenly created by the stroke of a wand, and allowed, to get a little dusty. . . . Within the space of a mile from its outskirts every irregularity of the soil was prehistoric . . . a Mediterranean lounging-place on the English Channel.

The mockery of the description is directed at the contrived and ephemeral triviality of the place. It stands in "humiliating contrast" to the ancient lands surrounding it. It is to this "pleasure city" that Alec has enticed Tess.

The only urban family of whom we know anything is that of the Stokes—or Stoke-d'Urbervilles—as they prefer to be known. The history of Mr. Simon Stoke, while perhaps not criminal, seems to be better left uninvestigated. He obviously wished for some sort of disguise, and the opportunity to start afresh in retirement:

> When . . . [he] had made his fortune as an honest merchant (some say money-lender) in the North, he decided to settle as a country man in the South of England, out of hail of his business district; and in doing this he felt the necessity of recommencing with a name that would not too readily identify him with the smart tradesman of the past.

The suggestion is simply that where there is business and money, there may be less honesty than is desirable.

Angel Clare resolves that if he is to become a farmer, the intelligent course of action will be to choose a wife who is skilled in farming matters. Social and spiritual sophistication are all very well, but are not very practical virtues:

> It seemed natural enough to him now that Tess was again in sight to choose a mate from unconstrained Nature, and not from the abodes of Art.

In contrast to "Nature" the word "Art" suggests artificiality, artifice, or artfulness. It does not here refer to the art of artists. The irony of the reference is that Clare believes he has found an idealised figure from pastoral "art" (poetry in particular), and it is in this incomplete, ambiguous judgment that he makes his mistake. Hardy's irony at the expense of the great world of fashion is also apparent in the phrase "abodes of Art"—those places where the people believe themselves to be accomplished in the "art" of living.

No coherent social commentary can be inferred from, nor is intended in, these various suggestions. We can see lurking in urban, educated society certain tendencies to dishonesty, prejudice and harshness. As far as Tess's experiences are concerned these suspicions are justified. Hardy does not refer to the wider picture.

Unnatural Society

The conclusion at which we can arrive with some certainty is the unnaturalness of society. It is in conflict with, and has a perverting influence upon simple, innocent human nature. It is alien to an existence in which human happiness is of first importance.

Determinism in *Tess*

Leon Waldorf

Critic Leon Waldorf argues in the following selection that Tess's fate is predetermined by the male characters in the book. Unable to reconcile the sexual with the maternal parts of Tess's character, neither Alec nor Angel can love her fully. Waldorf suggests that this conflict exists in many of Hardy's novels. Waldorf is associate professor of English at the University of Illinois at Urbana-Champaign. He has written a number of articles on the topic of psychology and the romantic poets.

The conception of tragedy in *Tess of the d'Urbervilles* rests on an assumption of inevitability. "The best tragedy—highest tragedy in short," Hardy thought, "is that of the WORTHY encompassed by the INEVITABLE." Throughout *Tess of the d'Urbervilles* Hardy invokes several discrete yet interrelated forms of determinism to make his heroine's fate seem inevitable. Heredity is the most obvious of these. Tess's ability to see or hear the d'Urberville Coach of the legend and her resemblance to the d'Urberville women of the portraits in the farmhouse at Wellbridge ("her fine features were unquestionably traceable in these exaggerated forms") suggest that she has the fateful blood of the ancient d'Urbervilles in her veins. A somewhat different form of determinism is in Hardy's use of the laws of Nature, particularly in the great pastoral scenes in which Angel and Tess first discover and resist their love for each other. "All the while," we are told, "they were converging, under an irresistible law, as surely as two streams in one vale." Tess with her sensuousness, is an embodiment of the principle in Nature of irresistible sexual attraction. Her flower-red mouth, her pretty face, her fine figure, and her unselfconscious affinity with all that is natural suggest how Nature is a force in her character and determinant of her fate. Still another form of determinism

Excerpted from "Psychological Determinism in *Tess of the d'Urbervilles*," by Leon Waldorf, in *Critical Approaches to the Fiction of Thomas Hardy*, edited by Dale Kramer. Reprinted by permission of Macmillan Ltd. (Footnotes in the original have been omitted in this reprint.)

may be seen in the use of omens to indicate the presence of a supernatural power behind the scenes: the text-painter, the cock that crows the afternoon of the wedding, the allusions to Satan in the characterisation of Alec, and so forth. The scene at Stonehenge is particularly evocative of a supernatural presence and seems to set the stage for the ironic suggestion of a divine hand in Tess's fate: "'Justice' was done, and the President of the Immortals, in Æschylean phrase, had ended his sport with Tess."

In considering these as well as other forms of determinism in the novel (the social code, for example), a question naturally arises as to what notion of psychological inevitability contributes to the design of the tragedy. For one thing, any determinism that has implications for human behaviour, as heredity, Nature, and the social code do, assumes some kind of psychology, though the rationale for it may not be made explicit. For another , a discussion of Tess's character and motivation would in any case involve psychological considerations. The great strength of the novel, it is widely acknowledged, is the characterisation of Tess. She haunts our imagination long after whatever confusions or inconsistencies we may find in the plot or narration have ceased to seem important. . . . In a novel where the heroine is so central to every important consideration, an understanding of how her character shapes her fate is essential for an interpretation of the meaning of her tragedy.

To a large extent the psychological considerations in the novel seem to resolve themselves into a paradoxical question of responsibility: Does Tess co-operate in her fate to an extent that makes her responsible for it? . . . In what way, it may be asked, does Tess fail to take the necessary trouble to ward off disaster? Is it her pride, her passionate nature, her passivity, or some combination of these that makes her fate inevitable?

Unfortunately, it is not possible to answer these questions about Tess's responsibility with anything like certainty. In fact, the uncertainty or indeterminacy in the novel is a major obstacle in the way of interpretation. There is an unresolved tension between the rhetoric of inevitability in Hardy's editorial commentary and a basic ambiguity at the heart of several crucial episodes. Because of the repeated emphasis on inevitability one expects a sense of certainty about the qualities in Tess's character that make her end tragic. Hardy is painstaking in his effort to link the forms of determinism to her character and fate. She is said to possess a "slight incautiousness of character inherited from her race" and her pride is thought to be "a symptom of that reckless acquiescence in chance too apparent in the whole d'Urberville family." In addition, the narration is everywhere buttressed by words such as "doomed," "destined," and "fated." But the crucial linking is never made and one remains uncertain about why Tess's fate is inevitable.

The ambiguity in two early episodes suggests the nature of the difficulty. Take, for example, the first occasion when the problem of responsibility becomes an important consideration, the scene in The Chase. It is a matter of some surprise to discover that there is still no general agreement about exactly what takes place after Alec returns from the slope. He finds Tess asleep. Most critics refer to the next event as a seduction, suggestive of a degree of responsibility on Tess's part, but others take it to be a rape.

Even in summary form the case for seduction is strong. When Car Darch's mother remarks "Out of the frying-pan into the fire!" after Alec's rescue of Tess from the hostility of the other women on the way home from Chaseborough, she seems to assume that Tess will be seduced by Alec and become his mistress. Car Darch's envy of Tess as the "first favourite with He just now" suggests that the mother's comment means that Tess will soon be dazed by Alec, as her daughters have been. Of course, her expectation is not necessarily an indication of what happens. But one of the functions of the scene, aside from establishing a situation in which Tess will have to be more receptive to Alec's affectation of concern for her than she so far has been, seems to be to foreshadow what will happen. With his cigar, black moustache, rolling eye, and provincial Byronism [in the style of poet Lord Byron] ("Well, my Beauty, what can I do for you?") Alec fascinates and seduces cottage girls. Tess is to become one of these. . . .

SPLITTING TESS'S CHARACTER

In going to some length to argue that there is an unresolved tension between the narrator's editorial insistence on inevitability and the ambiguity in his depiction of what happens to Tess, and why, my aim has been to call attention to a pattern of splitting in the novel. It is perhaps most evident in the characterisation, where essential feelings and attitudes are split into certain types of characters. I take the pattern to be a significant clue to the inevitability of Tess's fate. It is also a clue to the idea of tragedy in the novel. To anticipate and briefly summarise the rest of my argument, the decisive determinant of Tess's fate is a tendency in the fictional world in which she exists for men to have either sensual or spiritual feelings toward woman, but not both at the same time. The tendency is reflected not only in Alec and Angel, but in numerous characters in Hardy's other novels. Ultimately Tess is a victim of an ambivalent attitude towards woman that is traceable both to Hardy and to the culture in which he lived. The crucial determinism in the novel is therefore psychological, but the heroine's mind or character is not the place to look for it. It is rather to be sought in the nature of the imaginary world in which she and the other characters exist. Perhaps only because Tess is so sympathetically and convincingly drawn do we require a reminder that it is Hardy, not an indifferent Olympian, who presides over the fates of the mortals in this novel. The inevitability in the heroine's fate is not to be found in the various forms of determinism alluded to throughout the novel, but in the psychological nature of the existence that she and the other characters are imagined to have.

Numerous Hardy critics, among them some of the earliest, have attempted to identify the special features of Hardy's fictive world. One of the features noted most often, and one that throws some light on the psychology in *Tess of the d'Urbervilles*, is the idea of love at first sight. . . . The psychological basis of the idea is that the lover has in mind a prior, idealised image that the suddenly encountered object appears to match. . . . Angel is in love with an image of his own making. The image is one of rustic innocence and virgin purity. His first comment to himself about Tess is, "What a fresh and virginal daughter of Nature that milkmaid is!" When walking together in the midsummer dawn to do the milking, "She was no longer the milkmaid, but a visionary essence of woman—a whole sex condensed into one typical form. He called her Artemis, Demeter, and other fanciful names." When she says, "Call me Tess," he does, but he persists in idealising her. At the heart of his image of her is an expectation of virginity so strong as to be virtually a demand. After Tess's confession, he holds on to the image:

"Nothing so pure, so sweet, so virginal as Tess had seemed possible all the long while that he adored her, up to an hour ago." The discovery of what is later referred to as Tess's "unintact state" so alters her appearance in his eyes that she seems to be a different person: "You were one person; now you are another." Tess, in desperation, asks if he has stopped loving her. He answers that "the woman I have been loving is not you." "But who?" she asks. "Another woman in your shape."

ANGEL'S OBSESSION WITH TESS'S PURITY

Notwithstanding the various appeals to the forms of determinism we have already discussed, Angel's obsession with purity may be taken as a uniquely important determinant of Tess's fate. It is not going too far to say that without it there would have been no tragedy, especially of a "pure" woman. Purity would not have been an issue. The conflict of his image of woman with the real woman Tess becomes the turning-point in the novel. The characterisation of Angel is sufficiently plausible, in spite of a certain flatness, to make his attitude seem natural both to him and to the mental landscape of the novel. Although Joan Durbeyfield's letter to Tess suggests that many women approach marriage in Tess's state, her advice not to tell Angel may be interpreted as her awareness of the importance that the image (or illusion) of purity has. Farmer Groby's offhand but provocative comment is a similar indication that Angel's attitude is not thought to be an aberration.

With minor variations, it is an attitude that is a recurrent feature of the psychological world in which Hardy's characters are imagined to exist, and one which seems to increase in importance in the later novels. In *Desperate Remedies*, Miss Aldclyffe, on her deathbed, remains convinced that had Ambrose Graye known of the affair with her cousin and of the baby, "he would have cast her out." For that reason, she says of herself, she "withdrew from him by an effort, and pined." Henry Knight in, *A Pair of Blue Eyes* seems to prefigure Angel Clare in his obsession with purity. "Inbred in him," the narrator points out, "was an invincible objection to be any but the first comer in a woman's heart. He had discovered within himself the condition that if ever he did make up his mind to marry, it must be on the certainty that no cropping out of inconvenient old letters, no bows or blushes to a mysterious stranger casually met, should be a possible source of discomposure." In *The Trumpet-Major* Captain Robert Loveday is willing, even eager, to marry Matilda in spite of her reputation, but his brother John, who is the hero named in the title and the moral centre of the novel, prevents it. In *The Woodlanders*, Fitzpiers in spite of his claim in his letter to Grace that he could never feel estranged from her, even if she had slept with Giles' experiences "mental sufferings and suspense" and does not ask her to take him back until he learns from Marty South that Grace, contrary to her representation, had remained faithful.

In these and other instances where a woman's purity is in question, it is not difficult to distinguish Hardy's attitude from that of his characters. On the other hand, it may be doubted if his attitude is ever entirely out of sympathy with those of his characters, men and women, who are concerned about such matters. Most telling in this regard is the fact that the women in the novels are so often divided up into the two categories, pure and impure, that Angel invokes. "Of the two classes into which gentle young women naturally divide," the narrator of *The Hand of Ethelberta* tells us, there are "those who grow red at their weddings, and those who grow pale." On the morning of Tess's wedding, after she has discovered that Angel has not read her letter, "She was so pale when he saw her again that he felt quite anxious.". . .

FEMALE SEXUALITY

An important consideration in the conception of the female characters, and apparently crucial in the design of their fates, is the degree of sexuality attributed to them. Female characters with sexual experience prior to or outside of marriage usually do not survive, or do not fare well. In this tendency in Hardy's novels to divide the female characters in this way one can recognise a familiar theme in Western literature, the opposition between the fair maid and the *femme fatale*. . . .

In *Tess of the d'Urbervilles* it is not the image of woman that is split into two characters, although the tendency is represented in Angel's prolonged inability to reconcile his image of the innocent milkmaid with the reality of a sexually experienced woman. His remark to Tess that "You were one person; now you are another" might be interpreted as an attempt to deny or defend against the possibility that he might love her in spite of her experience. The double standard that he employs in judging Tess and not himself is both a curious and characteristic example of the kind of doubling one finds in the attitude toward woman in a great deal of fiction. The sleep-walking scene at Wellbridge, for example, when Angel attempts to bury Tess, might be interpreted as an extension of the doubling, an attempt to deny the sexual nature of woman. It is rather the attitude toward woman in *Tess of the d'Urbervilles* that is split into two characters, Alec and Angel, one taking an attitude that woman is primarily a sexual object, the other an attitude that denies her sexual nature through idealisation. The approximate representation of these two attitudes may be seen in an apparent doubling of male characters similar to the one of female characters, at least to the extent that the heroes or other principal male characters are frequently to be found in rivalry with a rake or other figure who has had a wider and often socially unacceptable sexual relationship with a woman, or whose relationship with women seems to be primarily sexual. . . .

Whatever else one might wish to say about the various thematic concerns and structural principles reflected in a recurrent opposition of such characters, it would seem clear that an irreconcilable conflict in the imaginary world of Hardy's novels is between the sexual and other (spiritual, intellectual, affectionate) feelings. The conflict functions throughout Hardy's novels as a virtual psychological law. It is an obvious determinant of the destinies of the characters in Hardy's last three novels. In each there is a central character created in a Shelleyan [the style of poet Percy Bysshe Shelley] mould and unable to achieve in a relationship with a beloved a reconciliation of sexual and spiritual feelings. Although in *Tess of the d'Urbervilles* Angel appears to overcome the difficulty of Tess's sexual impurity after the conversation with his travelling companion and confidant in Brazil, and after the death of Alec (something he had earlier insisted was a virtual precondition of any reunion: "How can we live together while that man lives? . . . If he were dead it might be different"), it is doubtful if such a reunion is possible in the psychological world of Hardy's novels. There is no precedent for it in the earlier novels. None of Hardy's major female characters is allowed to have premarital or extramarital sexual experience and survive. This is not the case with male characters. Lord Mountclere and Fitzpiers are both imagined as sexually promiscuous before marriage.

Fitzpiers is a conspicuous example of the double standard, for even after he is reunited with Grace he will not remain faithful to her. Hardy, it will be recalled, remarked that "the heroine is doomed to an unhappy life with an inconstant husband."

The prospects for a successful union between Tess and Angel were in fact never bright. Hardy revealed why in the interview published in *Black and White*:

> You ask why Tess should not have gone off with Clare, and "lived happily ever after." Do you not see that under *any* circumstances they were doomed to unhappiness? A sensitive man like Angel Clare could never have been happy with her. After the first few months he would inevitably have thrown her failings in her face. He did not recoil from her after the murder it is true. He was in love with her failings then I suppose; he had not seen her for a long time; with the inconsistency of human nature he forgave the greater sin when he could not pardon the lesser.

If this comment may be trusted, . . . then the phrase "under *any* circumstances" may be taken to mean that circumstances such as the misdirected letter or the chance reappearance of Alec were never to be taken as crucial determinants of Tess's fate. The decisive determinant was all along an attitude held by Angel. Here is the inevitability that encompasses Tess in tragedy: "he would *inevitably* have thrown her failings in her face." One may go on to doubt if all those coincidences, circumstances, and mishaps with which Hardy's novels are so replete, or the symbolic shape of them as a divine Crass Casualty, are as relevant for the fates of his characters as one is made to feel while reading. In any case, an important form of determinism in Hardy's fiction is psychological, one that structures the characters and plots of several major novels around the following question: Can one's sensuous and affectionate feelings be successfully united in a permanent relationship with another person? The answer implicit in the last three novels leaves little doubt as to the conclusion Hardy reached.

FREUD AND HARDY'S TESS

The question is one that [psychoanalyst Sigmund] Freud thought haunted the love life of men and women, but particularly men. In one of his papers on the psychology of love, written at the time Hardy was preparing the Wessex Edition, Freud discussed what he said was one of the most common disorders a practising analyst was likely to encounter, psychical impotence. In his discussion of the disorder, he expressed the view that "Two currents whose union is necessary to ensure a completely normal attitude in love, have, in the cases we are considering, failed to combine. These two may be distinguished as the *affectionate* and the *sensual* current." Freud traced the affectionate current to a man's primary object-choice and argued that in cases of psychical impotence the loved and idealised object in adult experience is modelled too closely on a maternal image. An unconscious conflict over incest prevents the man from approaching sexually a woman for whom the current of feeling is too profoundly associated with a maternal image, or a woman who seems in some way an embodiment of it. The tendency to split the feelings in this way exists in every man, as Freud discusses it, but becomes a problem only for some. "The whole sphere of love in such people," he writes, "remains divided in the two directions personified in art as sacred and profane (or animal) love. Where they love they do not desire and where they desire they cannot love." They may love many women, and desire many, but they cannot unite their sensuous and affectionate feelings in the love of one. Such a one would be too dear for possessing. . . .

When *Tess of the d'Urbervilles* is considered in the larger context of the world of Hardy's novels, with particular attention to the conditions that determine the course of love and marriage, it is clear that Tess's fate is to a large extent the result of a fierce psychological determinism at work in the imaginary world in which she exists. The psychological conditions of this imaginary world are as harsh and punishing as the physical conditions of Flintcomb-Ash or Egdon Heath. The men Tess knows represent totally opposing attitudes toward women. One sees her as a sexual object, the other as an idealised image of pastoral innocence and purity. While each is characterized as given to extremes, each experiences within himself the very division of attitudes represented as an irreconcilable conflict in the novel. Alec's religious conversion and Angel's "eight-and-forty hours' dissipation with a stranger" reveal the other sides of these two characters and suggest that the process of doubling extends into each character. In a sense Alec, Angel, and Tess are all victims of the conflict between the sensuous and affectionate feelings, but it is really the woman who pays. Ultimately, the novel reflects a conflict between a rational rejection of the unfair and sexist obsession with purity on Angel's part, a conscious meaning in the novel suggested by the subtitle, and Hardy's own irrational and unconscious sharing in that obsession in the design of his heroine's fate. This is in no way to deny Hardy's genuine and compelling sympathy with Tess, but it is to recognise that the sympathy was—inevitably—ambivalent.

Although Hardy was irritated by any suggestion of autobiography in his fiction, there seems to be wide agreement that certain novels are autobiographical. *A Pair of Blue Eyes*, for example, is usually thought to be partly based on Hardy's experience during his courtship of Emma. Like the young Hardy, the hero is an architect sent to plan and supervise the restoration of a village church. Another autobiographical element may be present in the striking similarity between the worsening domestic scene at Max Gate and the increasingly dark view of marital relations in the last novels—particularly *Jude the Obscure*, which seemed so offensive to Emma. In a more speculative vein one might attempt to relate the various heroines to the kind of woman to which Hardy was attracted and, ultimately, to Jemima Hand, his mother. . . .

At the time Freud attempted to analyse the tendency to split the sensuous and affectionate feelings, he laid the responsibility for this condition of the erotic life of civilised man on the incestuous tendencies of childhood and the frustration of the sexual instinct during adolescence. But he went on to speculate that "we may perhaps be forced to become reconciled to the idea that it is quite impossible to adjust the claims of the sexual instinct to the demands of civilization." It was this kind of bold speculation that would lead eventually to discoveries beyond the pleasure principle. Whatever value may be finally placed on the speculation, it gives recognition to a psychological condition, part of the ache of modernism, intuited by Hardy and thought by Freud to be a principal determinant in the fate of romance and marriage in the culture in which they both lived. The psychological determinism that Freud sees is certainly no darker than anything in *Tess of the d'Urbervilles* or *Jude the Obscure*, or that "mutually destructive interdependence of flesh and spirit" one finds in *The Return of the Native*. Perhaps only a determinism as dark as the one Freud posits does justice to the conception of Tess and the tragedy imagined for her.

Tess's Fate Is Not Predetermined

Bruce Hugman

In the following excerpt, Bruce Hugman asserts that
Tess's fate is not predetermined, but rather results
from consistency in her character that leads her to
make certain predictable choices. It is sadness and
suffering that is inevitable in this world, he concludes. Hugman is the author of *Hardy:* Tess of the
d'Urbervilles, from which this selection is excerpted.

It is sometimes suggested that Hardy's perception of the
pathos and misfortunes of life arises from a gloomy fatalism.
This is inferred from the fatalistic language he uses and
from a sentence in the last paragraph of the book:

> . . . the President of the Immortals, in Aeschylean [in the style
> of Greek playwright Aeschylus] phrase, had ended his sport
> with Tess.

This suggests that Hardy is taking the easy view that Tess's misfortunes are the result of the malevolent play of a supernatural
being. Its position so near the end of the book gives it considerable weight. But this is not what the book as a whole suggests.
Hardy made it clear in a reply to critics, that the "President of
the Immortals" was a personification of the vicissitudes of life,
a symbol, a secular reinterpretation of the Aeschylean deity.

In spite of its position in the book, and even without
Hardy's dismissal of the suggestion, it is unreasonable to in-
terpret this as a last minute succumbing to a supernatural
explanation. Nowhere else in the book is reference made to
malevolent deities, and there are no hints of divine intervention for which this sentence would be the final summary.
There is much talk of fate and doom—but those are different matters. Hardy relies on our responding to the spirit
rather than the letter of the phrase, and in it we should see
only the great unpredictability of life.

(We might note the possibility of a rejection of the Aeschylean scheme of things in a sentence at the end of the first Phase:

> But though to visit the sins of the fathers upon the children may be a morality good enough for divinities, it is scorned by average human nature; and it therefore does not mend the matter.

Visiting the sins of the fathers upon the children was a characteristic of the Old Testament Yaweh and of Aeschylus's Zeus alike.)

Such "fatalism" as there is, is more the property of the people's philosophy than of Hardy's. He records the

> . . . fatalistic convictions common to field folk and those who associate more extensively with natural phenomena than with their fellow creatures . . .

and the

> . . . lonely country nooks where fatalism is a strong sentiment. . . .

The inference from such observations is that in remote situations there is a strictly limited number of choices—possibly no choice—owing to the absence of a variety of people and opportunities which would provide alternative courses of action. If there is only one bachelor within ten miles of a girl's home farm, presumably she feels "doomed" to marry him.

After Tess's arrival at Flintcomb-Ash, when she has exhausted all other possibilities of employment in the neighbourhood she feels "doomed" to have gone there. It is, of course, only a chance outcome. But chance for humanity is so often mischance, and for that there seems to be no explanation:

> Why it was that upon this beautiful feminine tissue, sensitive as gossamer, and practically as blank as snow as yet, there should have been traced such a coarse pattern as it was doomed to receive; why so often the coarse appropriates the finer thus, the wrong man the woman, the wrong woman the man, many thousand years of analytical philosophy have failed to explain to our sense of order.

The village people were

> . . . never tired of saying among each other in their fatalistic way: "It was to be." There lay the pity of it.

HARDY IS NOT FATALISTIC

Hardy does not subscribe to this fatalistic view, although the overall pattern is a pessimistic one. It is the story of individuals at the mercy of forces they do not understand, and in the case of Tess, which ultimately destroy. For her, these forces take the form of the lust of Alec d'Urberville, an arbitrary social law, and finally the criminal law. That Tess was unavoidably the victim of these forces does not imply a fatalistic philosophy. It is not fatalistic to say that if one cuts oneself one will bleed, nor that if one steps in front of a moving bus one will be knocked down. These are simply facts which rely on accident for their realisation. Similarly it is not necessarily an indication of a predetermined scheme when people act in accord with their normal behaviour patterns. Most of us are likely to live and act in a more or less predictable way—not because we are divinely or diabolically imposed upon—but because we remain single persons with certain limits of capability.

For Tess these personal characteristics include a certain indecisiveness (e.g. her failure to confess to Clare before their marriage), and a "reckless acquiescence" to circumstance (e.g. her unquestioning acceptance of Clare's rejection of her). The chances are that she will act in a way more or less determined by those (and other) personal qualities, and that those dependent actions will (more or less) determine the pattern of her life.

To every action there is a reaction, which is inevitable in a certain sense, but strictly at the mercy of human choice and circumstance. Hardy suggests that human judgment often errs—owing to ignorance or prejudice—and that circumstances prove favourable or unfavourable for joy or tragedy in a quite unpredictable fashion.

Tess's ignorance of the "danger in men-folk" and Alec d'Urberville's lust are the ingredients of tragedy:

> Had she perceived this meeting's import she might have asked why she was doomed to be seen and coveted that day by the wrong man.

This "doom" was determined by the very ordinary facts of her family's poverty, their vain faith in their ancient lineage, and Tess's self-appointed responsibility to earn some money. The question of why she did not meet the "right" man is simply answered: there are a great number of people on the earth, and the odds against the "right" two meeting first time are very high. Her doom turns out to be a matter of human frailty and simple statistics.

This is a prosaic account of a highly charged subject. Tess

feels herself to be the toy of a malevolent power which hurries her irresistibly from one misfortune to another. She is weighed down to the point of despair by what seems to be an inescapable fate. But Hardy does not suggest that it is anything more than the result of the coincidence of miscellaneous factors. These are symbolically represented by the "President of the Immortals" and by the occasional reference to "doom" and "fate."

Human perception and judgment are not sufficiently refined to put to rights the confusion of existence:

In the ill-judged execution of the well-judged plan of things the call seldom produces the comer, the man to love rarely coincides with the hour for loving. Nature does not often say "See!" to her poor creature at a time when seeing can lead to happy doing; or reply "Here!" to a body's cry of "Where?" till the hide-and-seek has become an irksome, outworn game. We may wonder whether at the acme and summit of the human progress these anachronisms will be corrected by a finer intuition, a closer interaction of the social machinery than that which now jolts us round and along; but such completeness is not to be prophesied, or even conceived as possible. Enough that in the present case, as in millions, it was not the two halves of a perfect whole that confronted each other at the perfect moment.

The simple physical limitations of human beings "doom" them to misfortune more often than to fortune.

The student interested in biography and psychology may speculate endlessly about the significance of events in Hardy's life—the possibilities of sexual adventures in London, the tensions of his childless marriage to Emma, and so on, and their relationship to the certain bleakness of his outlook. What little evidence there is—in diaries and poems—has been given widely differing interpretations by critics. Even if there were more evidence such speculation is probably not of much value. The novels have an independent life of their own: our concern is with the art of the creation of that life, and the assumptions underlying that creation which can be inferred from it.

No philosophical or theological answers to the problems of life are suggested. The religious overtones of the book are certainly non-Christian, and very often pagan. The country people are "essentially naturalistic" in their outlook. With this view goes an instinctive superstitiousness. This results from the perception that there seem to be inherent correspondences between some separated events, and between

action and result, which conform to a pattern which is more
or less predictable. This arises from the occurrence of genuine coincidences and from the obvious fact that certain actions will almost inevitably provoke certain reactions. Furthermore it is often possible, in retrospect, to elicit what
appears to be a predetermined pattern, from what was a
random succession of events. Incidents to which no importance was attached at the time take an ominous significance
when seen from the present; when similar incidents recur
they are thought to herald similar results. This belief may
contribute to the repetition of the pattern, and so reinforce
the belief further.

There are many examples of such processes in *Tess* and
while Hardy discounts the physical truth of many of them,
their psychological effect cannot be disregarded.

Joan Durbeyfield with her *Compleat Fortune-Teller* and her

> . . . fast-perishing lumber of superstitions, folk-lore, dialect,
> and orally transmitted ballads . . .

is the most obviously superstitious character in the book.
Far from weighing her down with foreboding, it seems to
give her a remarkable elasticity of spirit which is equal to
the greatest of disasters. Aided by the occasional excursion
into the world of alcoholic fantasy, she faces life with exceptional equanimity.

TESS'S SUPERSTITIONS

In spite of Tess's "Standard" education she retains much of
her mother's superstitiousness without, however, her insensitive resilience. Tess is given to a belief in ill-omens, which
is common to many of the country people. When one of
d'Urberville's roses pricks her chin she is alarmed. (The sexual symbolism of this is powerful.) ". . . she thought this an
ill-omen—the first she had noticed that day." The interesting
thing is, that although the thorn prick is a fortuitous event, it
happens on a day which contains events that, to anyone but
Tess, were ominous in the most obvious and unsuperstitious
way. Her interpretation of the event as an "ill-omen" is an expression of her instinctive recognition of the strangeness and
danger of Alec d'Urberville's behaviour. The stubbing of her
toe, or any other such minor accident would have provoked
a similarly instinctive and "superstitious" interpretation.

In Clare's company Tess recalls that he had not danced

with her at the Marlott festival and remarks:

... O, I hope that is of no ill omen for us now!

Here her conjectured interpretation of the past event reflects her uncertainty of her worthiness to be Clare's lover. An incident which is altogether more sinister takes place at the Cross-in-Hand. D'Urberville asks her to place her hand upon what he believes to be an old, holy cross and to swear that she will never again tempt him. This she reluctantly does. Later she finds out from a local man that the supposed "cross" was a rude monolith marking the spot where a man was once tortured and killed: a man who had sold his soul to the devil. At this news Tess suffers a "petite mort." The least suggestive of persons might shudder at such an event. The association of her oath with violence and death is symbolically significant, as we later discover.

Besides Mrs. Durbeyfield, Dairyman Crick is the other explicitly superstitious character. He believes that the intervention of "conjurors" will solve his farming difficulties. He hears with distress the cock's crowing on the afternoon of Clare's marriage to Tess. The moderm reader at first discounts it as anything but coincidence: events later force him to adjust his attitude. Such a (contrived) event suggests disharmony in the created order, and shows human beings to be an integral part of that order. We see the imaginative and physical identification of the country people with their surroundings, and a "coincidence" such as this is a manifestation of that relationship. In Wessex sensibility is more highly developed than intellect, and these events are the realistic and artistic expression of their particular consciousness.

The woods of Wessex have a particularly sinister and powerful character:

> ... The Chase—a truly venerable tract of forest land, one of the few remaining woodlands in England of undoubted primaeval date, wherein Druidical mistletoe was still found on aged oaks, and where enormous yew-trees, not planted by the hand of man, grew as they had grown when they were pollarded for bows.

The trees assert their timelessness against the feeble and ephemeral nature of man's existence.

Even lands no longer forested keep some of their old arboraceous power:

> Superstitions linger longest on these heavy soils. Having once been forest, at this shadowy time it seemed to assert something of its old character, the far and near being blended, and every tree and tall hedge making the most of its presence. The

harts that had been hunted here, the witches that had been pricked and ducked.

Against such a primitive and haunting background the drama is played.

The sense of history which is suggested by the natural surroundings is sometimes much more specific:

> The Vale was known in former times as the Forest of White Hart, from a curious legend of King Henry III's reign in which the killing by a certain Thomas de la Lynd of a beautiful white hart which the King had run down and spared, was made the occasion of a heavy fine.

The purpose of these references is to establish in our minds that people have been living and dying in these lands for centuries within and beyond memory. However vivid and intense present experience may be, it is only a tiny, though essential, part in the history of mankind. The killing of a beautiful and innocent creature is of added artistic value to the story of Tess.

The land is by no means all sinister. The glories of the Froom Valley are those of a rich, productive, benign land. But, as Hardy implies, this is not necessarily the result of the benignity of the conventional—or any other God. As Tess enters the valley she is prompted to recite the *Benedicite.* Hardy comments:

> And probably the half-unconscious rhapsody was a Fetichistic utterance in a Monotheistic setting; women whose chief companions are the forms and forces of outdoor Nature retain in their souls far more of the Pagan fantasy of their remote forefathers than of the systematised religion taught their race at a later date.

Angel Clare once upset his father greatly by suggesting that:

> ... it might have resulted far better for mankind if Greece had been the source of the religion of modern civilisation, and not Palestine: and his father's grief was of that blank description which could not realise that there might lurk a thousandth part of a truth, much less a half truth or a whole truth, in such a proposition.

Clare's experience at Talbothays of the

> ... aesthetic, sensuous, pagan pleasure in natural life and lush womanhood ...

taught him the justice of these views:

> Latterly he had seen only Life, felt only the great passionate pulse of existence, unwarped, uncontorted, untrammelled by those creeds which futilely attempt to check what wisdom would be content to regulate.

The case for a simple, naturalistic, spontaneous and pagan philosophy as presented by Hardy through the experience of the novel is a very strong one.

INDIVIDUAL ACTION

The pagan view of life suggests that individuals are alone, and that responsibility for action lies finally with those who act. Sadness and suffering are inevitable parts of a life in which there are so many who act selfishly and wickedly. There is no god.

There are several references to the old sun religions. We see the sun as a generous life-giving force:

> His present aspect, coupled with the lack of all human forms in the scene, explained the old-time heliolatries in a moment. . . . The luminary was a golden-haired, beaming, mild-eyed, God-like creature, gazing down in the vigour and intentness of youth upon an earth that was brimming with interest for him.

We are reminded that the villagers go to church on the "Sun's day"—a pagan day—for what appear to be thoroughly pagan activities.

It is on the warm altar of the sun's temple that Tess meets her earthly fate. Stonehenge is the most magnificent, awesome setting for the last scene of her life. The starkness of the natural setting, with its ageless impassivity, accords perfectly with the beauty and simplicity of the lovers' mood. Tess feels she is at last "at home" in this heathen temple, "older than the centuries."

An enrichment of the pagan atmosphere is the frequent use of classical references. Classical mythology is a great deal more engaging and lively than even the best of the Christian myths. It embraces the whole of human experience, in deed not merely in theory. It is energetically concerned with performance and not hypothesis. Lessons were learnt (often painfully) by experience. Gods and mortals went about doing things, sometimes with happy, sometimes with sad results. They seemed to make it their business to explore their potential to the utmost. They lived to the full until they died. There was an arbitrariness, a great unpredictableness in their lives very much like that experienced by most mortals in most centuries. The emotions of those mythical beings had a passion and intensity which is lacking in the more austere Christian virtues. Hardy had found a rich store of parallels for the "passionate pulse of existence" which Clare and Tess felt beating within them.

The Destruction of Rural Life

Thomas Hinde

Thomas Hinde is a novelist and lecturer on nineteenth-century literature. In the following article, Hinde contends that the many improbable acts of fate that lead to Tess's demise reinforce a pervasive theme in the book. Hinde claims that Hardy's primary theme is that Tess is representative of the old rural ways of the English village and how they are being overturned by the inevitable march toward industrialization.

The plot of *Tess of the d'Urbervilles* turns on a succession of accidents and coincidences. Again and again Tess's tragic fate depends on some disastrous mischance. One or two of these may seem possible—life after all is full of mischance— but heaped on top of each other they produce a final effect of gross improbability. Does this matter? Are we to see them as blemishes on an otherwise fine novel; or are they such a pervasive part of it that they must either condemn it or form part of its success?

At its face value the novel suggests not only that these accidents and misfortunes are included by intention but that it is the author's view that life does give human beings just such a succession of kicks downhill to disaster. The refrain "where was Tess's guardian angel?" is more than an attack on the conventional Christian idea of a benevolent and protecting Almighty; it implies the exact opposite. Our problem, if we don't share this view, is that we see Tess as not so much the victim of Fate, nor as the victim of her own character and circumstances, but as Hardy's personal victim.

It is he who appears to make her suffer her improbable sequence of accidents. In criticizing this effect I do not imply that probability is a criterion by which we should univer-

Excerpted from "Accident and Coincidence in *Tess of the d'Urbervilles*," by Thomas Hinde, in *The Genius of Thomas Hardy*, edited by Margaret Drabble. Reprinted by permission of Weidenfeld & Nicolson.

sally or invariably judge. A novel sets its own standards, and no one, to take an obvious example, expects the same "realism" from [Franz] Kafka as from [Leo] Tolstoy. The problem with Hardy's novels is that in most other ways they set up expectations of a quite conventional realism. It is against this self-established standard that the plot of *Tess*, as much as that of any of his novels which came before it and which it otherwise excels, at first sight appears equally to offend.

I say at first sight because my purpose is to suggest a way of looking at *Tess* which sees its many accidents and coincidences neither as blemishes, nor as valid samples of Hardy's neither credible nor particularly interesting view of the part played in life by a persecuting fate; if encouragement were needed to search for such a view it would be provided by *Tess*'s many admirers who seem undismayed by its improbabilities, though these begin on the very first page and feature regularly throughout the book. . . .

The Destruction of the English Village

The plot of the novel turns on a succession of disastrous accidents which far exceeds realistic probability. But as in all such abstracts, vital elements which seem unrelated to the book's plot have been left out, in particular one to which Hardy persistently returns even though his attention is overtly directed towards Tess and her personal tragedy. This is the equally sure tragic destruction of the traditional society of the English village.

Twice he shows us mechanized agriculture at work; on the first occasion he describes how the reaping machine, with its red arms in the shape of a Maltese cross, gradually reduces the standing corn.

> Rabbits, hares, snakes, rats, mice, retreated into a fastness, unaware of the ephemeral nature of their refuge, and of the doom that awaited them later in the day when, their covert shrinking to a more and more horrible narrowness, they were huddled together, friends and foes, till the last few yards of upright wheat fell also under the teeth of the unerring reaper, and they were every one put to death by the sticks and stones of the harvesters.

It needs little intuition to see that Hardy is here describing by parallel the fate of the inhabitants of such a village as Marlott.

Humans themselves are the victims on the second occasion: Tess and her fellow workers who feed the monstrous

itinerant threshing machine at Flintcomb-Ash, with its dia-
bolical master.

> By the engine stood a dark motionless being, a sooty and
> grimy embodiment of tallness, in a sort of trance, with a heap
> of coals by his side: it was the engineman. The isolation of his
> manner and colour lent him the appearance of a creature
> from Tophet, who had strayed into the pellucid smokeless-
> ness of this region of yellow grain and pale soil, with which
> he had nothing in common, to amaze and to discompose its
> aborigines.

> What he looked he felt. He was in the agricultural world, but
> not of it. He served fire smoke; these denizens of the fields
> served vegetation, weather, frost, and sun. He travelled with
> his engine from farm to farm, county to county. . . . He spoke
> in a strange northern accent; his thoughts being turned in-
> wards upon himself, his eye on his iron charge, hardly per-
> ceiving the scenes around him, and caring for them not at all.

Still more symptomatic of the destruction of a village society by the new rich and their industrial money is the
chicken house where Tess keeps the Stoke-d'Urberville
chickens, once a copyholder's cottage.

> The descendants of these bygone owners felt it almost as a
> slight to their family when the house which had so much of
> their affection, had cost so much of their forefathers' money,
> and had been in their possession for several generations be-
> fore the d'Urbervilles came and built here, was indifferently
> turned into a fowl-house by Mrs Stoke-d'Urberville as soon
> as the property fell into her hand according to the law.

Apart from the implications of such incidents, Hardy as
author continually comments on the changing and deterio-
rating condition of rural Wessex. The May Day dance, for example, where we first meet Tess, is "a gay survival from Old
Style days when cheerfulness and May were synonyms."
The refreshments which the rural labourers of Trantridge
drink on Saturday nights are "curious compounds sold to
them as beer by the monopolizers of the once independent
inns." Still more important, it is the tenant farmers, deprived
of their independence, who are "the natural enemies of bush
and brake," and to whom Tess falls victim at the lowest point
of her decline at Flintcomb-Ash.

Economic Causes of Tess's Fate

And it is because Tess's family are victims of another aspect
of this destruction of rural independence that she is finally
exposed once more to Alec d'Urberville. As soon as her fa-

ther dies her mother loses her right to their cottage, and the family must join all those other labourers' families which take to the road on Lady Day, their worldly goods loaded on to hired waggons, to hunt for new jobs and homes. Oppressed by responsibility for her family, she no longer feels she has the moral right to resist his advances when they could bring with them the financial help she so badly needs.

Indeed, a good many of Tess's misfortunes turn out, on closer inspection, to have economic causes which seem almost as important as the random vengefulness of Fate to which Hardy attributes them. It is only a short step from realizing this to wondering whether Hardy is not consciously or unconsciously—concerned throughout the book not so much with Tess's personal fortune as with her fate as a personification of rural Wessex.

Just why Tess should be an appropriate figure to play this part is clearly explained in Chapter LI, in a passage which holds the clue to the book's social message.

The village had formerly contained, side by side with the agricultural labourers, an interesting and better-informed class, ranking distinctly above the former—the class to which Tess's father and mother had belonged—and including the carpenter, the smith, the shoe-maker, the huckster, together with nondescript workers other than farm labourers: a set of people who owed a certain stability of aim and conduct to the fact of their being lifeholders like Tess's father, or copyholders, or, occasionally, small freeholders. But as the long holdings fell in they were seldom again let to similar tenants, and were mostly pulled down, if not absolutely required by the farmer for his hands. Cottagers who were not directly employed on the land were looked upon with disfavour, and the banishment of some starved the trade of others, who were thus obliged to follow. These families, who had formed the backbone of the village life in the past, who were the depositaries of the village traditions, had to seek refuge in the large centres; the process humourously designated by statisticians as "the tendency of the rural population towards the large towns," being really the tendency of water to flow uphill when forced by machinery.

At once much that appeared arbitrary becomes logical. The destruction of the haggler's daughter no longer seems a cruel mischance, but inevitable. And many more of the accidents she suffers, which on a personal level seem so excessive and gratuitous, become those which her class *must* suffer.

The mail coach which runs down the haggler's cart and kills his horse is the vehicle which will destroy the livelihood of all hagglers, whether they are drunkards like John Durbeyfield, or sober and hard-working. Deprived of their former independence, the children of this village middle class will be driven downwards into just the sort of menial labouring jobs that Tess is forced to take. Her downward progress from milkmaid to arable worker of the lowest sort is the path ahead for all of them.

NEITHER UPPER NOR LOWER CLASS

In their distress they will turn to the new rich, as Tess's parents are driven to send Tess to call upon her "cousins," and these, represented by Alec d'Urberville, will offer only the further exploitation which Tess's job as poultry girl followed by her seduction represents. If they turn to the old upper middle class for relief, as Tess turns to Angel, they are again betrayed, and the mistaken (in Hardy's view) ethics of the Anglican church are employed as an additional moral stick to beat them with. Because, for all his superficial emancipation, Angel does represent this class and is basically not only priggish but as conditioned and conventional as his father and brothers. "With all his attempted independence of judgement, this advanced and well-meaning young man, a sample product of the last five-and-twenty years, was yet the slave to custom and conventionality when surprised back into his early teachings." As soon as we see him in this role, Tess's failure to confess her past to him ceases to seem an improbable accident and becomes merely the hook on which he happens to hang a betrayal which sooner or later is inevitable. She is not of his class and it can never accept her.

Much else now falls into place. Tess is rejected by the women of Trantridge on the night of her first seduction not just because they are jealous of the way Alec d'Urberville favours her but because she is not really a labourer of their kind. Farmer Groby ill-treats Tess not just because of the coincidental attack made on him by Angel but because tenant farmers *are* the destroyers of such families as Tess's.

Tess is of course many other things as well. She is, for example, the embodiment of "nature" and in particular of natural womanhood. "Women whose chief companions are the forms and forces of outdoor Nature retain in their souls far more of the Pagan fantasy of their remote forefathers than of the systematized religion taught their race at later date." And however much she may stand for a principle or a passing society, she remains a lost and frightened human being in a world which misleads then persecutes her. Scenes such as the splendid but appalling one in which she baptizes her dying child in her bedroom wash basin may indeed seem to establish her tragedy too clearly as a personal one for the interpretation I am suggesting.

But such a view of Tess becomes less and less satisfactory as Hardy inflicts on her a less and less probable sequence of accidental and coincidental misfortune. It is only when she is seen to some extent also to be a daughter of the doomed rural England which Hardy loved, and in particular of that class in the rural community from which Hardy himself came and which was once "the backbone of the village life" that her fate no longer seems arbitrary and author-imposed but inescapable.

CHAPTER 2

Imagery and Symbols in *Tess*

The Image of the Earth

Dorothy Van Ghent

Dorothy Van Ghent teaches English at City College in New York and is the author of *The English Novel: Form and Function*, from which this selection is excerpted. In it, Van Ghent traces the image of earth, mud, and roads in *Tess*, contending that they serve a symbolic function in the novel. The earth symbolizes the concrete, immovable, accidental universe in which events occur without humans in mind.

The dilemma of Tess is the dilemma of morally individualizing consciousness in its earthy mixture. The subject is mythological, for it places the human protagonist in dramatic relationship with the nonhuman and orients his destiny among preternatural powers. The most primitive antagonist of consciousness is, on the simplest premise, the earth itself. It acts so in *Tess*, clogging action and defying conscious motive; or, in the long dream of Talbothays, conspiring with its ancient sensuality to provoke instinct; or, on the farm at Flintcomb-Ash, demoralizing consciousness by its mere geological flintiness. But the earth is "natural," while, dramatically visualized as antagonist, it transcends the natural. The integrity of the myth thus depends, paradoxically, upon naturalism; and it is because of that intimate dependence between the natural and the mythological, a dependence that is organic to the subject, that Hardy's vision is able to impregnate so deeply and shape so unobtrusively the naturalistic particulars of the story.

In *Tess*, of all his novels, the earth is most actual as a dramatic factor—that is, as a factor of causation; and by this we refer simply to the long stretches of earth that have to be trudged in order that a person may get from one place to another, the slowness of the business, the irreducible reality of it (for one has only one's feet), its grimness of soul-wearying fatigue and shelterlessness and doubtful issue at the other end of the journey where nobody may be at home. . . . In *Tess* the earth is *primarily not a metaphor but a real thing* that one has to move on in order to get anywhere or do anything, and it constantly acts in its own motivating, causational substantiality by being there in the way of human purposes to encounter, to harass them, detour them, seduce them, defeat them.

In the accident of Prince's death, the road itself is, in a manner of speaking, responsible, merely by being the same road that the mail cart travels. The seduction of Tess is as closely related, causally, to the distance between Trantridge and Chaseborough as it is to Tess's naïveté and to Alec's egoism; the physical distance itself causes Tess's fatigue and provides Alec's opportunity. The insidiously demoralizing effect of Tess's desolate journeys on foot as she seeks dairy work and field work here and there after the collapse of her marriage, brutal months that are foreshortened to the plodding trip over the chalk uplands to Flintcomb-Ash, is, again, as directly as anything, an effect of the irreducible *thereness* of the territory she has to cover. There are other fatal elements in her ineffectual trip from the farm to Emminster to see Clare's parents, but fatal above all is the distance she must walk to see people who can have no foreknowledge of her coming and who are not at home when she gets there. Finally, with the uprooting and migration of the Durbeyfield family on Old Lady Day, the simple fatality of the earth as earth, in its measurelessness and anonymousness, with people having to move over it with no place to go, is decisive in the final event of Tess's tragedy—her return to Alec, for Alec provides at least a place to go.

The dramatic motivation provided by natural earth is central to every aspect of the book. It controls the style: page by page *Tess* has a wrought density of texture that is fairly unique in Hardy; symbolic depth is communicated by the physical surface of things with unhampered transparency while the homeliest conviction of fact is preserved ("The upper half of each turnip had been eaten off by the livestock"); and one is aware of style not as a specifically verbal quality but as a quality of observation and intuition that are here—very often—wonderfully identical with each other, a quality of lucidity. Again, it is because of the *actual* motivational impact of the earth that Hardy is able to use setting and atmosphere for a symbolism that, considered in itself, is so astonishingly blunt and rudimentary. The green vale of Blackmoor, fertile, small, enclosed by hills, lying under a blue haze—the vale of birth, the cradle of innocence. The wide misty setting of Talbothays dairy, "oozing fatness and warm ferments," where the "rush of juices could almost be heard below the hiss of fertilization"—the sensual dream, the lost Paradise. The starved uplands of Flintcomb-Ash, with their ironic mimicry of the organs of generation, "myriads of loose white flints in bulbous, cusped, and phallic shapes," and the dun consuming ruin of the swede field—the mockery of impotence, the exile. Finally, that immensely courageous use of setting, Stonehenge and the stone of sacrifice. Obvious as these symbolisms are, their deep stress is maintained by Hardy's naturalistic premise. The earth exists here as Final Cause, and its omnipresence affords constantly

---

TESS AND THE IMAGE OF NATURE

In the following excerpt from Tess of the d'Urbervilles, *the narrator implies that nature reflects Tess's moods.*

On these lonely hills and dales her quiescent glide was of a piece with the element she moved in. Her flexuous and stealthy figure became an integral part of the scene. At times her whimsical fancy would intensify natural processes around her till they seemed a part of her own story. Rather they became a part of it; for the world is only a psychological phenomenon, and what they seemed they were. The midnight airs and gusts, moaning amongst the tightly-wrapped buds and bark of the winter twigs, were formulae of bitter reproach. A wet day was the expression of irremediable grief at the weakness in the mind of some vague ethical being whom she could not class definitely as the God of her childhood, and could not comprehend as any other.

But this encompassment of her own characterization, based on shreds of convention, peopled by phantoms and voices antipathetic to her, was a sorry and mistaken creation of Tess's fancy—a cloud of moral hobgoblins by which she was terrified without reason. It was they that were out of harmony with the actual world, not she. Walking among the sleeping birds in the hedges, watching the skipping rabbits on a moonlit warren, or standing under a pheasant-laden bough, she looked upon herself as a figure of Guilt intruding into the haunts of Innocence. But all the while she was making a distinction where there was no difference. Feeling herself in antagonism she was quite in accord. She had been made to break an accepted social law, but no law known to the environment in which she fancied herself such an anomaly.

to Hardy the textures that excited his eye and care, but affords them wholly charged with dramatic, causational necessity; and the symbolic values of setting are constituted, in large part, by the responses required of the characters themselves in their relationship with the earth.

ACCIDENT AND COINCIDENCE

Generally, the narrative system of the book—that is, the system of episodes—is a series of accidents and coincidences (although it is important to note that the really great crises are psychologically motivated: Alec's seduction of Tess, Clare's rejection of her, and the murder). It is accident that Clare does not meet Tess at the May-walking, when she was "pure" and when he might have begun to court her; coincidence that the mail cart rams Tess's wagon and kills Prince; coincidence that Tess and Clare meet at Talbothays, *after* her "trouble" rather than before; accident that the letter slips under the rug; coincidence that Clare's parents are not at home when she comes to the vicarage; and so on. Superficially it would seem that this type of event, the accidental and coincidental, is the very least credible of fictional devices, particularly when there is an accumulation of them; and we have all read or heard criticism of Hardy for his excessive reliance upon coincidence in the management of his narratives; if his invention of probabilities and inevitabilities of action does not seem simply poverty-stricken, he appears to be too much the puppeteer working wires or strings to make events conform to his "pessimistic" and "fatalistic" ideas. It is not enough to say that there is a certain justification for his large use of the accidental in the fact that "life is like that"— chance, mishap, accident, events that affect our lives while they remain far beyond our control, are a very large part of experience; but art differs from life precisely by making order out of this disorder, by finding causation in it. In the accidentalism of Hardy's universe we can recognize the profound truth of the darkness in which life is cast, darkness both within the soul and without, only insofar as his accidentalism *is not itself accidental* nor yet an ideology-obsessed puppeteer's manipulation of character and event; which is to say, only insofar as the universe he creates has aesthetic integrity, the flesh and bones and organic development of a concrete world. This is not true always of even the best of Hardy's novels; but it is so generally true of the construction of *Tess*—a novel in which the accidental is perhaps more preponderant than in any other Hardy—that we do not care to finick about incidental lapses. The naturalistic premise of the book—the condition of earth in which life is placed—is the most obvious, fundamental, and inexorable of facts; but because it is the physically "given," into which and beyond which there can be no penetration, it exists as mystery; it is thus, even as the basis of all natural manifestation, itself of the quality of the supernatural. On the earth, so conceived, coincidence and accident constitute order, the prime terrestrial order, for they too are "the given," impenetrable by human *ratio*, accountable only as mystery. By constructing the *Tess*-universe on the solid ground (one might say even literally on the "ground") of the earth as Final Cause, mysterious cause of causes, Hardy does not allow us to forget that what is most concrete in experience is also what is most inscrutable, that an overturned clod in a field or the posture of herons standing in a water mead or the shadows of cows thrown against a wall by evening sunlight are as essentially fathomless as the procreative yearning, and this in turn as fathomless as the sheerest accident in event. The accidentalism and coincidentalism in the narrative pattern of the book stand, thus, in perfectly orderly correlation with the grounding mystery of the physically concrete and the natural.

THE FOLK AND THE EARTH

But Hardy has, with very great cunning, reinforced the *necessity* of this particular kind of narrative pattern by giving to it the background of the folk instinctivism, folk fatalism, and folk magic. If the narrative is conducted largely by coincidence, the broad folk background rationalizes coincidence by constant recognition of the mysteriously "given" as what "was to be"—the folk's humble presumption of order in a rule of mishap. The folk are the earth's pseudopodia, another fauna; and because they are so deeply rooted in the elemental life of the earth—like a sensitive animal extension of the earth itself—they share the authority of the natural. (Whether Hardy's "folk," in all the attributes he gives them, ever existed historically or not is scarcely pertinent; they exist here.) Their philosophy and their skills in living, even their gestures of tragic violence, are instinctive adaptations to "the given"; and because they are indestructible, their attitudes toward events authoritatively urge a similar fatalism

upon the reader, impelling him to an imaginative acceptance of the doom-wrought series of accidents in the foreground of the action.

We have said that the dilemma of Tess is the dilemma of
moral consciousness in its intractable earthy mixture;
schematically simplified, the signifying form of the *Tess*-
universe is the tragic heroism and tragic ineffectuality of
such consciousness in an antagonistic earth where events
shape themselves by accident rather than by moral design;
and the *mythological* dimension of this form lies precisely in
the earth's antagonism—for what is persistently antagonistic appears to have its own intentions, in this case mysterious, supernatural, for it is only thus that earth can seem to
have "intentions." The folk are the bridge between mere
earth and moral individuality; of the earth as they are, sepa-
rable conscious ego does not arise among them to weaken
animal instinct and confuse response—it is the sports, the
deracinated ones, like Tess and Clare and Alec, who are
morally individualized and who are therefore able to suffer
isolation, alienation, and abandonment, or to make others so
suffer; the folk, while they remain folk, cannot be individu-
ally isolated, alienated, or lost, for they are amoral and their
existence is colonial rather than personal. (There is no finer
note of this matter—fine in factual and symbolic precision,
and in its very inconspicuousness—than the paragraph describing the loaded wagons of the migrating families:

> The day being the sixth of April, the Durbeyfield wagon met
> many other wagons with families on the summit of the load,
> which was built on a well-nigh unvarying principle, as pecu-
> liar, probably, to the rural laborer as the hexagon to the bee.
> The groundwork of the arrangement was the position of the
> family dresser, which, with its shining handles, and finger
> marks, and domestic evidences thick upon it, stood impor-
> tantly in front, over the tails of the shaft-horses, in its erect
> and natural position, like some Ark of the Covenant which
> must not be carried slightingly.

Even in the event of mass uprooting, the folk character that
is preserved is that of the tenacious, the colonial, the instinctive, for which Hardy finds the simile of the hexagon of
the bee, converting it then, with Miltonic [the style of poet
John Milton] boldness, to its humanly tribal significance
with the simile of the Ark of the Covenant.) Their fatalism is
communal and ritual, an instinctive adaptation as accomo-
dating to bad as to good weather, to misfortune as to luck, to

birth as to death, a subject economy by which emotion is subdued to the falling out of event and the destructiveness of resistance is avoided. In their fatalism lies their survival wisdom, as against the death direction of all moral deliberation. There is this wisdom in the cheerful compassion of the fieldwomen for Tess in her time of trouble: the trouble "was to be." It is in Joan Durbeyfield's Elizabethan ditties of lullaby:

> I saw her lie do-own in yon-der green gro–ve;
> Come, love, and I'll tell you where

—the kind of ditty by which women of the folk induce maturity in the child by lulling him to sleep with visions of seduction, adultery, and despair. It is in the folk code of secrecy—as in Dairyman Crick's story of the widow who married Jack Dollop, or in Joan's letter of advice to her daughter, summoning the witness of ladies the highest in the land who had had their "trouble" too but who had not told. Tess's tragedy turns on a secret revealed, that is, on the substitution in Tess of an individualizing morality for the folk instinct of concealment and anonymity.

While their fatalism is a passive adaptation to the earthy doom, the folk magic is an active luxury: the human being, having a mind, however incongruous with his animal condition, has to do something with it—and if the butter will not come and someone is in love in the house, the coexistence of the two facts offers a mental exercise in causation (though this is not really the "rights o't," about the butter, as Dairyman Crick himself observes; magical lore is not so dainty); yet the magic is no less a survival wisdom than the fatalism, inasmuch as it does offer mental exercise in causation, for man cannot live without a sense of cause. The magic is a knowledgeable mode of dealing with the unknowledgeable, and it is adaptive to the dooms of existence where moral reason is not adaptive, for moral reason seeks congruence between human intention and effect and is therefore always inapropos (in Hardy's universe, tragically inapropos), whereas magic seeks only likenesses, correspondences, analogies, and these are everywhere. Moral reason is in complete incommunication with the "given," for it cannot accept the "given" as such, cannot accept accident, cannot accept the obscure activities of instinct, cannot accept doom; but magic can not only accept but rationalize all these, for the correspondences that determine its strategies are themselves "given"—like is like, and that is the end of the matter. As the folk fatalism imbues the foreground accidents with the suggestion of necessity, the folk magic imbues them with the suggestion of the supernaturally motivated; and motivation of whatever kind makes an event seem "necessary," suitable, fitting. The intricate interknitting of all these motifs gives to Hardy's actually magical view of the universe and of human destiny a backing of concrete life, as his evocation of the earth as Cause gives to his vision the grounding of the naturalistic.

The folk magic is, after all, in its strategy of analogy, only a specialization and formalization of the novelist's use of the symbolism of natural detail, a symbolism of which we are constantly aware from beginning to end. Magical interpretation and prediction of events consist in seeing one event or thing as a "mimicry" of another—a present happening, for instance, as a mimicry of some future happening; that is, magic makes a system out of analogies, the correlative forms of things. Poets and novelists do likewise with their symbols. [Poet Robert] Burns's lines: "And my fause luver staw my rose, / But ah! he left the thorn wi' me," use this kind of mimicry, common to poetry and magic. When a thorn of Alec's roses pricks Tess's chin, the occurrence is read as an omen—and omens properly belong to the field of magic; but the difference between this symbol which is an omen, and the very similar symbol in Burns's lines, which acts only reminiscently, is a difference merely of timing—the one "mimics" a seduction which occurs later, the other "mimics" a seduction and its consequences which have already occurred. And there is very little difference, functionally, between Hardy's use of this popular symbol as an *omen* and his symbolic use of natural particulars—the chattering of the birds at dawn after the death of Prince and the iridescence of the coagulated blood, the swollen udders of the cows at Talbothays and the heavy fertilizing mists of the late summer mornings and evenings, the ravaged turnip field on Flintcomb-Ash and the visitation of the polar birds. All of these natural details are either predictive or interpretive or both, and prediction and interpretation of events through analogies are the profession of magic. When a piece of blood-stained butcher paper flies up in the road as Tess enters the gate of the vicarage at Emminster, the occurrence is natural while it is ominous; it is realistically observed, as part of the "given," while it inculcates the magical point of view. Novelistic symbolism *is* magical strategy. In *Tess*, which is through and through symbolic, magic is not only an adaptive specialization of the "folk," but it also determines the reader's response to the most naturalistic detail. Thus, though the story is grounded deeply in a naturalistic premise, Hardy's use of one of the commonest tools of novelists—symbolism—enforces a magical view of life.

THE SUPERNATURAL

Logically accommodated by this view of life is the presentation of supernatural characters. Alec d'Urberville does not appear in his full otherworldly character until late in the book, in the episode of the planting fires, where we see him with pitchfork among flames—and even then the local realism of the planting fires is such as almost to absorb the ghostliness of the apparition. The usual form of his appearance is as a stage villain, complete with curled mustache, checked suit, and cane; and actually it seems a bit easier for the reader to accept him as the Evil Spirit itself, even with a pitchfork, than in his secular accouterments of the villain of melodrama. But Hardy's logic faces its conclusions with superb boldness, as it does in giving Angel Clare his name and his harp and making him a minister's son; if Alec is the Evil One, there will be something queer about his ordinary tastes, and the queerness is shown in his stagy clothes (actually, this melodramatic stereotype is just as valid for a certain period of manners and dress as our own stereotype of the gunman leaning against a lamppost and striking a match against his thumbnail). Alec is the smart aleck of the Book of Job, the one who goes to and fro in the earth and walks up and down in it, the perfectly deracinated one, with his flash and new money and faked name and aggressive ego. If he becomes a religious convert even temporarily it is because he is not really so very much different from Angel (the smart aleck of the Book of Job was also an angel), for extreme implies extreme, and both Angel and Alec are foundered in egoism, the one in idealistic egoism, the other in sensual egoism, and Angel himself is diabolic enough in his prudery. When Alec plays his last frivolous trick on Tess, lying down on one of the slabs in the d'Urberville vaults and springing up at her like an animated corpse, his neuroticism finally wears, not the stagy traditional externals of the Evil Spirit, but the deeply convincing character of insanity—of that human evil which is identifiable with madness. Both Angel and Alec are metaphors of extremes of human behavior, when the human has been cut off from community and has been individualized by intellectual education or by material wealth and traditionless independence.

Between the stridencies of Angel's egoism and Alec's egoism is Tess—with her Sixth Standard training and some anachronistic d'Urberville current in her blood that makes for spiritual exacerbation just as it makes her cheeks paler, "the teeth more regular, the red lips thinner than is usual in a country-bred girl": incapacitated for life by her moral idealism, capacious of life through her sensualism. When, after Alec's evilly absurd trick, she bends down to whisper at the opening of the vaults, "Why am I on the wrong side of this door?" her words construct all the hopelessness of her cultural impasse. But her stabbing of Alec is her heroic return through the "door" into the folk fold, the fold of nature and instinct, the anonymous community. If both Alec and Angel are spiritually impotent in their separate ways, Tess is finally creative by the only measure of creativeness that this particular novelistic universe holds, the measure of the instinctive and the natural. Her gesture is the traditional gesture of the revenge of instinct, by which she joins an innumerable company of folk heroines who stabbed and were hanged—the spectacular but still anonymous and common gesture of common circumstances and common responses, which we, as habitual readers of newspaper crime headlines, find, unthinkingly, so shocking to our delicate notions of what is "natural." That she goes, in her wandering at the end, to Stonehenge, is an inevitable symbolic going—as all going and doing are symbolic—for it is here that the earthiness of her state is best recognized, by the monoliths of Stonehenge, and that the human dignity of her last gesture has the most austere recognition, by the ritual sacrifices that have been made on these stones.

Hardy's Use of Nature Reveals His Narrative Flaws

David Lodge

David Lodge is an English critic and novelist and the author of several novels, including The British Museum Is Falling Down *and* Ginger, You're Barny. *In the following article, Lodge argues that while nature imagery in* Tess *seems to indicate that Tess is at one with nature, his narrative commentary suggests otherwise. This inconsistency distracts from the art of the novel, Lodge concludes.*

Hardy's undertaking to defend Tess as a pure woman by emphasizing her kinship with Nature perpetually drew him towards the Romantic view of Nature as a reservoir of benevolent impulses, a view which one side of his mind rejected as falsely sentimental. Many Victorian writers, struggling to reconcile the view of Nature inherited from the Romantics with the discoveries of Darwinian [from Charles Darwin] biology, exhibit the same conflict, but it is particularly noticeable in Hardy.

A passage which seems especially revealing in this respect is that which describes Tess's gloomy nocturnal rambling in the weeks following her seduction, where she is explicitly shown entertaining the pathetic fallacy, and her mistake explicitly pointed out by the author:

> On these lonely hills and dales her quiescent glide was of a piece with the element she moved in. Her flexuous and stealthy figure became an integral part of the scene. At times her whimsical fancy would intensify natural processes around her till they seemed a part of her own story. Rather they became a part of it; for the world is only a psychological phenomenon, and what they seemed they were. The midnight airs and gusts, moaning among the tightly-wrapped buds and bark of the winter twigs, were formulae of bitter re-

proach. A wet day was the expression of irremediable grief at
her weakness in the mind of some vague ethical being whom
she could not class definitely as the God of her childhood,
and could not comprehend as any other.

But this encompassment of her own characterization, based
on shreds of convention, peopled by phantoms and voices
antipathetic to her, was a sorry and mistaken creation of
Tess's fancy—a cloud of moral hobgoblins by which she was
terrified without reason. It was they that were out of harmony
with the actual world, not she. Walking among the sleeping
birds in the hedges, watching the skipping rabbits on a
moonlit warren, or standing under a pheasant-laden bough,
she looked upon herself as a figure of Guilt intruding into the
haunts of Innocence. But all the while she was making a distinction where there was no difference. Feeling herself in antagonism she was quite in accord. She had been made to
break an accepted social law, but no law known to the environment in which she fancied herself such an anomaly.

Here we have two paragraphs, one describing Tess's subjective
state of mind, and the second describing the objective "reality."
We are meant to feel that the second cancels out the first, that
"guilt" is a fabrication of social convention, something unknown to the natural order which Tess distorts by projecting
her own feelings into it. It seems to me, however, that there is
an unresolved conflict in Hardy's rhetoric here. Not only are
the "midnight airs and gusts, moaning amongst the tightly
wrapped buds and bark of the winter twigs" images of sorrow
and remorse too moving and impressive to be easily over-
thrown by the rational arguments of the second paragraph; we
are explicitly told that "the world is only a psychological [i.e.
subjective] phenomenon," in which case the view expressed in
the second paragraph is as "subjective" as that expressed in
the first, and has no greater validity. If Tess felt herself in antagonism she *was* in antagonism. But in fact "antagonism" is a
clumsy formulation of the experience so delicately expressed
in the first paragraph. That Nature should present its most
sombre aspect to Tess when she is most desolate is, in a way,
evidence of how deeply she is "in accord" with Nature. There
are many other places in the book where Hardy "intensifies
natural processes around Tess till they seem part of her story,"
without suggesting that she is deceiving herself, e.g.—

She was wretched—O so wretched. . . . The evening sun was
now ugly to her, like a great inflamed wound in the sky. Only
a solitary cracked-voiced reed-sparrow greeted her from the
bushes by the river, in a sad, machine-made tone, resembling
that of a past friend whose friendship she had outworn.

There is further ambiguity about the "actual world" of nature with which, according to the author, Tess is in accord without realizing it. Is she mistaken in thinking herself guilty, or Nature innocent, or both? Elsewhere in the novel it is true to say that when Nature is not presented through Tess's consciousness, it is neither innocent nor guilty, but neutral; neither sympathetic nor hostile, but indifferent. When Tess and her young brother are driving their father's cart through the night, "the cold pulses" of the stars "were beating in serene dissociation from these two wisps of human life." The birds and rabbits skip happily and heedlessly

Not a Great Writer

When we are considering Hardy's power of creating men and women . . . we become most conscious of the profound differences that distinguish him from his peers. We look back at a number of these characters and ask ourselves what it is that we remember them for. We recall their passions. We remember how deeply they have loved each other and often with what tragic results. . . . But we do not remember how they have loved. We do not remember how they talked and changed and got to know each other, finely, gradually, from step to step and from stage to stage. Their relationship is not composed of those intellectual apprehensions and subtleties of perception which seem so slight yet are so profound. In all the books love is one of the great facts that mould human life. But it is a catastrophe; it happens suddenly and overwhelmingly, and there is little to be said about it. The talk between the lovers when it is not passionate is practical or philosophic, as though the discharge of their daily duties left them with more desire to question life and its purpose than to investigate each other's sensibilities. Even if it were in their power to analyse their emotions, life is too stirring to give them time. They need all their strength to deal with the downright blows, the freakish ingenuity, the gradually increasing malignity of fate. They have none to spend upon the subtleties and delicacies of the human comedy.

Thus there comes a time when we can say with certainty that we shall not find in Hardy some of the qualities that have given us most delight in the works of other novelists.

Virginia Woolf, "The Novels of Thomas Hardy," in *The Second Common Reader*. New York: Harcourt Brace, 1932.

round the defenceless Tess at her seduction; and the Valley of the Var has no interest in her arrival. Is not Tess more human in preferring a sad but sympathetic Nature to a gay but indifferent one?

Hardy, then, here undermines our trust in the reliability of Tess's response to Nature, which is his own chief rhetorical device for defending her character and interesting our sympathies on her behalf. Without this winterpiece, which the author dismisses as a delusion of Tess's mind, we would lose the significance of Tess's renewal of energy in the spring which urges her towards the Valley of the Var and her "rally":

> A particularly fine spring came round, and the stir of germination was almost audible in the buds; it moved her, as it moved the wild animals, and made her passionate to go. . . . Some spirit within her rose automatically as the sap in the twigs. It was unexpended youth, surging up anew after its temporary check, and bringing with it hope, and the invincible instinct towards self-delight.

But of course the instinct is, in the event, vincible . . . and so we return to the basic contradiction pointed out by [literary critic] Ian Gregor, of which he says: "the small measure in which this confusion, which is central to the theme of the novel, really decreases its artistic compulsion, suggests how effectively the latter is protected against the raids of philosophic speculation." I find myself in some disagreement with this verdict for, as I have tried to show, the confusion is not merely in the abstractable philosophical content of the novel, but inextricably woven into its verbal texture.

[Critic] John Holloway has also noted the duality in Hardy's view of life, and defends him on the grounds that "Hardy has a good deal more to say about the quality of events, the feel of them, than about their course." In a novel, however, no representation of reality can be entirely neutral and objective: it must always be mediated through the consciousness of a character or a narrator. The reader must be able to identify this consciousness, and he does so by responding correctly to the language used. The case against Hardy is that he regularly confuses the reader with a number of conflicting linguistic clues. I shall offer one further illustration of the difficulties of interpretation and evaluation this creates.

In Chapter XIX there is a description of Tess walking in the garden of Talbothays Dairy at dusk:

It was a typical summer evening in June, the atmosphere being in such delicate equilibrium and so transmissive that inanimate objects seemed endowed with two or three senses, if not five. There was no distinction between the near and the far, and an auditor felt close to everything within the horizon. The soundlessness impressed her as a positive entity rather than as the mere negation of noise. It was broken by the strumming of strings.

Tess had heard those notes in the attic above her head. Dim, flattened, constrained by their confinement, they had never appeared to her as now, when they wandered in the still air with a stark quality like that of nudity. To speak absolutely, both instrument and execution were poor; but the relative is all, and as she listened Tess, like a fascinated bird, could not leave the spot. Far from leaving she drew up towards the performer, keeping behind the hedge that he might not guess her presence.

The outskirt of the garden in which Tess found herself had been left uncultivated for some years, and was now damp and rank with juicy grass which sent up mists of pollen at a touch; and with tall blooming weeds emitting offensive smells—weeds whose red and yellow and purple hues formed a polychrome as dazzling as that of cultivated flowers. She went stealthily as a cat through this profusion of growth, gathering cuckoo-spittle on her skirts, cracking snails that were underfoot, staining her hands with thistle-milk and slug-slime, and rubbing off upon her naked arms sticky blights which, though snow-white on the apple-tree trunks, made madder stains on her skin; thus she drew quite near to Clare, still unobserved of him.

Tess was conscious of neither time nor space. The exaltation which she had described as being producible at will by gazing at a star, came now without any determination of hers; she undulated upon the thin notes of the second-hand harp, and their harmonies passed like breezes through her, bringing tears into her eyes. The floating pollen seemed to be his notes made visible, and the dampness of the garden the weeping of the garden's sensibility. Though near nightfall, the rank-smelling weed-flowers glowed as if they would not close for intentness, and the waves of colour mixed with the waves of sound.

I am particularly concerned, here, with the meaning of the third of these four paragraphs, of which John Holloway has said, "This passage is almost uniquely significant for understanding Hardy. The scene is centrally important in *Tess* itself, and among the most intensely realized the author ever wrote." . . .

To me, the remarkable feature of the paragraph, the source of that "unexpected" equality noted by Mr. Holloway, is that in it the conventional response (of revulsion) invited by concepts like "rank," "offensive smells," "spittle," "snails," "slug-slime," "blights," "stains," etc., is insistently checked by an alternative note which runs through the language, a note of celebration of the brimming fertility of the weeds and the keen sensations they afford. This note is conveyed cognitively in words like "juicy," "mists," "blooming," "dazzling," "profusion"; but it also seems to invade the very language in which the conventionally noisome features of the garden are described. There is a kind of sensuous relish, enforced by the rhythm and alliteration, in the thickening consonants of "cuckoo-spittle," "cracking snails," "thistle-milk," and "slug-slime," which is strangely disarming. A linguist would no doubt regard this argument with suspicion; and it is indeed difficult to give a satisfactory account of verbal effects at this depth. But it must be conceded, I think, that if Hardy intended to stress the *unpleasantness* of the garden, he has gone about his task in a curious way.

Even if the reader recoils from the overgrown garden, there is no suggestion that Tess does. She seems at home in it. She moves through the undergrowth "as stealthily as a cat"—an image which, taken in conjunction with the "fascinated bird" simile in the preceding paragraph, catches up the whole web of natural imagery and reference applied to Tess throughout the novel. The participles *gathering, cracking, staining,* and *rubbing off,* of which the grammatical subject is Tess, as well as imitating her physical movement, stress the active nature of her relationship with the natural world. She seems to collaborate in the transformation of her appearance rather than suffer it. . . .

This interpretation becomes more attractive as soon as we consider the differences between the characters of Tess and Clare, the nature of their relationship, and the part played in its development by the natural environment.

Talbothays is situated in "the Valley of the great Dairies, the valley in which milk and butter grew to rankness," "a green trough of sappiness and humidity." When Clare, returning from a visit to his parents,

> began to descend from the upland to the fat, alluvial soil below, the atmosphere grew heavier; the languid perfume of the summer fruits, the mists, the hay, the flowers, formed therein a vast pool of odour which, at this hour, seemed to make the very bees and butterflies drowsy. . . . He could not help being

aware that to come here, as now, after an experience of home-
life, affected him like throwing off splints and bandages.

The "note" of the valley is, then, one of fertility running almost to excess, indulging the senses, relaxing or suspending
conscience. In this environment humanity is helpless in the
grip of its instincts and passions. In Tess, conscience and
scruple are inexorably overwhelmed by "'the appetite for
joy' which pervades all creation"; and "Amid the oozing fatness and warm ferments of the Froom Vale, at a season
when the rush of juices could almost be heard below the
hiss of fertilization, it was impossible that the most fanciful
love should not grow passionate." There is a relishing of
sound in the language of these passages which associates
them with the "weeds" paragraph.

The "fanciful love" is, of course, Clare's, and the qualification is important. "He loved her dearly, though perhaps
rather ideally and fancifully than with the impassioned thoroughness of her feeling for him." We are told of Clare's father that "to the aesthetic, sensuous, pagan pleasure in natural life and lush womanhood which his son Angel had
lately been experiencing in Var Vale, his temper would have
been antipathetic in a high degree." In fact this pleasure is
always something of an affectation on the part of Angel, a
kind of compensation for his exclusion from the busy civilized world of the nineteenth century, a swaggering adver-
tisement of his free-thinking. His reaction to Tess's confession later in the novel demonstrates conclusively that his
temperament is essentially puritanical and conventional—
"'My position—is this,' he said abruptly. 'I thought—any
man would have thought—that by giving up all ambition to
win a wife with social standing, with fortune, with knowledge of the world, I should secure rustic innocence as surely
as I should secure pink cheeks;. . . .'" From the beginning it
is clear that Tess is an assurance to Angel that the "aesthetic,
sensuous, pagan pleasure" of the Var valley is respectable
and innocent in the conventional moral sense. "'What a
fresh and virginal daughter of Nature that milkmaid is,'" he
thinks on first taking notice of Tess. Later, "It seemed natural enough to him now that Tess was again in sight to
choose a mate from unconstrained Nature, and not from the
abodes of Art," and yet he is constantly trying to dignify the
homely pastoral in which he is involved—the country wooing
of a milkmaid—by Art, by talking to her about "pastoral life in

ancient Greece" and calling her by classical names, thus demonstrating that he is not really prepared to accept a mate from unconstrained Nature.

The paragraph describing the overgrown garden might be aptly described as an image of "unconstrained nature." It reminds us of the wild, exuberant, anarchic life that flourishes on the dark underside, as it were, of the cultivated fertility of the valley. Does it not reveal something similar about Tess— that she is "a child of Nature" in a sense that extends far beneath the surface of conventional pastoral prettiness and innocence which that phrase denotes to Angel? Let us examine one item in the description in the light of this interpretation:

> . . . rubbing off upon her naked arms sticky blights which, though snow-white on the apple-tree trunks, made madder stains on her skin.

There is clearly an antithesis here between *snow-white* and *madder*, which is given a cautionary or ironic note by the *though*: i.e., though the blights looked pretty and pure on the tree trunks, they produced a red stain on Tess's naked arms when she rubbed against them. *Snow-white* has associations with chastity and virginity. Red (the colour of some of the weed-flowers earlier in the passage) is the colour of passion, and of blood (with which Tess is ominously splashed at the death of the horse, Prince.) And it is difficult to avoid seeing an Empsonian [relating to poet and critic Sir William Empson] ambiguity in the word *madder*—no doubt many readers have, like myself, taken it to be the comparative form of *mad* on first reading, not the name of a vegetable dye. Thus, although one cannot paraphrase meanings so delicately hinted, I submit that the force of this connection between Tess and the natural world is to suggest the "mad" passionate, non-ethical quality of her sensibility.

This dimension of Tess's character makes her life a peculiarly vulnerable one. It lays her open to seduction by d'Urberville—it is important to realize that she is seduced, not raped; and Tess herself is frightened by the intensity of her passion for Angel:

> Her idolatry of this man was such that she herself almost feared it to be ill-omened. She was conscious of the notion expressed by Friar Lawrence: "These violent delights have violent ends." It might be too desperate for human conditions —too rank, too wild, too deadly.

Yet this vulnerability is something we value in Tess. Ironically it is valued by Clare, without his understanding the reason. He is intrigued and impressed by a quality of imaginative thoughtfulness in her speech which he finds surprising in one so young. "Not guessing the cause," comments Hardy, "there was nothing to remind him that experience is as to intensity, and not as to duration. Tess's passing corporeal blight had been her mental harvest." The play on "blight" and "harvest" here, and the metaphorical application of "rank" and "wild" to Tess's passion in my previous quotation, give further encouragement for a reading of the weeds paragraph as a metaphorical expression of Tess's character. . . .

One's reading of the whole paragraph depends very importantly on whether we take the observing consciousness to be primarily Tess's or primarily the author's. But it is very difficult to decide. The information that the garden had been uncultivated for some years, and the comparison of the weeds with cultivated flowers must come from the narrator. But the lines "damp and rank with juicy grass which sent up mists of pollen at a touch; and with tall blooming weeds emitting offensive smells" seem to describe directly the sensations of Tess; it is surely her touch which sends up the mists of pollen, and her eye which observes them.

The opening sentence of the succeeding paragraph seems to favour a view of the weeds paragraph as authorial, for we are told that Tess was conscious of neither time nor space. Yet reading on, we discover that this state of mind did not exclude observation of the physical attributes of the overgrown garden, but included and transfigured them through the pathetic fallacy: "The floating pollen seemed to be his notes made visible, and the dampness of the garden the weeping of the garden's sensibility. Though near nightfall, the rank-smelling weed-flowers glowed as if they would not close for intentness, and the waves of colour mixed with the waves of sound." This introduces quite a new view of the overgrown garden—an image neither of soiling nastiness nor of wild, unconstrained nature, but of beauty perceived through emotion. This can be seen as an extension of either of the two former views (but scarcely of both), depending on our evaluation of Tess's ecstatic response to the music. The poor quality of the instrument and the musician is twice remarked upon. Are we, then, to see Tess as "taken in" by Clare's musicianship, as she is taken in subsequently by his declaration of love? In which case we are meant to "see through" the pathetic fallacy at the end of the passage, to feel that the transfiguration of the, in fact, noisome weeds is an index of her delusion. Or is her ecstatic experience to be valued independently of the music which provokes it? Is her inclusion in this experience of the homely and conventionally unaesthetic particulars of her environment a moving testimony to an "undissociated sensibility" to which nothing natural is alien? Hardy's aside "but the relative is all" (like his earlier comment that "the world is a psychological phenomenon") does not help us to decide.

There is no end to such questions, because Hardy presents us with such a confusion of linguistic clues. What an astonishing diversity of tone is displayed in the four paragraphs! The first shows Hardy in his most ponderous, generalizing authorial style, with which Tess herself is incongruously saddled in the penultimate sentence. The second paragraph establishes her keen sensuous response to the music with the striking image of nudity, and the simile of the fascinated bird, but qualifies this effect by some slightly patronizing reference to the absolute and the relative. The third paragraph assaults us with an astonishing *tour de force* of concretely realized sensation. And the final paragraph leads us into a world of romantic synaesthesia. It is as if Hardy, bewildered by the rich possibilities of the scene, has confused himself and us by trying to follow out all of them at the same time.

Hardy is a peculiarly difficult novelist to assess because his vices are almost inextricably entangled with his virtues. We value him for the breadth, variety, and unexpectedness of his vision; his mind plays over his characters and their actions so as to place them in constantly shifting perspectives which are never without interest. The nature of the undertaking provokes comparison with the very greatest writers, but it creates enormous demands upon his control of his verbal medium which he does not consistently satisfy. That is, he shows himself capable, on different occasions, of realizing all the effects for which he was striving, but he cannot be relied upon to do so. Sometimes his various "voices" subtly make their points and modulate smoothly into one another; at other times they seem to be interrupting and quarrelling between themselves. Alternately dazzled by his sublimity and exasperated by his bathos, false notes, confusions, and contradictions, we are, while reading him, tantalized by a sense of greatness not quite achieved.

Humanist Philosophy in *Tess*

Jagdish Chandra Dave

Jagdish Chandra Dave is the author of *The Human Predicament in Hardy's Novels*, from which the following selection is excerpted. In it, Dave contends that Hardy is advocating a humanist position throughout the novel that is exemplified in the characters of Tess and Angel. Tess has an almost instinctive humanism: Abandoned by the Christian god, Tess nevertheless acts in the best interest of others, even sacrificing herself to do so.

Tess of the d'Urbervilles embodies Hardy's anguish of the social absurd most disturbingly. Tess stands for an individual human being left alone in the midst of the society which scorns her misfortune. Moving about in a state of undesired pregnancy after dusk amid the hills and dales adjoining her village "She had no fear of the shadows; her sole idea seemed to be to shun mankind—or rather that cold accretion called the world, which, so terrible in the mass, is so unformidable, even pitiable, in its units." That "cold accretion," the organized mass of individuals, is the social world which instead of becoming a structure of fortification to a poor pitiable "unit" against the neutral ways of the natural universe, turns stifling and hostile. Tess fears it, not the shadows, the self-projected spirits and invisible princes of the world. Compared to the cold cruelty of conventional society the spectacle of life in the primal harmony of Nature is positively refreshing, for hate is unknown there. . . .

Hardy's own ethics, dissociated from theology and metaphysics, worked out in response to the secular human need to be happy, is represented . . . in Angel and Tess.

Angel welcomed the new light of scientific thought which exploded the very foundation of obscurantist dogma. That is what alienated him from the vicarage, his father's residence, which symbolizes the traditional Christianity: "Its transcendental aspirations—still unconsciously based on the geocentric view of things, a zenithal paradise, a nadiral hell—were as foreign to his own as if they had been the dreams of people on another planet." But Angel is not an impatient revolutionary wishing to do away with the past altogether or disown Christianity entirely. He merely aims at moderate reform. He tells his father:

> I love the Church as one loves a parent. I shall always have the warmest affection for her. There is no institution for whose history I have a deeper admiration; but I cannot honestly be ordained her minister, as my brothers are, while she refuses to liberate her mind from an untenable redemptive theolatry.

And again:

> My whole instinct in matters of religion is towards reconstruction; to quote your favourite Epistle to the Hebrews, "*the removing of those things that are shaken, as of things that are made, that those things which cannot be shaken may remain.*"

Both Angel and his father are at one as far as the moral aspect of Christianity is concerned. Hardy comments:

> Now, as always, Clare's father was sanguine as a child; and though the younger could not accept his parent's narrow dogma he revered his practice, and recognized the hero under the pietist. [. . .] Indeed, despite his own heterodoxy, Angel often felt that he was nearer to his father on the human side than was either of his brethren.

OLD AND NEW FAITH

In the father and the son are contrasted the essential old faith and the new humanism. The new is significantly the child, not the enemy, of the old. When the father, grieved at the son's atheistic doctrines, said: "What is the good of your mother and me economizing and stinting ourselves to give you a University education, if it is not to be used for the honour and glory of God?" the son's simple answer is "Why, that it may be used for the honour and glory of man, father." This is the clear pronouncement of humanism.

Angel has recognized the human situation in the world without God. But he is still a growing humanist who has yet to reorganize his moral thought on a new basis. He is not aware that his "good morals" include also, and largely, crude customary notions of virtue which are as worthless as the dogma he has disavowed. That is why Tess's confession of her seduction by Alec entirely changes his view of her although he himself could not claim to have immaculate chastity. Her tears and mortification could not melt to pity the hard-heartedness which he showed to her. Hardy comments:

> With all his attempted independence of judgment this advanced and well-meaning young man, a sample product of the last five-and-twenty years, was yet the slave to custom and conventionality when surprised back into his early teachings. No prophet had told him, and he was not prophet enough to tell himself, that essentially this young wife of his was as deserving of the praise of king Lemuel as any other woman endowed with the same dislike of evil, her moral value having to be reckoned not by achievement but by tendency.

But Angel undergoes in Brazil, away from Tess, home and the moral clime of his country, a process of purification.

> During this time of absence he had mentally aged a dozen years. What arrested him now as of value in life was less its beauty than its pathos. Having long discredited the old systems of mysticism, he now began to discredit the old appraisements of morality. He thought they wanted readjusting. Who was the moral man? Still more pertinently, who was the moral woman? The beauty or ugliness of a character lay not only in its achievements, but in its aims and impulses; its history lay, not among things done, but among things willed. . . .

TRUE VIRTUE DEFINED

Now in the character of chastened Angel are combined his own earlier atheism with the essential Christian spirit of love, compassion and forgiveness, the combination that Hardy stood for. The pagan freedom and generosity are not inconsistent with the Christian virtue. In fact, they alone can make it truly a virtue as distinguished from mere conformity to the customary norms. Angel becomes at the end an accomplished humanist of Hardy's persuasion and treats Tess with extreme kindness and love in their hide-out before she is arrested for murdering Alec.

Tess is not learned in books like Angel. Yet her humanism right from the start is more authentic than his. She tells Angel that before she killed Alec in a fit of anger, "I never could bear to hurt a fly or a worm, and the sight of a bird in a cage used often to make me cry." The awareness of sorrow pervading all sentient existence makes her compassionate towards all creatures. The religion of loving-kindness and morality of the Sermon on the Mount . . . are to be founded

on an uncompromising atheism and an absolute regard for human responsibility.
Her second surrender to Alec is to be viewed in the light of the above. When on the eve of their departure from Marlott, the children are singing to care-worn Tess,

> Here we suffer grief and pain,
> Here we meet to part again;
> In Heaven we part no more.

Tess turned from them, and went to the window again. Darkness had now fallen without, but she put her face to the pane as though to peer into the gloom. It was really to hide her tears. If she could only believe what the children were singing; if she were only sure, how different all would now be; how confidently she would leave them to Providence and their future kingdom! But, in default of that, it behoved her to do something; to be their Providence; for to Tess, as to not a few millions of others, there was ghastly satire in the poet's lines—

> Not in utter nakedness
> But trailing clouds of glory do we come.

To her and her like, birth itself was an ordeal of degrading personal compulsion, whose gratuitousness nothing in the result seemed to justify, and at best could only palliate.

A GREATER SACRIFICE

The children are singing inside the home with continued regard on "the centre of the flickering fire," it is the eve of their expulsion, and outside there is darkness and uncertainty. A little reflection will reveal that apart from Tess's inward conflict and determination to help the young ones stated clearly in the passage quoted above, every detail in the situation has a symbolic meaning. Tess's ancestral home suggests the home our forefathers have built us with the light and fire of faith inside, the fire which seems to be at its last flicker near the end of the nineteenth century. Children, or those who are intellectually so, or poets like [William] Wordsworth, can still sing songs of hope in Heaven. But for the adult and enlightened like Tess there is no meaning in such babble and bubbles of religious emotion, for they look courageously to the darkness outside, darkness beyond life and behind the universe. The life of man has no meaning, the world has no reasons for its being there, and philosophy is a futile attempt at inventing meaning and reasons which exist nowhere in the roll and rush of time. But suffering is genuine so long as it lasts, and something must be done to mitigate it. It is the common bond that binds all humanity and all beings so to say into a fraternal community. Self-sacrifice for others' good, therefore, is meaningful even in the irrational universe. It constitutes a value in itself and has not to depend for its justification on any Super-mundane Being or hope for personal happiness after death. The darkness of metaphysical nihilism itself has to become the light and guide for our moral endeavour. Man has to learn to be man's Providence in the absence of any other Providence. Tess's loyalty to Angel, even if it brought sorrow and starvation only to her individual self, might perhaps be vindicated as a virtue. But it was no longer a virtue since it brought misery to her whole family. She could not abdicate her responsibility to them for the luxury of her "dumb and vacant fidelity" to Angel whose return seemed to her now impossible. Therefore, the humanist in her led her to surrender to Alec and sacrifice herself thus. She is spiritually dead after this, and continues to live merely for her family. Angel, when he returns, is quick enough to perceive "that his original Tess had spiritually ceased to recognize the body before him as hers—allowing it to drift, like a corpse upon the current, in a direction dissociated from its living will."

RECONSTRUCTING MORALITY

All this largely resembles atheistic existentialist ethics. The central problem in it, as also in Hardy's philosophy, is the reconstruction of morals on a new basis. [Literary critic] C.I. Glicksberg observes: "[French novelist and existentialist Jean-Paul] Sartre's tragic humanism rests on an atheistic premise. Since God does not exist, man must give up the futile search for standards outside himself. There is nothing disheartening in the discovery that man is alone in the universe." The same applies literally to Hardy's tragic humanism as well. Hardy has not attempted, has not thought worth attempting, the phenomenological description of the world. But his perception of the metaphysical and social absurd is unmistakable. In a well-considered response to it Tess offers herself as a sacrifice on the altar of duty. Hardy is a pessimist, if he is one at all, in the existentialist sense, and he is certainly not a determinist, for a determinist can logically claim to have no ethics. "I ought," as [philosopher Immanuel] Kant contended, implies "I can," and the determinist, being unable to accept the power and freedom of will, can prescribe no "oughts" or ideals of ethics. Both the existentialists and Hardy regard freedom, limited though it is, as an inescapable characteristic of man.

There is, yet, a vital difference between Hardy's ethics as we derive it from his novels, and atheistic existentialist ethics as represented chiefly and popularly by Jean-Paul Sartre. Sanity, compassion and renunciation, which make the one as gentle as it is bold, are a singular want in the other. The human being in existentialism means basically an individual's "being-for-itself" (pour-soi), and anything that curbs or curtails its spontaneous volitional flow, even when it seems criminal towards his fellow-beings, is to be dismissed as a taboo, for other men, to him, are little more than objects. All ideals, and moral injunctions, consequently, are no more than inhibitions, and society is a vast mass of irreconcilable freedoms seeking to encroach upon one another, exploit one another for self-fulfilment, and united together only in the irremediable relationship of hatred. As [existentialism scholar] James Collins observes:

> Sartre is especially insistent on the impossibility of overcoming hatred through motives of love, personal respect or belief in God. It is just as natural to desire a loving, interpersonal, human community as to desire to become God—and just as impossible of fulfilment.

There can be no sound humanism without recognizing the ideal of love to unite a "for-itself" with other "for-themselves," to moderate his freedom by renunciation for their welfare. That is precisely what an existentialist cannot enjoin if he has to maintain his basic position, and must illogically advocate if he has to be a humanist. The paradox is irresoluble. It weakens existentialist humanism.

Hardy would agree that hate, the result of the ruthless pursuit of self-interest, characterizes the human community in the actual, else why should the coarse appropriate the fine, the wrong man the woman, the wrong woman the man, the phenomenon which no analytical philosophy can explain satisfactorily to our sense of moral order or harmony? But he does not confuse the actual with the ideal, does not think that this hate cannot be overcome. A perfect community interpenetrated by the spirit of selfless love may be inconceivable. But there are sure to be exceptional individuals, who lay down even their lives for the gratuitous love for others. It is within our power to become, or at least to try to become, such men. Hardy's great characters are not self-seeking brutes liberated from all restraint that theology had imposed on man previously. They are like Tess and with loving-kindness they freely choose to appoint themselves as Providence to guard their unfortunate fellows against sorrow so far as possible, even at the cost of self-delight. The disappearance of God binds them all the more steadfastly to humanity but does not lead to the perverted love of self.

CHAPTER 3

Men in *Tess*

The Character of Alec

H.M. Daleski

H.M. Daleski is a prolific critic whose books include
works on D.H. Lawrence, Charles Dickens, and
Joseph Conrad. In the following selection, Daleski
analyzes the character of Alec, claiming that Tess
begins to turn against and hate Alec because she is
afraid of her own sexuality.

Alec d'Urberville is the last of the rakes in the novels, and
Hardy takes the figure to extremes. Whereas the rakes who
precede him, such as Troy [from Hardy's *Far from the Maddening Crowd*] or Fitzpiers [in *The Woodlanders*], possess a
compelling sexual magnetism, this is magnified in Alec to
blatant sexual power, to a drive for mastery and conquest.
He is a "handsome, horsey young buck," and when Tess first
meets him, his sensuality is manifest in his "full lips . . . red
and smooth" and in his eyes. But what is most distinctive
about him is the force he exudes: "Despite the touches of bar-
barism in his contours, there was a singular force in the gen-
tleman's face, and in his bold rolling eye." "Despite" seems to
be the wrong word here; it is precisely Alec's capacity for un-
restraint, a readiness to let go, come what may, that is one of
the conditions of his singular force. He has a "reputation as a
reckless gallant and heart-breaker," and both his reckless-
ness and his force are concretized in the manner in which he
drives Tess in his smart gig on the way to Trantridge.

The ride also figures the sort of relationship Alec wishes
to impose on Tess. When they reach a long, steep descent
and he begins to drive recklessly down it, it seems at first as
if this is merely an expression of his natural flamboyance
and high spirits: "Why, Tess," he says in response to her request that he slow down, "it isn't a brave bouncing girl like
you who asks that? Why, I always go down at full gallop.
There's nothing like it for raising your spirits." The ride, we
see, is a replay of Troy's sword exercise, in which Alec both

Excerpted from *Thomas Hardy and Paradoxes of Love*, by H.M. Daleski. Copyright ©
1997 by the Curators of The University of Missouri. Reprinted by permission of University of Missouri Press. (Footnotes in the original have been omitted from this
reprint.)

tests Tess and shows his own skill. It soon becomes apparent, moreover, that there is more to his driving than a raising of spirits. For one thing, the horse is a mare; and as the dashing young male urges it into a full gallop, the description of the pell-mell drive downhill, with "the figure of the horse rising and falling in undulations before them," takes on insistent sexual overtones. These are still further emphasized when, before the end of the drive, Tess is reduced to desperation and "her large eyes [stare] at him like those of a wild animal." For another, the mare is no ordinary horse but "has killed one chap" and has also "nearly killed" Alec himself on another occasion. Consequently, the drive downhill also becomes a question of Alec's pitting himself against the horse, of his testing his power over it and demonstrating his mastery: "If any living man," he tells Tess, "can manage this horse I can:—I won't say any living man can do it—but if such has the power, I am he." The scene becomes more and more uncannily evocative of the episode in [D.H. Lawrence's novel] *Women in Love* in which Gerald Crich subdues the mare at the railway crossing in the presence of Gudrun Brangwen.

Once Alec has loosened the rein and given the mare its head, what he demonstrates in the ride is the degree to which he can impel it to a wild abandon while he himself coolly—if high-spiritedly—retains control of it. The motif of abandon, so sharply concretized in the mare's plunge downhill, is of central importance in Tess's story, as becomes clear subsequently. But as the gig speeds along, alternative possibilities in the development of her relationship with Alec are nicely juxtaposed.

With the horse knowing well "the reckless performance expected of her," they go shooting wildly down the first hill they come to. In her alarm Tess clings to Alec, and it is only when they safely reach the bottom of the hill that she disengages herself and realizes how completely she has given way to impulse: "She had not considered what she had been doing; whether he were man or woman, stick or stone, in her involuntary hold on him." She expresses her anger, with "her face on fire," but it is not only anger that her fiery face suggests. Alec then "[loosens] rein" again, they go rocking down a second hill, and the only way she can persuade him to stop is by agreeing to let him kiss her. She implores him not to claim his due, but he is "inexorable" and gives her "the kiss of mastery," a phrase that draws together related significances of the drive. When they come to "yet another descent" and Alec ties to extort another kiss, Tess defeats him by allowing her hat to blow off and refusing to get back into the gig after she has retrieved it. Her eyes light up "in defiant triumph" at this point. In the power struggle that is joined between them on this ride, Tess shows her capacity for resistance, and, demonstrating that she can take a stand, she walks the rest of the way.

Tess, however, is not always prepared to walk, and her behavior on another occasion is premonitory of what is to come. One night she is drawn into a fierce quarrel with the Queen of Diamonds when suddenly Alec appears on horse back. He urges her to jump onto the horse, and, seeing a chance of "triumphing" over "the contentious revellers," Tess (in a vivid phrase) "[abandons] herself to her impulse" and "[scrambles] into the saddle behind him." This episode immediately precedes the crucial scene in The Chase and, being a striking instance of Tess's capacity for abandon in relation to Alec, would strongly seem to suggest that what follows is a seduction. But, as is well known, critical opinion is sharply divided on this issue. Among others, [literary critic] Tony Tanner, in perhaps the best study of the novel, repeatedly refers to what happens as a rape. [Critic] Leon Waldorf, among others, thinks the evidence points to a seduction. [Critic] Ian Gregor, straddling these views, says that the "encounter" in The Chase is "both a seduction *and* a rape." In the murk in which Hardy encompasses the episode, only one thing seems clear: the opposed critical views are the result of a thoroughgoing ambiguity in the presentation of this crucial event in Tess's life, as a number of critics have noted. The real issue is what lies behind the ambiguity and how it is constituted.

It seems to me that the ambiguity is the culminating instance in the novels of divergent views between the seer and the see-er. From the moment Alec returns to the sleeping Tess, the tones of the seer are very much in evidence. It is not for nothing that the prophet Elijah is at once invoked: lamenting the absence of Tess's "guardian angel," the narrator says, "Perhaps, like that other god of whom the ironical Tishbite spoke, he was talking, or he was pursuing, or he was in a journey, or he was sleeping and not to be awaked." And in the page or so before the novelist drops the curtain on what eventuates in The Chase, the seer unremittingly evokes a rape. Suggestions of violation are strong: Tess is a "white muslin figure" that seems to be swallowed up in the "darkness" and the "'blackness" that "[rule] everywhere around"; the epitome of innocence, hers is a "beautiful feminine tissue" that is "practically blank as snow as yet," but it is "doomed" to have "traced" on it "a coarse pattern." Indeed, it is asked why the coarse should (in a key term) *appropriate* the "finer thus." And though the seer declares that "to visit the sins of the fathers upon the children" is a "morality" that should be "scorned," he nonetheless adds this dimension to what he is clearly presenting as a rape: "One may, indeed, admit the possibility of a retribution lurking in the present catastrophe. Doubtless some of Tess d'Urberville's mailed ancestors rollicking home from a fray had dealt the same measure even more ruthlessly towards peasant girls of their time." Furthermore, the description of Alec's return to Tess ended, in the first edition of the novel, with the following passage (subsequently omitted from later editions):

> Already at that hour some sons of the forest were stirring, and striking lights in not very distant cottages; good and sincere hearts among them, patterns of honesty and devotion and chivalry. And powerful horses were stamping in their stalls, ready to be let out into the morning air. But no dart or thread of intelligence inspired these men to harness and mount, or gave them by any means the least inkling that their sister was in the hands of the spoiler; and they did not come that way.

This pronouncement is echoed in the edition we now have in the comments of a villager on Tess's baby: "A little more than persuading had to do wi' the coming o't, I reckon. There were they that heard a sobbing one night last year in The Chase; and it mid ha' gone hard wi' a certain party if folks had come along."

There are a number of reasons for the seer's insistence on rape. In the preceding novels he has time and again presented passion as being destructive; in making the act of passion a rape, a brutal and violent destruction of Tess's innocence, he gives a final turn of the screw to this motif. Second, the seer has shown consistent animosity to the rake figures in the novels, subjecting them to a continuing vein of hostile commentary; in presenting Alec as a rapist, he pushes animus against the type as far as it can go, exposing what might be regarded as a compelling sexual attractiveness as consisting in blatant force, a ruthless exercise in power: it is this that Alec's mastery of a horse is represented as becoming when transposed to a woman. Third, and most important, that Tess should be raped and not seduced is essential to the seer's presentation of her as a victim. Taking on the mantle of prophet to a stiff-necked people, he thus casts his "pure woman" in their teeth.

Given the quoted pronouncements of the seer in the scene in The Chase, it is astonishing that, outside the novel, Hardy should so nonchalantly have lent himself to a very different view of the matter. Writing to a correspondent at about the time the novel appeared in book form, he said: "Clarc's char acter [in the serial version] suffers owing to a mock marriage having been substituted for a seduction pure & simple of the original MS—which I did for the sake of the Young Girl. The true reading will be restored in the volumes." Perhaps this statement is not so astonishing after all, for it is to "a seduction pure & simple" that the novel, of course, also points.

ALEC IS NOT A RAPIST

Prior to the scene in The Chase, Alec is certainly not presented as a rapist. For "near three mortal months" he has pursued Tess and, though riled by her "trifling" with him, has accepted her rebuffs. On the night in question he tells her that he loves her and asks whether he may not treat her "as a lover." He also reveals that on that day he has presented her father with "a new cob" to replace Prince and given toys to the children of the family. Most revealing of all, when he leaves Tess to try to find out where they are, he is compassionate to her: "'Nights grow chilly in September. Let me see.' He pulled off a light overcoat that he had worn, and put it round her tenderly. 'That's it—now you'll feel warmer,' he continued. 'Now, my pretty, rest there; I shall soon be back again.'" It is the see-er, the meticulous recorder of concretized action, who quietly presents this little vignette and who makes us see that neither Alec's concern nor his tenderness casts him as a rapist. He makes us see too that Tess is not quite the innocent victim she is purported to be by the seer. We are told that she has "never quite got over her original mistrust" of Alec, but she nonetheless falls asleep when he leaves her, just as she let herself sleep when Prince is killed. She is also remarkably compliant as the episode unfolds, When Alec asks her whether he has often offended her "by love-making," she replies "sometimes"; and when he presses her as to whether it has been "every time," she is "silent." She does not "perceive" that Alec has "not taken the Trantridge track." When he asks whether he may treat her as a lover, she does not say no, and musters no more than a "murmured 'I don't know—I wish—how can I say yes or no when—,'" allowing him to "[settle] the matter by clasping his arm round her as he [desires]" while she expresses "no further negative."

Nor is Tess's behavior after the night in The Chase easily reconcilable with her having been raped. One can conceive how a novelist such as Hardy could lead us to imagine that a woman might fall in love with her rapist; but Tess, both before and after the crucial episode, states that she does not love Alec. However, though the episode takes place on "a Saturday in September," it is not until "a Sunday morning in late October" that she leaves him, having freely lived as his mistress, that is, for about a month after it. This period is crucial: it is once again Tess who freely chooses to do what she does. It is as a responsible tragic agent, not helpless victim, that in this most important of matters, we must once again view her.

LOATHING ALEC

What is most striking about Tess's feeling when she leaves Alec is her self-loathing, her self-disgust. When he catches up with her, she says to him: "if I had ever sincerely loved you, if I loved you still, I should not so loathe and hate myself for my weaknesses I do now! . . . My eyes were dazed by you for a little, and that was all." And when her mother tells her she should have gotten Alec to marry her, she reflects bitterly how little her mother knows the feeling toward him that has made her "detest herself":

> She had never wholly cared for him, she did not at all care for him now. She had dreaded him, winced before him, succumbed to adroit advantages he took of her helplessness; then, temporarily blinded by his ardent manners, had been stirred to confused surrender awhile: had suddenly despised and disliked him, and had run away. That was all. Hate him she did not quite; but he was dust and ashes to her, and even for her name's sake she scarcely wished to marry him.

Tess loathes and hates herself so strongly, it appears, because she now despises and dislikes Alec. Her feeling for him fills her with revulsion from her own body as well as his. She herself, as well as Alec, is reduced to "dust and ashes" because she now feels that what she gave Alec was a body devoid of the love that could truly animate it—and that could alone redeem it in her eyes. Though her eyes were "dazed" and "blinded" by him, they see clearly enough now. Her surrender, moreover, was "confused," we are to understand, because it was not wholehearted, because (as she later maintains) there was not at least a strong physical passion to move her to it: when Alec begins to pursue her for a second time and says, "Here I am, my love, as in the old times!" she answers: "Not as then—never as then—'tis different! . . . And there was never warmth with me!"

The see-er indicates what cold bodies are like in the superb scene of the parting of Alec and Tess, which encapsulates all the elements in their relationship:

> Alec d'Urberville removed his cigar, bent towards her, and said—"You are not going to turn away like that, dear? Come!"

> "If you wish," she answered indifferently. "See how you've mastered me!"

> She thereupon turned round and lifted her face to his, and remained like a marble term while he imprinted a kiss upon her cheek—half perfunctorily, half as if zest had not yet quite died out. Her eyes vaguely rested upon the remotest trees in the lane while the kiss was given, as though she were nearly unconscious of what he did.

Tess's coldness here may seem to support [Hardy critic] John Bayley's contention that "Hardy conveys with a total delicacy and accuracy the repulsion this unawakened girl feels for the sexuality of Alec." Bayley further maintains that to suggest that Tess's "real appetite and affiliation are with Alec" is to "vulgarise" a "sex dogma . . . from [novelist] D.H. Lawrence, and [impose it] upon a situation to which it has not the smallest relevance." It seems to me, however, that we have been made to see that Tess has not only been awakened sexually by Alec but that she has been touched more deeply by him than she is willing to admit: she may have been "blinded" by his "ardent manners," but she has also been "stirred" into surrender, and that implies a passionate response on her part. Moreover, when she says she would not so loathe herself if she had "ever sincerely loved" him or if she loved him "still," that ambiguously suggests that she has had some genuine feeling for him. Since Bayley refers to Lawrence, it is well to note what Lawrence himself has to say about the relationship: "Alec d'Urberville could reach some of the real sources of the female in a woman, and draw from them. . . . And, as a woman instinctively knows, such men are rare. Therefore they have a power over a woman. They draw from the depth of her being."

However we may choose to explain the nature of the power Alec exerts over Tess, it seems indisputable that she is overcome by it. She may speak ironically in the farewell scene, but we must assume that she in fact "succumbed" to Alec because he "mastered" her. If such mastery implies a subduing of her spirit, that in turn implies (in the end) the marble flesh that she now indifferently yields to him, as if she is "nearly unconscious" of him—and the taste of dust and ashes. Not that she alone is cold. Her marble is matched by the coldness that underlies his will to dominance, for coolness, as we have seen in the episode with the mare, is a condition of such mastery. But like Tess in regard to herself, Alec too is not fully aware of what impels him. His drive for mastery is more complex than he realizes, and he is a more complex character than is generally recognized, for the drive coexists with the authentic tenderness toward Tess that he exhibits on occasion and with the sincere concern for her that is evident even after she has run away from him: "And if certain circumstances should arise—you understand—" he says to her, "in which, you are in the least need, the least difficulty, send me one line, and you shall have by return whatever you require." There is in Alec an unacknowledged force of feeling that will later draw him back to Tess, scattering his evangelical pretensions like so much chaff in the wind, even if at this stage of the relationship, he is, for the most part, more concerned with his own needs.

The needs of the body alone are soon sated, though Alec is slower in reaching satiety than Tess, and the narrator beautifully captures the last flicker of his half-extinguished desire as he kisses Tess "half perfunctorily, half as if zest [has] not yet quite died out." Since, his desire is fueled not by love but by a will to mastery, it is fired by opposition, not submission; and it is Tess's very yielding that dooms it to extinction, as is suggested by a passage in the manuscript (italicized in the following quotation) that the novelist inserted into his description of Alec's kiss and then deleted (possibly because it was too specific about the length of Tess's stay with him as his mistress): "he imprinted a kiss upon her cheek—half perfunctorily, half as if zest had not yet quite died out *for only a month had elapsed since she had ceased to defend herself against him.*"

Angel Clare

Virginia R. Hyman

In the following article, Virginia R. Hyman argues
that Angel Clare is a sympathetic character who re-
acts to Tess in a realistic way. Angel is merely a human, with human flaws, who bravely changes his
attitudes throughout the novel to come to a deeper
understanding of love and spirituality. Virginia R.
Hyman has written the book *Ethical Perspective in
the Novels of Thomas Hardy,* from which this selection is excerpted.

Most readers see Angel Clare as being placed as far ahead of
Tess as Alec is behind her, for Angel Clare is presented as
the "intellectual" who holds "modern views." And since we
believe that the intellectual stage is the highest level of
achievement, we cannot understand why Hardy makes his
hero so unattractive. . . .

While we assume that the intellectual stage comes at the
end of human development, we must remember that for
Hardy, as for the other ethical evolutionists, the intellectual
stage was a median one. It was preceded by the theological
or mythic stage and followed by the sociological one. It was
this last stage where the egotism of the earlier stages was finally overcome and the latent altruistic potential fully developed. This is the hierarchy that Hardy endorses when he
says that the "higher passions" must be "ranked above the
inferior," the "intellectual above the animal," and that above
the intellectual were the "moral tendencies.". . .

ANGEL AND TESS

It is necessary to note the way Hardy characterizes Angel,
for it is the very reverse of his characterization of Tess. Tess
is created by positive strokes; her development is one of accretion. Angel, on the other hand, is developed by negative

effects; his development is marked by losses rather than gains. Similarly, while Angel thinks of himself as clearly superior to those "less advanced" than he, Hardy takes great pains to show the similarity between him and others, especially his brothers and his parents. This negative shading is important to note, for it prevents us from being taken in either by Angel's view of himself or by Tess's idealized view of him. Furthermore, it accounts, in part, for our negative reactions to him.

What Hardy makes clear is that, at the time they meet, both Angel and Tess are at the same level of development, although they have arrived at it by different routes. They both believe themselves more free of the past than they actually are; they both try to escape from their sense of drift by fixing on the abstract and the idealized. When the two meet, they have arrived at the same median, or metaphysical, stage, although coming from different directions. When they separate, they go in different directions. While we have seen how Tess's direction is charted by her devotion to Angel, we have yet to see how Angel's direction is affected by Tess. . . .

ANGEL AND HIS FAMILY

Although he is vaguely conscious of the similarities between himself and his father, he prides himself on the differences which make his father "the last of the old Low Church sort" and himself a "sample product of the last five-and-twenty years." He considers himself more liberated and therefore more advanced than his father. . . . He refuses to accept ordination, for, he asserts "although [he] loves the Church as one loves a parent" he cannot be her minister "while she refuses to liberate her mind from an untenable redemptive theolatry." His father believes that a university education should be used for "the honour and glory of God"; Angel insists that "it may be used for the honour and glory of man." His "whole instinct in matters of religion is towards reconstruction." Angel considers his own attitudes more socially oriented and more positive than his father's. In quoting from his father's favorite Epistle to the Hebrews to define his position, he betrays, however, its negative side: "the removing of those things that are shaken as of things that are made, that those things which cannot be shaken may remain." Although he is critical of the negative aspect of his father's Paulinism [belief in the theology of the epistles], he is unaware of the negative aspect of his own more liberated and advanced views. . . .

ANGEL'S OTHERWORLDLINESS

Angel prides himself on his lack of concern with his material future. In his "unworldliness" he sees himself "nearer to his father than was either of his brethren." What he cannot see is that this "unworldliness" has its negative, as well as its positive side. He is aware that his father's unworldliness "had necessitated Angel's getting a living as a farmer, and would probably keep his brothers in the position of poor parsons for the term of their activities." But he can see nothing wrong with his father's abiding by his principles, even when it means the sacrifice of their future. He himself will repeat his father's actions with even more dire consequences. By insisting on his own principles, he will place Tess in even more straitened circumstances than those in which his father's unworldliness had placed himself and his brothers.

The one positive feature that distinguishes Angel from both his father and his brothers is his openness to the future. When he first appears as a traveler in the company of his brothers, the difference between them is marked. The very amorphousness of his appearance implies that, unlike his brothers, Angel has not yet achieved the stage of development that will eventually characterize him. . . .

ANGEL'S REACTIONS TO TESS

The appearance of Tess, however, seems to cause a strange kind of intellectual relapse in Angel. For while he had begun to look at the people around him as individuals, he sees Tess as a type, indeed, almost as an archetype. He prefers to think of her as a goddess or as a symbol of Rustic Innocence. He prefers to see her at dawn, for then her features are changed from being "simply feminine" to "those of a divinity." He prefers to call her Artemis or Demeter rather than Tess, and although he is amazed at her "advanced views," he dismisses their significance, preferring to believe that "such a daughter of the soil could only have caught up the sentiment by rote."

It would seem, then, that Tess's initial effect on Angel is to cause him to regress intellectually to the position of a romantic. But what seems like regression on the intellectual level can be seen as development on the emotional one. That is, Tess's presence evokes feelings in Angel that he had previously been unaware of. And these feelings are shown to develop in a way that corresponds to what Hardy saw as the necessary steps toward altruism. They are remarkable in that they also reveal some degree of psychological insight. And because Angel's feelings are essentially reactions to Tess, who is also the focus of our own attention, they tell us something about our own reactions as readers. . . .

As Angel's desires become more clearly defined, his view of Tess shifts. He shifts from the "pagan" to the romantic view: He sees her as Rustic Innocence, as symbol of an idealized Nature he knows does not exist. From having been a fructifying mother figure she becomes the unattainable Beloved. And when she proves, after all, attainable, and destroys his illusions of her innocence, "the new-sprung child of nature" becomes the "belated seedling of an effete aristocracy." This negative reaction is as subjective, or, as we would say, as adolescent, as Angel's earlier idealization. It is as much a defense against his accepting her objective reality as his earlier attitudes had been.

Although it is easy for us as modern readers to discount Angel's reactions to Tess's confession as conventional Victorian prudishness based on a false and outmoded social standard, his reactions do, in fact, have a good deal of psychological validity. Angel's desire for purity, which had led him to reject the complexities of the church and the social world, now lead him to reject the complex and impure Tess. And just as his earlier desire for purity had been shown in its negative aspect as a delusive attempt to escape from the past, so his rejection of Tess is also an attempt to escape from complexities that threaten to enmesh him. He finds in Tess the very things he had attempted to escape from. . . .

Tess, then, who had first called forth Angel's desires for bliss and upon whom he had projected his need for purity and escape, now forces him to confront himself. Having admired "spotlessness," "though he himself could lay no claim to it," and "hating impurity," though it is part of himself, in loving Tess, Angel had been able to have the best of both worlds. But if Tess is as impure as he himself, there is no other world and hence no escape from having to confront the aspect of imperfection in himself. Angel cannot place his faith and hope in God, as his parents do, nor project them onto another, as Tess does. There is nothing in objective reality different from what is in himself. And what is now within himself is only part of what had been there formerly, for his confrontation with Tess has effectively destroyed his belief and his hope that he can find something "out there" that will correspond to his needs and his desires. In a way not unlike Hardy's method in *The Hand of Ethelberta*, by telling her story, Tess has defictionalized Angel's world.

Although Angel rejects Tess, he begins to accept, almost immediately, the new knowledge she brings. His dream that the "pure" Tess had died and that he is burying her reflects his unconscious acceptance of this new knowledge. He acts more like one bereaved than one who is morally outraged, and indeed he is bereft; for in burying the "pure" Tess he is burying that part of himself which the real Tess had destroyed. And the world which he awakens to is bleak, for it is devoid of the projections of the ego. . . .

CHANGES IN ATTITUDE

For Hardy, then, Angel's new perspective, his ability to "look on his own existence as an outsider," is a step in the right direction. He returns to life "like a ghost" and looks back at the pattern of his life from another perspective. And memory, which usually abstracts and idealizes, now defictionalizes. With the ideal Tess dead and his own sense of self diminished, the real Tess comes to life in a way Angel had discounted when he had been with her: she returns in his memory as a very real physical being: "He almost talked to her in his anger, as if she had been in the room. And then her cooing voice, plaintive in expostulation, disturbed the darkness, the velvet touch of her lips passed over his brow, and he could distinguish in the air the warmth of her breath.". . .

Further distance in space as well as in time finally gives him a clearer perspective. . . . In Brazil, Angel comes to a "more just" conclusion:

> During this time of absence he had mentally aged a dozen years. What arrested him now as of value in life was less its beauty than its pathos. Having long discredited the old systems of mysticism, he now began to discredit the old appraisements of morality. He thought they wanted readjusting. Who was the moral man? Still more pertinently, who was the moral woman? The beauty or ugliness of a character lay not only in its achievements, but in its aims and impulses; its true history lay not among things done, but among things willed.

How, then, about Tess?

Viewing her in these lights, a regret for his hasty judgement began to oppress him. Did he reject her eternally, or did he not? He could no longer say he would always reject her, and not to say that was in spirit to accept her now.

Having proceeded this far, he needs, as Tess had needed, another human being to carry him farther. Luckily, he encounters a stranger with the kind of "large-mindedness" Tess had expected from Angel. The large-mindedness of the stranger is, in turn, the result of "sojourn[ing] in many more lands and among many more peoples than Angel." He tries to give Angel the benefit of his experience. He espouses the kind of moral relativity held by the Positivists:

> To his cosmopolitan mind such deviations from the social norm, so immense to domesticity, were no more than are the irregularities of vale and mountain chain to the whole terrestrial curve. He viewed the matter in quite a different light from Angel, thought that what Tess had been was of no importance beside what she would be, and plainly told Clare that he was wrong in coming away from her.

Significantly, the stranger's words do not take effect until after he dies. They are "sublimed by his death" and then "influence Clare more than all the reasoned ethics of the philosophers." Just as the memory of Tess had affected Angel more than her presence, so the memory of the dead traveler exerts a greater influence than his presence. At this stage, experience alone is not enough. For the kind of advance Angel is to make, reflection upon experience is also required.

By contrasting himself with one more advanced than he, Angel sees his own "parochialism" and is "ashamed." He also begins to see the inconsistency between his "objective" view of history and his subjective judgment of Tess. He had preferred the relative freedom of pagan Hellenism to the "inherited creed of mysticism" of Christianity. Yet he had chosen to judge Tess by the values of that very creed of mysticism. He had despised Mercy Chant for embodying "the curiously unnatural sacrifice of humanity to mysticism." Now that judgment must devolve upon himself.

Having reached this stage of what Hardy would term the "devolution" of his moral arrogance, Angel moves from consideration of historical parallels and contrasts to more personal memories. He remembers Izz Huett's selfless admission of Tess's love. He remembers how Tess had appeared on the day of the wedding, "how her eyes had lingered upon him; how she had hung upon his words as if they were a god's!" This memory is followed by his recollection of her utter faith in him and reliance upon him "during the terrible evening over the hearth." As a result of a reconsideration of these experiences, "from being her critic he grew to be her advocate." He recognizes his "mistake" in "allowing himself to be influenced by general principles to the disregard of the particular instance." Later, he wonders why he had not judged her "constructively, by the will, rather than by the deed." This shift of emphasis from general principles to specific instances, and to reliance upon motive rather than act, is clear evidence that Angel is coming closer to what [French philosopher Auguste] Comte would have called the "sociological" stage of development. His experience with Tess and his reconsideration of that experience has brought him to the point where he can, unlike Tess, move into the future. . . .

CLARE'S PROGRESSION

Clare returns as if from the grave to confront the echoes of his former life. When his mother tries to console him in the same terms that he had formerly used, he rejects the reassurance, seeing new meanings in the old terms: "'Child of the soil'! Well, we are all children of the soil." Later, he accepts the justice of the charges that Tess makes against him in her angry letter. And the Tess Angel finds is a kind of mocking echo of his former judgment of her. She is neither the Tess he had first imagined nor the one he had later remembered and forgiven. She is now in fact what he had formerly accused her of being: she is Alec's mistress by choice. She is, besides, a shadow of her former self: "Tess had spiritually ceased to recognize the body before him as hers, allowing it to drift, like a corpse upon the current, in a direction disassociated from its living will." Angel accepts the change and assumes the responsibility for it: "Ah! I am at fault," is all that he says.

When Tess catches up to Clare and tells him that she has murdered Alec, his response is quite different from his earlier reaction of horror when he had first suspected her of destructiveness:

> It was very terrible if true; if a temporary hallucination, sad. But, anyhow, here was this deserted wife of his, this passionately fond woman, clinging to him without suspicion that he

would be anything to her but a protector. He saw that for him to be otherwise was not, in her mind, within the region of the possible.

Rather than responding with horror or imposing moral judgment, Angel sees through the act to the motive behind it, and through the motive to its essence: Tess's utter dependence on him. His initial judgment is twice qualified: "it was very terrible if true; if a hallucination, sad." But he shifts from *his* judgment to perception of *her* need with the words, "but, anyhow," and goes on: "here was this deserted wife of his. . . ." This perception of her utter reliance upon him arouses his own feelings, which are, at last, adequate to the situation: "Tenderness was absolutely dominant in him at last." His vow to protect Tess "whatever [she] may or may not have done" follows and is proved valid by his subsequent actions.

The scene is, of course, a reversal of the earlier one when he had rejected Tess for much less. And the congruity in this scene between Clare's perceptions, feelings, words, and actions are in direct contrast to the earlier discordance between his perceptions and his actions. For earlier, Angel had perceived that "Tess was no insignificant creature to be toyed with and dismissed, but a woman living her precious life—a life which possesses as great a dimension as the life of the mightiest." And later, on the morning of their marriage, he had promised himself "never to neglect her, or hurt her, or even to forget to consider her." This perception and vow, however, had been unrelated to his feelings and detached from the real Tess. Now the words are felt as well as thought, and acted upon after they are spoken. At last Angel's feelings have caught up to his perceptions; his original perception of Tess's needs and fears as being different from his own is validated by his experience, and he accepts her on her own terms. Recognizing his own part in bringing her to her present position, he assumes full responsibility. His sympathetic response to Tess proves he has "passed the test" and reached the altruist position. He has become in fact what Tess had seen in him from the first. . . . In Angel, Tess's wishes are at last realized.

But in fulfilling Tess's expectations, in responding to her needs and desires rather than to his own, in becoming the altruist Tess had assumed he was, Angel experiences no sense of satisfaction. For, in reaching the altruist level he has transcended Tess; he is at a greater distance from her than ever before. And while Tess is happy with their union, Angel is essentially alone, for while he now responds to her, Tess is incapable of responding to him—to his new attitudes, feelings, and perspectives. We see the distance between the two in Clare's relation to her all during the last episode. . . .

CLARE'S PERSPECTIVE MATURES THE READER'S

The position that the reader is left in at the end of the novel coincides with Clare's perspective and his reactions. We know, as Tess does only partially, that the demands she makes both of the world and of Angel are incapable of full realization, and though we sympathize with her, we can no longer identify with her. We accept her death as both inevitable and painful—as a loss of something that is also within us, for she embodies those things we also cherish: the desire for happiness, the belief in absolute purity and goodness, and the need to project these desires onto something outside of ourselves—a God, a Utopia, or a Beloved. The depth and strength of her commitment to these values give her the stature of a tragic heroine. We see, with Angel, "the full depth of her devotion, its single-mindedness, its meekness; what long suffering it guaranteed, what honesty, what good faith." But these very values, which make her a latter-day Saint Theresa, disqualify her for life. We see, with Angel, that her faith, hope, and charity are too simple and "single-minded" for the secular world. The world is not heaven, nor human beings gods. We know, as we have known from the beginning, that Tess's Angel does not exist. The real Angel is very much less than what Tess imagines him to be. He has been defined more by what he is *not* than by what he is, by what he rejects rather than by what he accepts. By contrast to Tess, he is diminished in stature. That diminution is, however, a matter of choice, and is compensated for by more subtle responses and broader perspectives. As the projections of the ego are withdrawn, more of objective reality is allowed to enter. As the self becomes invisible, the pattern is allowed to emerge. Thus, as Tess, with all that she embodies, is distanced from us and placed in the past, we are left, like Angel, with a sense of a diminished self confronting a diminished world.

Tess Is a Victim of Men

T.R. Wright

Critic T.R. Wright is a lecturer in English at the University of Newcastle upon Tyne in England. In the following selection, Wright argues that the men of the novel—Alec, Angel, and even the narrator—doom Tess. He cites various passages to prove that Tess is incapable of standing on her own and expressing her own sense of self and that the male characters in the novel are unable to listen or care about her individuality.

The erotic world of Hardy's fiction has so far been found to contain little in the way of purity. It will not therefore be surprising that the subtitle, "A Pure Woman," added to the first edition of *Tess* but absent from the expurgated, more conventionally decent serial version of the novel, was part of a wider campaign to challenge such contemporary values which involved Hardy in a number of late manuscript alterations. Many critics have balked at attributing purity to a fornicator, unmarried mother, religious sceptic, adulterer and murderess, but Hardy renewed the attack in the preface to the "fifth" edition, accusing such critics of

> an inability to associate the idea of the subtitle adjective with any but the artificial and derivative meaning which has resulted to it from the ordinances of civilization. They ignore the meaning of the word in Nature, together with all aesthetic claims upon it, not to mention the spiritual interpretation afforded by the finest side of their own Christianity.

Tess, in other words, is purely natural and purely woman (the essence of the feminine), pure in beauty and in her motives. Hardy conceded ... that she lost "a certain purity in her last fall," in returning to Alec, but insisted nevertheless that she retained her "innate purity" in spite of her traumatic sexual experiences.

Hardy's preface claims that the novel says "something more in fiction than had been said" before, giving expression to "tacit opinion" rather than "the merely vocal formulae of

Excerpted from *Hardy and the Erotic*, by T.R. Wright. Copyright © T.R. Wright 1989. Reprinted with permission from Macmillan Ltd. (References in the original have been omitted in this reprint.)

society," embodying "views of life prevalent at the end of the nineteenth century." He is clearly aware of the "potentially subversive" nature of entering "areas of experience hitherto fenced off because of the explosive material apprehended as buried there." He continues, as we shall see, to write indirectly rather than openly about subconscious drives only beginning to be recognised, "the necessary laws of loving" as outlined by [psychoanalyst Sigmund] Freud. But in presenting Tess as a victim of male splitting of women (Angel idealising and Alec debasing her) and of a perpetual and inescapable struggle between nature and civilisation, Hardy points to similar phenomena as those described more "scientifically" by Freud.

At the height of the controversy over his "Tessism" Hardy defined his understanding of tragedy in these terms, as "the WORTHY encompassed by the INEVITABLE." The novel portrays not only Tess but also her fellow-milkmaids, all infatuated with Angel Clare, as victims of irresistible drives common to their whole sex and race:

> They writhed feverishly under the oppressiveness of an emotion thrust on them by Nature's law—an emotion which they had neither expected nor desired. . . . The differences which distinguished them as individuals were abstracted by this passion, and each was but portion of one organism called sex. . . . The full recognition of the futility of their infatuation, from a social point of view; its purposeless beginning; its self-bounded outlook; its lack of everything to justify its existence in the eye of civilization (while lacking nothing in the eye of Nature); the one fact that it did exist, ecstasizing them to a killing joy; all this imparted to them a resignation, a dignity, which a practical and sordid expectation of winning him as a husband would have destroyed.

It is a paragraph which virtually summarises the novel, encapsulating Tess's tragic and passionate struggle to reconcile the demands of nature and civilisation.

THE OBJECT OF DESIRE

Tess, of course, is more the object than the subject of desire, a victim, of male visions that sexual "succulence" of which contemporary critics complained. Not only in the eyes of the characters but in those of the narrator, more recent critics have agreed, she is altogether too edible, "an object of the reader's consumption." Readers of this novel more than any other seem to divide along sexual lines, male critics too often repeating the mistakes of the male characters and falling in love with an image of their construction. "Is it not . . . the strong, passionate, impure Tess we understand and love?" asks one disbeliever in her purity. Feminist critics, on the other hand, have found "an unusually overt maleness in the narrative voice":

> Time and again the narrator seeks to enter Tess, through her eyes—"his [eyes] plumbed the ever-varying pupils, with their radiating fibrils of blue, and black, and gray, and violet"— and through her flesh—"as the day wears on its feminine smoothness is scarified by the stubble, and bleeds." The phallic imagery of pricking, piercing and penetration which has been repeatedly noted, serves not only to create an image-chain linking Tess's experiences from the death of Prince to her final penetrative act of retaliation, but also to satisfy the narrator's fascination with the inferiority of her sexuality, and his desire to take possession of her.

At the beginning of the novel the narrator hides behind a few passing "strangers" who "would look long at her in casually passing by, and grow momentarily fascinated by her freshness" to excuse the detail in which he describes Tess's physical charms. He even dwells on her lips when supposedly describing her accent, the characteristic intonation "approximately rendered by the syllable UR":

> The pouted-up deep red mouth to which this syllable was native had hardly as yet settled into its definite shape, and her lower lip had a way of thrusting the middle of her top one upward, when they closed together after a word.

The narrator, then, is at least as interested in the shape of her lips as in the words they utter. He stresses, however, that not only as a subject but as an object, the image she presents is neither coherent or unified:

> Phases of her childhood lurked in her aspect still. As she walked along today, for all her bouncing handsome womanliness, you could sometimes see her twelfth year in her cheeks, or her ninth sparkling from her eyes; and even her fifth would flit over the curves of her mouth now and then.

THE NARRATOR BOTH OBJECTIFIES AND SUBJECTIFIES

The narrator, it needs to be recognised, is interested in Tess as both subject and object. He notices, with male eyes and customary euphemistic circumlocution, the size of her breasts (being accused by contemporaries of indecent directness in this respect). But he notices too the failure of her body to express her feelings. "One day she was pink and flawless; another pale and tragical," he writes of her last days at Marlott before leaving for Talbothays: "When she was pink she was feeling less than when pale; her more perfect beauty accorded with her less elevated mood; her more intense mood with her less perfect beauty." The "dominant scopic regime of the novel" may at times reveal the narrator to be "the speaking subject, the one whose desires structure our view of Tess." But the narrator also claims the right to speak for Tess, to enter her subjective consciousness and its struggle both to express her own feelings and to escape the imprisoning objectification of male desire.

From the passing strangers at the beginning of the novel to the sixteen patient policemen who wait for her to awake at Stonehenge at its end, Tess is the object of the erotic male gaze, which "never innocently alights on its object" but "constructs it in the image, of its own desires." Her body is the pure blank surface on which men inscribe or trace a variety of patterns, from Alec's coarse design to Angel's more ethereal portrait. There is a whole chain of related metaphors involving "the tracing of a pattern, the making of a mark, the carving of a line or sign, and the act of writing," all of which embody a recognition of the way men "write" women, inscribing their deepest needs on this beautiful surface.

It is part of Tess's tragedy that her history is written, her identity formed, by the wrong man. She is first seen by Angel Clare, whose "eyes lighted" on her only at the end of the dance on Marlott Green, just as he has to hurry away. It is left therefore to Alec d'Urberville to construct her in his more brutal fashion. His "bold rolling eye" immediately settles on his pretty cousin at their first meeting, when his forcing of a strawberry through her reluctantly parted lips signals quite clearly his designs upon her. For the moment, however, he is content merely to watch "her pretty and unconscious munching," fascinated by the same physical development which attracted the passing strangers:

> She had an attribute which amounted to a disadvantage just now; and it was this that caused Alec d'Urberville's eyes to rivet themselves upon her. It was a luxuriance of aspect, a fullness of growth, which made her appear more of a woman than she really was.

COVETED BY THE WRONG MAN

The episode ends with the narrator ruminating ominously on her being "doomed to be seen and coveted that day by the wrong man," her destiny decided by an accident of timing.

At their next encounter in the gig, when Alec frightens Tess into holding his waist, bargaining for a kiss as the price for slowing down, it is made even clearer that he is attempting to stamp her with his own desire. She finally agrees to the kiss and he is "on the point of imprinting the desired salute" when she dodges aside. The "kiss of mastery" to which she eventually submits, however, causes her to flush with shame and "unconsciously" to remove "the spot on her cheek that had been touched by his lips." His "imprint" is

---

A VICTIM OF HER SENSUALITY

This is the true tragedy of Tess Durbyfield—not a girl's loss of virginity, or even a woman's murder of a man when goaded past endurance. Only a despairing soul allows itself to be destroyed by someone else, to be subtly led away from its true self, not only by the threats or persuasions of another, but by an inner, unconscious consent more treacherous than the act of any hired lackey. . . . Tess was not only the victim of Fate, Circumstance, a malign progenitor, of shiftless, cowardly or bestial people, she was also the victim of her own strong sensuality, and of an insidious need to immolate herself under the deceptive guise of benefiting others. . . . Tess is alienated from her true self, and the portrait of her may be called that of a human sacrifice. In choosing Stonehenge as the setting for her last hours with Angel, Hardy stressed the sacrificial elements involved, but he looked upon Tess as having been destroyed by "the letter of a law that killeth." I do not think he was fully aware of the significance of his symbolism, of that which he had rightly apprehended with his intuition. As Virginia Woolf says:

> It is as if Hardy himself were not quite aware of what he did, as if his consciousness held more than he could produce, and he left it for his readers to make out his full meaning.

But there is so much beauty in this book, both in the descriptions of the heroine and in those of nature, we are led away from the contemplation of suffering, over and over again. When Hardy is moved by his creation Tess assumes divine proportions; she is enlarged symbolically until she towers above us like one of the great Byzantine Saints or Empresses.

Evelyn Hardy, *Thomas Hardy, A Critical Biography.* London, 1954, pp. 231–235.

clearly felt as a "stain," her reluctance to accept his intimacies being increased as part of the late revision of the manuscript. She had earlier been presented as more naive and trusting, allowing Alec to kiss her four times and showing none of the "fire" with which she now expresses her anger at Alec's trick, nor the "defiant laugh" at the success of her own manoeuvre, losing her hat in order to escape from the gig. Even her anger, however, is portrayed in an erotic light, for it leaves her "face on fire" while the act of opening her mouth to say "no" merely inflames him further by revealing "the red and ivory" within. What Tess says carries little weight against what Alec sees in her.

The most indelible mark inscribed by Alec upon Tess's body, of course, occurs in The Chase. Even his fingers disfigure her pure body and sink "into her as into down." She is once more surrounded by symbols of masculine strength and natural fecundity, "the primeval yews and oaks," their "roosting birds" and their "hopping rabbits and hares." The natural context of this decisive event runs completely contrary to the "civilized" morality which causes an "immeasurable social chasm . . . to divide our heroine's personality" from her earlier innocent self. The narrator asks, without hope of adequate answer,

> Why it was that upon this beautiful feminine tissue, sensitive as gossamer, and practically blank as snow as yet, there should have been traced such a coarse pattern as it was doomed to receive.

THE NARRATOR VIEWS HER AS PURE

Tess herself, for the narrator at least, remains as pure as her skin, for the coarse pattern is not of her design.

What precisely is supposed to have happened in The Chase is left tantalisingly vague and unclear. Tess later reproaches herself for her "weakness," telling Alec that "My eyes were dazed by you for a little," implying at least some willingness and responsibility on her part. It is, in Hardy's terms, a tribute to her beauty that his desire to leave his mark on her remains alive even after possession. He demands a final kiss:

> She thereupon turned and lifted her face to his, and remained like a marble term while he imprinted a kiss upon her cheek half perfunctorily, half as if zest had not yet quite died out.

At this point the manuscript initially continued: "for only a month had elapsed since she had ceased to defend herself against him," which suggests force on his part. But this too is ambiguous, the main point seeming to be that he might have been more "zestful" had the interval been longer. Tess meanwhile rests her eyes "upon the remotest trees. . . as though she were nearly unconscious of what he did." She remains entirely passive, turning her head for him to kiss the other cheek, which feels "damp and smoothly chill as the skin of the mushrooms in the fields around." The narrative consciousness, as so often, identifies with the male point of view, the desiring subject, even to the feel of her cheeks. But Tess remains pure, associated with sculpted artefacts and other objects of natural beauty.

When Tess confesses to her mother, in a passage added in 1892, to a "confused surrender" to the "adroit advantages he took of her helplessness," having been "blinded by his ardent manners" but then having "suddenly despised and disliked him," her complicity in her downfall seems clear enough. Her mother, however, draws a similar conclusion to the narrator (even if her theology is different): "'Tis nater, after all, and what do please God!" One of the field-women confuses her "surrender" still further in another 1892 addition: "A little more than persuading had to do wi' the coming o't." Whatever the "truth" of the matter—and Hardy himself seems never finally to have decided—the narrative continues to stress Tess's oneness with nature throughout. Her guilty conscience, which makes her see the rain as nature weeping over her folly, is seen to be a "mistaken creation" of her fancy, not an integral part of her consciousness. It is a cultural product, an intertextual artefact, "based on shreds of convention, peopled by phantoms and voices antipathetic to her":

> It was they that were out of harmony with the actual world, not she. Walking among the sleeping birds in the hedges, watching the skipping rabbits on a moonlit warren, or standing under a pheasant-laden bough, she looked upon herself as a figure of Guilt intruding into the haunts of Innocence. But all the while she was making a distinction where there was no difference. Feeling herself in antagonism she was quite in accord. She had been made to break an accepted social law, but no law known to the environment in which she fancied herself such an anomaly.

Tess herself, misled by social conventions, fails to recognise the extent to which her actions have been "purely" natural.

This oneness with nature is presented as a particularly female characteristic, part of Tess's being "purely" woman. In binding the corn during harvest, the narrator insists, a woman

> becomes part and parcel of outdoor nature, and is not merely an object set down therein as at ordinary times. A field-man is a personality afield; a field-woman is a portion of the field; she has somehow lost her own margin, imbibed the essence of her surrounding, and assimilated herself with it.

Tess, too, in helping with the harvest, loses her superficial cultural "personality," mingling with the deeper forces of nature as in the sexual act itself. She is depicted "holding the corn in an embrace like that of a lover" while the "feminine smoothness" of her unprotected skin, in one of the phallic images already noted, "becomes scarified by the stubble and bleeds." As she continues to help with the harvest she recovers confidence in her own "innate sensations" as opposed to the "conventional" feelings responsible for her misery. Her beauty as she baptises her dying baby is "immaculate." Her strength and health too survive even its death. For, as she comes to recognise, "the recuperative power which pervades organic nature was surely not denied to maidenhood alone." The return of spring moves her, "as it moved other wild animals," bringing with it a resurgence of the pleasure principle, "the invincible instinct towards self-delight." She travels to Talbothays with renewed vigour which finds expression in the familiar words of the psalms praising all living things upon earth, transformed on her lips into a pagan celebration of the "forces of out-door Nature."

In moving to Talbothays, then, as well as in falling in love there, Tess is seen to be in tune with natural forces deeper than conventional social morality. Her first sight of Angel Clare stirs subliminal memories whose meaning "suddenly flashed upon her," a sense shared more feebly by Clare, who is unable to recall where he met her. The force of this repetition has been likened to Freud's analysis of "hysterical trauma":

> For Freud, the first episode is sexual but not understood as such at the time. The second event is innocuous, but is experienced as a repetition of the first, liberating its traumatic effect.

Angel's Observations

Tess, so innocent of her sexual nature on their first encounter, now experiences a "flood of memory" which her more recent experiences help to explain. Angel, observing her closely at breakfast and discerning in her "a fresh and virginal daughter of Nature," is also transported "into a joyous and unforeseeing past." It is ominous, however, that he should spend so much time observing and "regarding her," forcing her to behave "with the constraint of a domestic animal that perceives itself to be watched." For the scopic drive can be seen to dominate Angel as it dominated Alec, causing him also to create her in the image of his desire.

For a time, though, the two lovers inhabit an Edenic world of unrestrained natural instincts. The garden through which Tess creeps as "stealthily as a cat" to listen "like a fascinated bird" to Angel's harp "had been left uncultivated for some years" and is now "rank with juicy grass which sent up mists of pollen." Her pure limbs are once more marked and stained with entirely natural deposits as she gathers

> cuckoo-spittle on her skirts, cracking snails that were underfoot, staining her hands with thistle-milk and slug-slime, and rubbing off upon her naked arms sticky blights which, though snow-white on the apple-tree trunks, made madder stains on her skin.

"Madder" stains, of course, are bright red, "blood-red" in the manuscript, part of a web of red imagery pervading the novel, indicative of both the beauty and the suffering of nature.

Angel and Tess are seen gradually to converge "under an irresistible law, as surely as two streams in one vale." Isolated in the early hours of the morning, they feel "as if they were Adam and Eve," or even the new Adam in the hour of resurrection with the Magdalen by his side. Tess once again merges with all women to become "a visionary essence of woman—a whole sex condensed into one typical form." She needs no artificial decoration: "diamonds of moisture from the mist" hang from her eyelashes "and drops upon her hair, like seed pearls." She is at her most beautiful in natural settings, as when Angel observes her in the dairy with the sun shining "upon her pink-gowned form and her white curtain-bonnet, and upon her profile, rendering it keen as a cameo cut from the dun background of the cow." The narrative dwells on his response:

> How very lovable her face was to him. . . . And it was in her mouth that this culminated. Eyes almost as deep and speaking he had seen before, and cheeks perhaps as fair; brows as arched, a chin and throat almost as shapely; her mouth he had seen nothing to equal on the face of the earth. To a young man with the least fire in him that little upward lift in the

middle of her red top lip was distracting, infatuating, maddening. It is difficult to tell whether this is Angel's self-justification . . . or the narrator's male sympathy. Either way, Angel spends so much time studying the "curves of those lips" that he can "reproduce them mentally with ease." On this occasion he jumps up from his seat, goes quickly towards "the desire of his eyes" and clasps her in his arms. Tess's response is relatively subdued, toned down in the process of purifying revision. In the manuscript she "panted" and "burst into a succession of quick sobs." In the text as it now stands she merely "sank upon him in her momentary joy, with something like an ecstatic cry." It is altogether more sedate, but still unquestionably sexual.

Tess continues to be seen very much as a part of nature, a warm-blooded animal. When Angel surprises her yawning he sees the "red interior of her mouth as if it had been a snake's," admires the "satin delicacy" of her skin and finds her the embodiment of "pure" and natural sexuality:

> The brim-fulness of her nature breathed from her. It was a moment when a woman's soul is more incarnate than at any other time; when the most spiritual beauty bespeaks itself flesh; and sex takes the outside place in the presentation.

The purity of her incarnate soul does not involve a disembodied spirituality; it is expressed in physical beauty which Angel clearly longs to possess, like the penetrating male sun which he feels

> slanting in by the window upon his back, as he held her tightly to his breast; upon her inclining face, upon the blue veins of her temple, upon her naked arm, and her neck, and into the depths of her hair.

She is purely a natural creature, "warm as a sunned cat," regarding him "as Eve at her second waking might have regarded Adam," while he longs yet again to enter her mysterious depths, to plumb the "deepness" of her "ever-varying pupils."

Their love-making at the dairy continues to be depicted as purely natural. When they skim the milk together he cleans her finger "in nature's way." When they break up the curds, against whose "immaculate whiteness" Tess's hands display "the pinkness of the rose," Angel takes advantage of her sleeves being rolled "far above the elbow" to kiss "the inside vein of her soft arm." And though her arm, like the cheek Alec kissed, feels "as cold and damp . . . as a new-gathered mushroom," her accelerated pulse drives the blood to her "finger-ends, and the cool arms flushed hot." When they drive together to deliver the milk to the railway station, where she stands with "rainy face and hair" in "the suspended attitude of a friendly leopard at pause," bewildered by the advance of civilisation and asking innocent questions about the sophisticated Londoners, she proves her love in the way that comes naturally to her:

> She clasped his neck, and for the first time Clare learnt what an impassioned woman's kisses were like upon the lips of one whom she loved with all her heart and soul, as Tess loved him.

Her consent to marriage comes as a final victory for those natural instincts which obey the pleasure principle above all else, that "'appetite for joy' which pervades all creation," and nature is seen once more to triumph over civilisation.

It becomes increasingly evident, however, that Angel's love for Tess is not so purely natural. The narrator, even at the height of their passion, calls him "more spiritual than animal,"

> less Byronic than Shelleyan; could love desperately, but with a love more especially inclined to be imaginative and ethereal; it was a fastidious emotion which could jealously guard the loved one against his very self.

THE NATURE OF ANGEL'S LOVE

"Imaginative and ethereal" are alterations in the manuscript which emphasise the erotic, cultural, unnatural elements in Angel's affection. Again, even as he hastens the preparations for their wedding, it is stressed that he loves her "rather ideally and fancifully than with the impassioned thoroughness of her feeling for him." Tess herself, kneeling in her room before their departure from Talbothays, is frightened both by the depth of her own love and by the unreal elements she detects in his idealisation of her, "for she you love is not my real self, but one in my image; the one I might have been." After their marriage but before her confession he is depicted as "looking at her silently" as if "deciding on the true construction of a difficult passage," unsure how to read her properly. And when she finally tells him of the events at Trantridge he positively denies that she is the same person as the one he had loved: "You were one person; now you are another." He sees her for the first time "without irradiation" while she tries to convince him that it "is in your own mind what you are angry at."

What Tess's confession does, in fact, is "to call into question the absolute authority of his gaze to construct her" and to disclose "the gap separating desire from the ostensible object." He is forced to acknowledge that her eyes could be "seeing another world" to his. She continues to look "absolutely pure" and to love him with perfect Pauline [relating to the theology of the epistles] charity. But she is no longer the ideal image he had painted her, "so pure, so sweet, so virginal," the word "virginal" being new in the first edition. The "fifth" edition drives home Hardy's increased anger at his character's (and his critics') refusal to accept the purely natural:

> *Some might risk the odd paradox that with more animalism he would have been the nobler man. We do not say it.* Yet Clare's love was *doubtless* ethereal to a fault, imaginative to impracticality. With these natures, corporeal presence is something less appealing than corporeal absence, the latter creating an ideal presence that conveniently drops the defects of the real. . . . The figurative phrase was true: she was another woman than the one who had excited his desire.

That Angel's rejection of the "un-intact" Tess involves a repression of his own "natural" feelings emerges quite clearly in the sleepwalking sequence in which he manages to "negotiate the dangers of turbulent water," symbolising the raging passions beneath, in order to lay her body in the empty stone coffin of the Abbey-church, thereby burying the sexual instinct. Tess derives some comfort from the fact that his subconscious self still recognises her as his wife, but is frightened to wake him lest his "daytime aversion" recur. She refrains the following morning from telling him of the escapade since it would only "anger him . . . to know that he had instinctively manifested a fondness for her of which his commonsense did not approve." Angel accordingly remains firmly under the control of his unbending conscience or superego, which occupies "the remote depths of his constitution" as "a hard logical deposit, like a vein of metal in a soft loam." Completely out of touch with his deeper feelings, he allows her to return to her parents "and hardly knew that he loved her still." Her "cooing voice" continues to haunt his night-time consciousness, when he can still feel "the velvet touch of her lips" and "the warmth of her breath." He insists to his parents that she is indeed spotless while the terms of his proposal to Izz Huett show that he is already beginning to question the values of the "civilization" that would condemn it, "Western civilization that is."

REDUCED TO AN OBJECT

Angel's departure exposes Tess once more to the dangers of the male-dominated world in which she is reduced to an erotic and economic object. Nature now reveals its harsh side in the form of the wounded pheasants, so "unmannerly" treated by the hunters, whom she puts out of their misery. In comparison with these, she realises, her own suffering appears slight, "based on nothing more tragic than a sense of condemnation under an arbitrary law of society which had no foundation in Nature." She resolves nevertheless to reduce her attractiveness as an object of male lust, clipping her eyebrows and covering her face with a handkerchief. Even the landscape she traverses, however, is sexualised, "bosomed with semi-globular tumuli." Flintcomb-Ash itself is covered with "myriads of loose white flints in bulbous, cusped, and phallic shapes" at which Marian shrieks with laughter while Tess remains "severely obtuse."

Try as she may to resist and to repress her sexuality, Tess cannot escape her role as an object of erotic fascination. When she stumbles on Alec at his preaching she observes the "electric" effect she still has on him. She immediately turns to go, only to feel his "fancied gaze" on her back. He, of course, pursues her and continues to fix his eyes upon her, "contemplating her." He complains of being unable to rid himself of her "image," confessing to a "burning desire" to see the woman he once despised but who remained "unsmirched in spite of all." He no longer, in Freudian terms, debases her but he continues to blame her for her beauty: "never was such a maddening mouth since Eve's." He casts himself in the role of Satan, complete with fork, coming to tempt Eve in her parents' allotment and she falls a second time, returning to live with him in repayment for his kindness to her family. Having killed him, she enjoys a brief taste of paradise with Angel which is described in purely natural terms, as on the morning when they are discovered by the cleaning lady, her "lips being parted like a half-open flower near his cheek." Nothing, it appears, can sully her innate natural purity.

Tess dies, at the end of the novel, a victim of fate, of civilisation, and above all of male desire, having learnt "the cruelty of lust and the fragility of love." She never fully succeeds in becoming a subject rather than an object. In many of the most important scenes in the novel, it has been pointed out, her consciousness is all but edited out. Tess is asleep, or in a reverie, at almost every crucial turn of the plot: at Prince's death, at the time of her seduction by Alec, when the sleepwalking Angel buries his image of her, at his return to find her at the Herons, and when the police take her at Stonehenge.

When she tries to speak to Angel, "He silenced her by a kiss" and when she studies Alec too closely he exclaims, "Don't look at me like that!" Even the narrator, as we have seen, is often less concerned with what she says than with the shape of her lips. The texts, in fact, remain confused over her diction, varying between dialect and Standard English. She is split partly by her education: having "passed the Sixth Standard in the National School," she "spoke two languages: the dialect at home, more or less; ordinary English abroad and to persons of quality." Later, of course, she picks up Clare's vocabulary and accent along with fragments of his knowledge.

But Tess is also split in the way . . . all women are split: between desire and language, attempting to express their own subjectivity and sexuality in a language dominated by men. She is split too by the two men, Angel and Alec, who idealise and debase her simultaneously; and by the narrator, who both describes her with erotic fascination and attempts to purify her. Even her two lips are made to speak different languages, the top one lifting invitingly when she smiles while the other remains "severely still." Eventually, in a passage added in 1892, she disowns her body altogether, Clare recognising on his return that "his original Tess had spiritually ceased to recognise the body before him as hers." Her tragedy can in this sense be said to lie in her failure "to *possess herself*, to make her body and the languages that it speaks her own." Her much-vaunted purity cannot prevent her image and eventually her body being appropriated by others.

CHAPTER 4

Tess

Tess: Poor and a Woman

Anne Z. Mickelson

In this excerpt, Anne Z. Mickelson argues that
Hardy realistically portrays the life of a peasant
woman in Victorian society. Tess's struggle with
poverty, her second-class status as a woman, and
her attempts to maintain her self-worth and dignity
are the crux of the novel, according to Mickelson.
Mickelson is the author of *Thomas Hardy's Women
and Men*, from which this article is excerpted.

In *Tess of the d'Urbervilles* the clash between society/culture
and nature becomes a passionate defense of Tess as beautiful nature (the natural self, love, fertility, tenderness) and an
indictment of a culture which degrades the poor, regards
woman's virtue as a commodity to be delivered to the husband on the wedding night, and upholds the double standard. Culture, here, is also the beginning of a mechanical social order in which men and women become dehumanized
work machines, like the driver of that red, ticking reaper in
the Flintcomb-Ash scene who ruthlessly forces Tess to keep
up with his machine without giving her any respite. . . .

Tess is seen as a nineteenth-century woman whose personality development as a woman becomes blighted by cultural pressures. Trained from childhood to fit herself for an
inferior role, she becomes early in life a prisoner to her
sense of responsibility and duty to family. Later, stigmatized
by society as a "fallen woman" and conscious of this stigma-
tization, her negation of self becomes even more pronounced in the love relationship with Angel. Her words to
Angel: "I will obey you like your wretched slave, even if it is
to lie down and die," are offered as a powerful example of
the psychic self-damage caused by attrition of self-esteem. In
the end, looking like a "corpse upon the current," as Hardy

Excerpted from *Thomas Hardy's Women and Men: The Defeat of Nature*, by Anne Z.
Mickelson (Metuchen, NJ: Scarecrow Press, 1976). Copyright © 1976 by Anne Z. Mickelson. (Footnotes and references in the original have been omitted from this reprint.)

describes her, the only way she can prove her worth as a woman is through an act of murder.

Hardy leaves little doubt in the reader's mind that the process of wearing away of self-esteem begins at birth. For Tess, is born not only into a weak and shiftless family (it had once been part of the aristocratic d'Urbervilles, and is now a decaying peasant family known as The Durbeyfields), but she has two other great disadvantages. She is a woman and she is a peasant. Pervasive to the novel's materials is the background of Victorian society. Tess is part of a class-conscious society which regards the peasant as an inferior member of society and woman as inferior to man. Tess's duty is laid out for her from cradle to grave—submission and obedience to parents, then to husband, and always to society. As a peasant woman, Tess must work, which she does for most of her brief life. Yet, though she is a functioning member of the economy and the breadwinner in her family, Victorian society demands that she obediently turn over her earnings to her feckless father, thus making her economically dependent. In this way, she is made to contribute to the myth of the man as breadwinner and woman as homemaker. As field worker, she can expect her wages to be lower than those of the man working alongside her. If she marries a man of her own class, she will have to bear many children with little respite from hard physical work in the fields.

VICTORIAN MEN AND WOMEN

The lot of the peasant woman was, in most respects, more difficult than that of the man. A woman living in 1850 bore thirteen children, seven of whom survived. For most of the time she worked in the field for eleven hours a day at haytime and harvest. During gleaning time, she would leave her home at 2 a.m. and not return until seven that night. Often she had to walk as far as seven miles back and forth to the job, taking her daughters with her. "For this effort, she would reckon six bushels of corn a very good reward."

In other places, women were paid eight pence a day and at harvest time received a shilling plus two quarts of ale or cider. In addition to field work, the woman had to tend to her husband when he got home. Home life was frequently a casualty of such conditions. Husbands of working wives finding no supper, fire, nor comfort at home (if the wife were detained at work) would go to the beershop for relief, squandering the few pennies so sorely needed at home. In Tess's home the problem is even more acute, for both parents frequent the local pub and spend Tess's hard-earned money there.

The special problems of the individual who is both poor and a woman are an important element to the background of *Tess of the d'Urbervilles*, making the novel more than "a moral fable . . . of the destruction of the peasant world," as [literary critic] Arnold Kettle once said. Hardy makes it clear that his book is about a woman—a beautiful and intelligent woman for whom marriage to a man of her own class offers nothing more than a life of work in field and home, the breeding of many children, and death, perhaps, at an early age. The only alternative to marriage is domestic service or factory work. Like thousands of other village girls, Tess can obtain work in some middle-class household in which she will polish, scrub, clean, fetch and carry, in return for meager room and board and appallingly low wages. Or she can try to find work in some bleach and dye works, or lace works, or a pottery factory—and work long hours under unsanitary conditions and for low pay. Tess, a cottager's daughter, with a little more education (up to the Sixth Standard) than that possessed by her parents, is forced by family poverty to put away her dreams of becoming a teacher and yield to her mother's urgings that she go into service for the d'Urbervilles. In keeping with her peasant skills, Tess accepts a job tending the d'Urbervilles' fowls. The d'Urbervilles are a rich merchant family, no kin to Tess, living in a district called "The Chase," in a manorial house known as "The Slopes." They have been able to buy the aristocratic name of d'Urbervilles and annex it to the more plebeian title of Stoke.

THE PLOT

The downward trend of Tess's life begins symbolically with her ride down a steep, mile-long incline in Alec d'Urberville's dog cart. Alec, scion of this rich merchant family, decides to exercise the unspoken . . . *droit du seigneur* [right of the lord]. Singular beauty in a peasant girl has always marked her as prey for the upper class man, as Daniel Defoe, Samuel Richardson, and other British novelists have demonstrated. Alec proves no exception to his class. It is no accident that Hardy gives him the background of "The Chase" and "The Slopes" and has him ride in a dog cart.

Characteristically, Alec's language to Tess contains animal imagery ("You are as weak as a bled calf "), or the language of commerce ("worth your weight in gold"). Also, Hardy makes it very clear that Alec is the lord and master in his realm. "If you meet with any difficulties and want help here," he instructs Tess, "don't go to the baliff, come to me." It to no surprise to learn that Tess is soon raped. She leaves Alec after a few months, finds out she is pregnant, gives birth to a child which dies, and finds herself outside the pale of society—a "fallen woman" at the age of eighteen. Hoping to love, be loved, and live down the past, she marries Angel Clare after unsuccessfully attempting to tell him about Alec. Angel leaves her a few days after the confession on the wedding night. Tess has to work at hard farm labor until her parents' eviction from their home for reasons of Tess's "promiscuity" and their own shiftlessness forces her to return to Alec as his mistress. Upon Angel's repentance and return, she kills Alec and is executed for murder. . . .

Tess copes with the hard realities in every way she knows how, by back-breaking manual work, or caring for her many brothers and sisters, or taking charge of her parents staggering home from the pub. As for the passivity exhibited sometimes not only with family, but with Alec and later to a greater degree with Angel, it is not only the result of guilt feelings. It is impressed upon her by the inhibition of woman's right to aggression prescribed by society. I will have more to say about this in connection with her love relationship with Alec and then with Angel.

This, then, is the Victorian society into which Tess is born, and by which she is conditioned and then executed at an early age for the murder of Alec d'Urberville, the man who seduces her, and continues to make emotional demands on her for the rest of her life. Since the book begins and ends with the family relationship, and family plays as important a role for Tess . . . , it is necessary to look briefly at this relationship first and then explore at greater length how the complexities of family feeling and the special loyalties it evokes affect the love relationship. . . .

Tess's Family

Important for Hardy's picture of women in this novel, Joan Durbeyfield becomes an example of the evolutionary process which turns the woman callous when she accepts her inferior status. Long since unhampered by a troubling conscience, Joan is animated only by self-preservation and sees in her daughter's beauty a stepping stone to family prosperity. She is an illustration of the way woman will exploit woman as a result of a sexist society which constantly attempts to strip woman of her dignity. With a moral code consisting of one aphorism, "'Tis nater, after all, and what do please God," Joan believes in deception as the only means to marriage. Man must be trapped into marriage; woman must seek to have some man keep her, and Joan is indignant that Tess is so "foolish" as to neglect forcing Alec to marry her or keeping her. The stoppage of presents from Alec to the Durbeyfield home fills Joan with real anguish ("See what he has given us," she cries to Tess). It is the only time in the book that Joan is "ready to burst into tears" from sheer vexation over her daughter's "stupidity."

Central to the novel's materials is Hardy's concern with family environment and societal influences on character. Tess's misfortune obviously, is to be born of weak parents and to be the eldest of seven children. Both factors force her into a position of responsibility. Coupled with her character, which is proud, conscientious, strong and loving, this makes her vulnerable to the family's deep needs. But her pride is constantly being chipped away. The process is evident in a series of carefully-built scenes: the Cerealia rites when the villagers howl at her father's drunken boasts that he has aristocratic blood; her resolve to transport the beehives to Casterbridge with the help of her little brother so that none of the villagers will know that her father is too drunk to do it himself; her awareness of the family cottage's shabbiness. Her constant euphemizing of her parents' weaknesses to people reveals that though she may appear at ease among her peers, hers is a precarious ease. It is always being undermined by the apprehension that one or the other parent will, in some way, reveal the growing seediness of the family.

Ironically, any attempt to preserve her dignity militates against her and results in some kind of catastrophe. The drive to Casterbridge causes the horse's death—no small tragedy for a poor family like the Durbeyfields—and her refusal to walk home with Car and the other villagers who have had too much to drink is the reason why Alec is able to overtake her and subsequently violate her. Hardy seems to give the impression that even fate is against Tess here, but what becomes apparent is that the fault is not in the stars but in the social and economic conditions surrounding Tess.

Hardy's concern with family enables the reader to see that Tess's heroic efforts in behalf of the family can do no more than palliate the poverty to a small extent. Furthermore, all her efforts to do even this much constantly come up against the parents' backsliding. Very frequently, we see her in tears of frustration at her inability to keep her mother from contributing to the father's delinquency. What becomes obvious is that though Tess is forced to assume responsibility, she does not control her parents. She is by mechanism of guilt concerning her duty as daughter and by vulnerability of character compelled to play roles which enable her parents to manipulate her.

The proliferation of roles into which Tess is induced becomes an outgrowth of the friction within her caused by her dual role of substitute parent and dutiful daughter. Awareness of the parents' shortcomings and recognition of the fact that she must keep them from making fools of themselves continually rubs against the concept of the love and respect she has been taught is due them. Also, she appears torn between her realization of their inadequacies and the vain hope that they possess some buried common sense upon which she can rely. Hardy tells us of her "most touching and urgent letter" to her mother asking for advice as to whether she should tell Angel about her past. Later, after her confession, she seizes upon her mother's words as defense against his stony anger: "She knows several cases where they were worse than I, and the husband has not minded it much—has got over it at least."

The rubric of Tess's life, then, is complications caused not only by her refusal to subscribe to solipsistic reasoning, but also by her efforts to move out of the ambiance of her parents' folk culture. She struggles against acquiring the attitudes toward love and marriage displayed by them and others around her. . . .

The values that Hardy builds into this novel and represents as Tess's values are his indictment of woman as sexual object, of deceit as a necessary basis for marriage, and the concept that a woman who is not a virgin is damaged goods to be offered to the lowest bidder. He approves of Tess's thinking on Alec after her rape: "even for her name's sake she scarcely wished to marry him.". . .

INDEPENDENCE

Hardy makes it clear that a woman's bid for independence results in great trouble. Having defied ecclesiastical authority in baptizing her illegitimate child, burying it in the churchyard, and placing flowers at the head of the grave, Tess leaves home to find work in Talbothays. The place is a dairy farm not far from the d'Urberville estates and her forefathers' country. It is here that Tess meets Angel Clare, falls in love with him, and is rejected by him because of her "past." By relating to a man whose background and training must lead him to reject her, Tess is demonstrating the deep wish of those who are constantly rejected but keep hoping that this *one* time things will be different.

Hardy feels it necessary to make some defense for Angel's treatment of Tess. Angel is a minister's son; his love for Tess has more "radiance" than "fire"; he is an idealist; he lacks "animalism," etc. Eventually, Hardy's honesty forces him to indict Angel as "slave to custom and conventionality." Stripping layer after layer of personality away from Angel, he reveals that the "liberal" man is a very ordinary and conventional person under the patina of pseudo-liberalism. He is a man, says Hardy, who needs a prophet to tell him that Tess is deserving of love and respect. No such prophet comes forth, unfortunately for Tess, until months later when Angel, weakened by disease in Brazil, listens to a man expounding on the question—who is good? But before Angel has his epiphany, he succeeds in violating Tess's spirit as thoroughly as Alec rapes her body. Indeed, he acts like one of [novelist Nathaniel] Hawthorne's crazed Puritans after hearing Tess's story. We read that his face "withered" and that he breaks into a laugh "ghastly as a laugh in hell." Later when he meets the pious Mercy Chant, he finds himself whispering "fiendishly" in her ear "the most heterodox ideas he could think of" and laughing at the horror in her face.

Angel demonstrates that he is the product of a culture which allows a man sexual freedom as long as he is discreet about it and observes appearances. . . .

ANGEL AND ALEC

Actually, there is little doubt that the two men in Tess's life, Angel and Alec, are one and the same man. Their concept of woman reflects society's view of her and the myths constructed about woman. For Alec, Tess is at first a victim whose body it is his obligation and right to plunder. Later, when he gets religion, he seems to become confused as to who is victim and who is victimizer, and accuses Tess of being a "temptress." He goes so far as to ask her to swear that "you will never tempt me—by your charms or ways," which Tess in her fright does. However, his male ego will not permit him any rule but that of the aggressor. Soon he drops religion, but not without telling Tess that she is responsible for his fall from grace. He begins referring to himself as "Satan" come to tempt Eve ("You are Eve, and I am the old Other One come to tempt you").

There is authorial irony in the way Alec's physical hopping in and out of hedges, tombstones, hayricks parallels his mental gymnastics. It is as if Hardy wants us to understand the ridiculousness of the various socially-approved, stereotyped roles Alec plays. For, in contrast, Hardy presents Tess brushing aside the view of Alec as either tempter or tempted: "I never said you were Satan, or thought of it," she says simply. "I don't think of you in that way at all."

Clearly, Tess refuses to stereotype man or woman in any one mythical role. This is evident in her relations with Angel. When Angel in the happy days of courtship sententiously refers to her in classical terms, Tess cuts through this rhetoric with: "Call me Tess." She wants to be neither victim, temptress, nor goddess. She just wants to be a woman and be allowed to develop as a woman.

Unfortunately, neither Hardy's fictional world nor the real world in which the author lived permits Tess her request. A statesman's wife went so far as to declare that not only did Tess deserve hanging, but "they ought all to have been hanged." It is not clear by what she meant as "all," but her heated rhetoric attests to the strong feelings the novel aroused. As for Angel, Tess's social fall from goddess to mortal woman is indeed great. She is vile to him after he hears of the experience with Alec and he is incredulous the morning after the confession that Tess still looks "pure.". . .

THE VICTORIAN MAN

Angel represents to Hardy the Victorian man who wants as wife a creature of piety, submissiveness, and purity—all "proper" feminine virtues. Tess is damaged property for him because she is not a virgin. He expresses the concept of Tess as "property" several times; for example, when he speaks of their coming marriage: "I should carry you off as my property." Certainly, Angel's language to Tess is mercantile and it has the ring of the economics of sexuality even more so than Alec's language. By giving up marrying money, he tells her, he believed he "should secure rustic innocence as surely as I should secure pink cheeks."

Earlier he tells Tess that she is his consolation "prize'" for not going to the university. Without a doubt, Angel is the outraged merchant who feels robbed. In the sleep-walking scene with Tess, he keeps looking at Tess and exclaiming: "Dead, dead, dead. . . . My wife—dead, dead." Tess is never a person to Angel any more than she is to Alec. For Alec she is all body and for Angel she has to fit a composite picture of purity, goddess, and calico prettiness. Angered when he learns that Tess is not what he thought, the disappointed Angel sets forth on a new life after almost destroying the woman he "loves." He dumps her off near her parents' home and tells Tess in so many words, don't call me, I'll call you ("until I come to you it will be better that you should not try to come to me").

The psychic self-damage to Tess, who lives in a society operated by men who act as a policing force to keep her believing that she is first inferior, then "fallen," is most evident in her relationship with Angel. Though she tries to assert her dignity ("I am only a peasant by position not by nature") when he accuses her of being an uncomprehending peasant woman, her love for him and her desire to be loved reduce her to abasement and slavishness. Everything in her environment—low social and economic status, family shiftlessness, her violation by Alec, the view of society of her as "fallen"—contributes to her intense urge for love. Her emotional dependency is so great that she cannot bear the rejection of the man she loves. Hence, there is her offer to kill herself, and Angel loftily replying that he will not add murder to his other follies (one of them presumably, Tess). She suggests divorce to appease him, but his reply is what will people think (very much what her mother says when she returns first from Alec, then from Angel). Her self-esteem is so low that when Angel carries her in that sleep-walking scene across the narrow footbridge over a river she is "pleased . . . to think he was regarding her as his absolute possession, to dispose of as he should choose."

Hardy is not indulging in male fantasy here, but indicating to what extent Tess's self-esteem has sunk. Nothing in Tess's experience has given her any protection against her disabling experience. Nothing has taught her to think of self. Hardy emblematizes this in the sleep-walking scene, in which he comments that Tess's feet are bare and cold and stones hurt her feet, "but Clare was in his woolen stockings, and appeared to feel no discomfort." In the end, Tess submits not to Angel's unhealthy Puritanism, but bows to his statement that children born of their marriage would share in the mother's stigma. Tess, remembering her own childhood and the slurs and ridicule surrounding her parents, can only nod miserably when Angel tells her of his decision.

Tess of the d'Urbervilles is a penetrating study of a woman who battles to be recognized as a person in her own right, but who never gets the chance to realize her womanhood. Considered inferior as a woman and as a peasant, her self-esteem is constantly eroded by a society which brands her as socially, economically, and morally unacceptable. The hunted of predatory men like Alec and others, the scorn of the morally-righteous like Angel, the victim of family loyalty, it is no wonder that toward the end she looks like a woman out of whose body all the blood has run. The black flag which goes up on the prison roof as signal that her execution for murder is over becomes a symbol of a blighted life. The most poignant thing about Tess, though, is not her death but her loneliness in life—the special loneliness which comes from not being known by others. At no time can she expect understanding from Angel.

After her death, we get the impression that he will mourn like [William Shakespeare's title character] Othello over Desdemona: "Oh the pity of it—the pity of it," but Angel can afford pity for Tess now. For Angel, unlike Tess, gets a second chance at happiness with a dream girl who appears to be everything he has always wanted. This is Liza-Lu, Tess's young sister, described as "a tall budding creature—half girl, half woman—a spiritualized image of Tess." Hardy's message is clear. With Tess the sensual woman dead, Angel can walk into the sunset with the young and virginal Liza-Lu. It is an ironic ending which speaks eloquently of the lack of even a rough egalitarianism for woman in society.

The novel is a high point of maturity in Hardy's fiction. He deals with poverty and the woman, the double standard of morality, the role of passivity forced upon woman, and how woman's chances for happiness are eventually blighted.

Tess Is at Odds with Nature

Marjorie Garson

Unlike many critics, Marjorie Garson in the following excerpt claims that Tess is not representative of a character who is at one with nature—rather, it is her fight against nature that marks her character. Garson concludes that Hardy is not entirely in control of the nature imagery that surrounds Tess, leaving the work flawed. Marjorie Garson is the author of *Hardy's Fables of Integrity: Woman, Body, Text,* from which this article is excerpted.

Tess of the d'Urbervilles teaches us to read it in terms of its ending. From the opening pages, the novel's effect depends upon a strong sense of sequence, on Hardy's ability to suggest that Tess is caught in time and doomed to be destroyed as certain temporal patterns unfold. The kinds of devices upon which critics used to focus so heavily—ironies of timing, coincidences—suggest Tess's entrapment in a number of inexorable sequences. Her fate seems predetermined both by heredity (the narrator emphasizes that she has her mother's nubility and sensitivity to music, and implies she shares her father's quixotic pride) and by a historically specific environment. The cycle of nature is presented as analogous to her own experience: as her fatal love for Angel develops, the sequence of Tess's emotions is echoed, and exacerbated, by the waxing summer heat, so that the unfolding season itself seems to announce her fall. Then, too, as the novel's title suggests, Tess is mysteriously fated to expiate the crimes of her aristocratic ancestors. Finally, the motif of Druidical sacrifice locates Tess's fate within a still more distant English past and implies that there is some ancient mythic pattern which she is doomed to repeat, some demonic sequence in which she is doomed to be yet another term. . . .

Tess is a woman with a past: the statement has two different meanings, and it is from the gap between these meanings that some of the ironies of the plot emerge. When Tess, on the verge of telling Angel the secret of her pregnancy, loses her nerve at the last moment, she pretends that what she was going to confess was her aristocratic background. Angel responds to both secrets, when he knows them, in ways which are inappropriate, given his advanced and free-thinking pretensions. He ought not to have been impressed by Tess's lineage, but he was; he ought to have forgiven Tess her mistake, but he did not. The two secrets both function as tests which Angel fails to pass, and their structural identity is thus underscored.

Angel's self-contradictory reactions point, indeed, to the fundamental dichotomy between the two different kinds of narrative which Hardy is combining in this novel. The foundling romance is a form which endorses the existing social order, in that the transcendent virtue of the apparently lower-class heroine is explained when she turns out to be the daughter of a king, or of a rich man. The novel Hardy is claiming to write is one which challenges the existing social order: a defence of the fallen woman as a victim of social prejudice. There seem to be two impulses here which are at odds with one another, and some of the contradictions in the novel may be illuminated by an awareness of the conflict.

To see Tess as the heroine of a foundling romance makes sense of some of the details of her nature which are less realistic than Hardy tries to make them sound. Tess seems not really to be her parents' child. Despite a perfunctory attempt to establish traits which she shares especially with her mother, Hardy does not convince us that the sensitive, introspective, flower-like maiden owes very much to her biological connection with Joan and Jack Durbeyfield. Tess is characterized by fine and subtle intuitions, which seem not to have been learned in Marlott; by a highly articulate world-weariness, which owes more to her creator's own pessimism than to concepts aired in the Durbeyfield household; and by articulate, indeed eloquent, language, which seems scarcely to have been marked by a local accent. And most important of all, perhaps, she is distinguished from her fellows by the exceptional beauty for which jewels and fine clothes are the natural complement. The special pathos of her victimization by Farmer Grobie and his demonic ma-

THE DEEPER REALITY OF NATURE

In the following excerpt from his diary, Thomas Hardy describes his view of the meaning of nature while looking at a landscape painting.

After looking at the landscape ascribed to Bonington in our drawing-room I feel that Nature is played out as a Beauty, but not as a Mystery. I don't want to see landscapes, *i.e.*, scenic paintings of them, because I don't want to see the original realities—as optical effects, that is. I want to see the deeper reality underlying the scenic, the expression of what are sometimes called abstract imaginings.

The "simply natural" is interesting no longer. The much decried, mad, late-[painter Joseph] Turner rendering is now necessary to create my interest. The exact truth as to material fact ceases to be of importance in art—it is a student's style—the style of a period when the mind is serene and unawakened to the tragical mysteries of life; when it does not bring anything to the object that coalesces with and translates the qualities that are already there,—half hidden, it may be—and the two united are depicted as the All.

Thomas Hardy, January 1887.

chinery derives not only from Hardy's generalized indignation at the sexual and economic vulnerability of rural women, but from his particular and erotic sense of Tess's unique fineness and fragility. . . .

TESS IS ODDLY INCOMPETENT

Although Tess is associated with cyclical nature, and perceived as caught in a series of chronological patterns, she herself exhibits an odd blankness about sequence. She is improbably incompetent, for example at predicting chains of cause and effect. It is hard to believe that an adolescent girl brought up by Joan Durbeyfield would be as ignorant as Tess seems to be of the nature of the threat posed by Alec, yet Tess reluctantly surrenders to a number of overtures without any apparent sense of where they are leading. Then, too, despite her obsessive fear of Angel's learning her history, Tess is unrealistically unable to predict his response when he does—improbably naïve in her jubilation that her transgression is "just the same" as his. What has been called her passivity is often an unwillingness or inability to stop chains of consequences once they have begun to unroll. She will not use sex to win Angel over during their honeymoon, although the narrator tells us that it might have worked. She decides not to ask her in-laws for money because her feelings are hurt when Mercy Chant mocks her boots. (The ultimate consequence of this decision is her vulnerability to Alec's overtures—a consequence to which Hardy himself seems blind, as he does nothing to rationalize her responsibility for this particular chain of events.)

Tess's peculiar relationship to time can be read by assuming that she is a coherent "character" and by attempting to set up a paradigm into which such reactions will fit. Recently it has been read as the result—irritating or impressive, depending on one's point of view— . . . [of Hardy's] desire to make Tess more innocent than she was in the first drafts of the narrative, more purely and pathetically a victim. I see Tess's relationship to time in terms of a larger project: that dehistoricizing of her which is necessary if she is to serve as a resolution of the tension between nature and aristocracy which I believe underlies the narrative.

TESS'S ARISTOCRATIC PAST

Tess can be loved for her aristocracy only if she is felt as innocent of it—innocent of and indeed the victim of history itself. It is, I think, her innocence of history which makes readers feel she has a mythic dimension. Her epithet—"of the d'Urbervilles"—expresses precisely that connection in separation which links Tess with her aristocratic forebears, in such a way as to skip over her actual parents and erase all local, specific identities and allegiances. Tess inherits aristocratic glamour without being implicated in aristocratic guilt. She is like her mother but not like her father, from whom she nevertheless inherits a superiority he himself does not have. She is linked in a mystified synchronic way with her remote ancestors and condemned to suffer for their crimes; the doom does not make very much moral sense and has to be handled in a slightly unreal Gothic fashion—through winking portraits, sinister omens, and local legends. Hardy seems to be suggesting, by his discussion of Tess's rapacious ancestors, that the aristocracy of the past condemned the poor to suffer in the present; but since the figure of Tess contains both the contemporary victim and the historical victimizer, it short-circuits any serious social criticism of the contemporary class structure.

It is interesting that Tess is harassed by social forces: by a man whose family has bought its tide with new money; by the brutal technology—exemplified by the threshing machine—which bends human life to its inhuman rhythm. But precisely how this newness is connected to history is blurred. Clearly Alec's family's interest in adopting an ancient family name derives from the value such a name has acquired in a process which is not delineated. Again Alec serves as a scapegoat—mocked precisely for his newness, while the "oldness" on which alone this newness could be parasitical is exonerated (in the figure of Tess herself) from any responsibility for creating him. The class from which Tess descends creates Alec as surely as it destroys Tess (or, one might also say, as surely as Tess destroys him)—but is not in the novel to receive the blame. It is significant that Tess is not harmed by any contemporary "real" aristocrat: she herself usurps that position, and precludes the presentation of an old family with *contemporary* power.

Tess has value for Hardy because she is associated with the glamour of the real aristocracy; but she must not be implicated in its crimes. She must expiate them with her death, but without ever having been besmirched by them. She must retain, in the context of an implicating history, the "purity" Hardy insists on in the subtitle. She must not operate in time—she must not operate time—but be operated upon. She must be destroyed, and yet not destroyed—victimized, and yet preserved intact. The ways in which Tess is disconnected from her past are necessary if she is to figure the unity he desires.

Hardy has set up his narrative in terms of the dangers of misreading his heroine. The novel as a whole is a plea for a specific reading of Tess: Alec and Angel destroy her because they read her wrongly, and Hardy's purpose is to analyse and expose their misreadings, place these misreadings, culturally and historically, and dramatize their destructiveness.

TESS'S RELATIONSHIPS

Implicit in the notion of misreading is the concept of a real Tess who must be differentiated from the false images which Alec and Angel have of her. Both men are presented as insensitive to this Tess, the inner Tess, the Tess as she herself experiences herself, to which we as readers are apparently given a privileged insight. This is not the only Hardy

novel in which the problem of personal identity, the question
of the relationship between subject and object, the "Me" and
the "Not Me," becomes a subject of speculation, nor is Tess
the only character of whom the narrator says things like:

> Upon her sensations the whole world depended, to Tess:
> through her existence all her fellow creatures existed, to her.
> The universe itself only came into being for Tess on the par-
> ticular day in the particular year in which she was born.

But the question of subjectivity becomes an especially crucial one in the structure of this novel. Hardy makes Tess's
selfhood a central issue, allows his heroine to protest pas-
sionately against being misconstrued, and encourages us to
feel that she has been systematically violated and victimized
by not being recognized for what she really is. The question
remains, however, to what extent he himself is implicated in
the very attitudes he exposes in his male characters. . . .

Hardy implicates himself . . . in Angel's idealization of
Tess as a "fresh and virginal daughter of Nature." There are
no virgins in nature; and Hardy shows clearly how destructive to Tess this idealizing will be—makes Tess protest
against it—has her recognize that "she you love is not my
real self, but one in my image; the one I might have been."
And he makes clear that Angel is deceiving himself—that he
is attracted to Tess precisely because she is *not* a child of nature in any simple way, because she is so much superior to
the other milkmaids. Indeed it is Tess's felt alienation from
nature which draws Angel to her in the first place: her mus-
ings deeply appeal to him, because they express in naïve
terms precisely his own overbred pessimism. Angel exploits
Tess by using her to confirm the Romantic vision of a natural life which he believes that he himself, in withdrawing
from the public arena, has chosen. His outrageous treatment
of her is itself a comment on the irresponsibility of the
dream of pastoral innocence.

Yet Hardy, even while criticizing Angel for what he does
to Tess, is at the same time using Angel to do the same thing
on his own behalf. Through Angel, Tess is endowed by the
text with some of the very attributes which she herself explicitly disowns. By attributing to Angel an idealized vision
of Tess as nature-goddess which Tess herself repudiates,
Hardy is able to have it both ways. In those early mornings
when the couple feel like Adam and Eve, and Angel insists
on addressing Tess as Artemis and Demeter, when she be-

comes for him "a visionary essence of woman—a whole sex condensed into one typical form," Hardy establishes a vision of Tess, which does not fade merely because Tess protests against it. Indeed, her protest confirms her status: what better proof that she is indeed nature's child than her uneasiness with Angel's culture-bound metaphors? The text, aware that "nature" is itself a cultural construct, nevertheless allows the figure of Tess to draw power from the Romantic illusion. . . .

Evidently Alec has possessed Tess's body but not her soul. Angel's sin against Tess is his failure to realize this. His repudiation of her causes—or deepens—a radical split in Tess, makes her separate herself from her body; it constrains Tess to define herself—while it *enables* the narrator to redefine her—along the lines of pure spirit. It is Angel's very rejection of her, in other words, which allows the text—or the narrator, or Hardy—to expiate the fascination with Tess's body expressed in the first half of the novel, and this is what it proceeds to do. Tess is increasingly spiritualized as the novel goes on. The narrator emphasizes her growing dissociation from her own body, so that by the time she gives herself to Alec she has "ceased to recognize the body before him as hers—allowing it to drift, like a corpse upon the current, in a direction dissociated from its living will." But the imaginative effect of this theoretical *division* is actually to *unify* Tess, who becomes pure spirit, pure voice. Her final speech to Alec, a disembodied "soliloquy" heard through the door by Mrs. Brooks, is almost operatic in its stylization; and her final statement—"I am ready"—seems intended to have the resonance of Shakespearian tragedy. It is as if the "real" Tess, Tess as she herself experiences herself, has become identical with soul: her body has virtually become invisible before her execution. . . .

Tess and Nature: Contradictions

In defining self as soul, however, Hardy leaves a surplus of body, and that surplus gets back into the novel through the natural imagery for which it is so celebrated. Hardy uses "nature" in this novel in two ways: as a brooding physical presence and as a polemical principle, an abstraction or norm invoked again and again to the same end: to persuade the reader that Tess is indeed what he calls her in his subtitle: "A Pure Woman." Both these methods, however, self-destruct. When Hardy, defending his subtitle, complains in his 1892 Preface that Tess's critics ignore "the meaning of the word in Nature," the epistemological naïveté of the phrase points to some of the problems he gets himself into. By insisting that Tess, in surrendering to Alec, is only behaving naturally, Hardy establishes the principle upon which he repeatedly defends her: that those who condemn her do so on the basis of "an arbitrary law of society which had no foundation in Nature." When, for example, the narrator insists that the evening woodland does not (as Tess imagines) condemn her, when he emphasizes that emotional regeneration is natural to a "fallen woman" and that therefore social regeneration ought also to be possible, when he implies that Tess's natural impulse to praise nature is a lot saner and more truly religious than the Christian impulse to insist on her damnation, when he sets up the pathetic analogy between his victimized heroine and the murdered pheasants—in all these instances he implies that Tess is a natural creature and should not be condemned by society's "arbitrary law."

But, as many critics have pointed out, this argument is self-contradictory. The text makes clear that specifically human excellence involves more than a surrender to "nature." If Tess's behaviour is merely natural, and to be defended on that ground, why should Alec's be condemned? If nature is the norm, what about the dairymaids, natural creatures right enough, who in their lovesick misery "writhed feverishly under the oppressiveness of an emotion thrust on them by cruel Nature's law"? It is precisely because Hardy, more consciously than any of his characters, posits "nature" as inanimate, indifferent, and amoral that we are disconcerted when he puts his narrator's argument into the mouths of characters whose point of view he disavows—when he has Joan Durbeyfield conclude complacently that Tess's pregnancy is "nater, after all, and what do please God" and Angel insist that Alec is Tess's husband "in Nature." Their facile use of the abstraction as polemical counter parodies the narrator's, and reveals the theoreticalness and arbitrariness of his reasoning as well as of theirs.

Hardy's use of nature as setting is equally problematical. The most impressive and memorable natural scenes in the novel are those which mirror the growing love of Tess and Angel at Talbothays—notably the celebrated description of the "rank" garden through which Tess moves towards the sound of Angel's harp in Chapter 19. The detail in this passage is as rich and circumstantial as the purpose is transparent: to suggest that since Tess, in particular, is part of nature, her desire for life and love will be irresistible, her surrender to Angel inevitable. The heavy, sticky ripeness of the garden suggests the pressure on her of sheer sexuality —as, indeed, do all of the other evocations of growing summer heat in Phase Three of the novel. However, what makes this particular scene stand out from the others is that there is a gap between the narrator's and the character's points of view here so sharp as to be slightly disconcerting, and to seem to call for interpretative commentary. Tess moves through this very sensuous and even threatening garden apparently oblivious to it, "conscious of neither time nor space." She has, indeed, recently been criticized for this unconsciousness, which is seen as a symptom of her culpable idealism, her dangerous attempt to rise above the body, and is linked with her uncritical awe of Angel's sexual purity as well as with her irresponsible desire for incorporeality. Yet such a reading, does not account for the peculiar intensity of the description itself, the note of fascinated disgust which informs the tone of the narrator. . . .

NATURE AND ALEC AND ANGEL

I see the gap, rather, as revealing what most of the time remains concealed—that *all* the natural imagery mirroring the relationship between Tess and Angel is displaced. It is precisely because Tess does not define her attraction for Angel as sexual that the sultry weather "tells": the imagery would lose its point if the overt relationship between them were as sultry as the weather. It is the repression of the sexual nature of the attraction between them that makes the natural imagery so powerfully metaphorical. (I want to remain ambiguous about who is doing the repressing.) And it is also, perhaps, the suppression of the whole story of the relationship between Tess and Alec, which as it were gets told for the first time, in a kind of ponderous slow-motion, through the Talbothays imagery—as if Tess, though Alec's mistress and the mother of a child, had never been through this process before. Indeed, she declares she has not: Tess defends herself to Angel (and constitutes herself to herself) through a myth of plenitude and presence, which depends, however, on a radical dehistoricization: "What was the past to me as soon as I met you? It was a dead thing altogether. I became another woman, filled full of new life from you. How could I be the early one?"

Natural imagery, I would argue, bears so much weight in the novel because, while apparently mirroring Tess's experience, it in fact restores the sequence, the temporality, the physicality, repressed in the figure of Tess herself. The suggestion that Tess *should* have acknowledged the reality figured by the garden seems from this perspective irrelevant: Tess cannot "see" the fissures which she herself is created to close. But there is a paradox here: Tess can be read as a pure child of nature not in spite of but *because* of her alienation from it. It is precisely because she *does not* feel what nature figures that she deserves the epithet. Attempting to constitute a "real" Tess, a Tess who will exist to herself, Hardy has got her caught in an explicable relation with an Other which mirrors the "body" which this "self" represses. "Nature" reveals the inadequacy of Tess as a figure of unity, and perhaps reflects less the relationship between the main characters than the anxieties and concerns of the author which these characters are invented to resolve.

Such concerns emerge also in the famous description of the landscape around Flintcomb-Ash, the demonic anti-Wordsworthian [rejecting the style of poet William Wordsworth] vision of earth and sky as "upper and nether visages" mirroring each other, "the white face looking down on the brown face, and the brown face looking up at the white face"—and neither looking at the human figures who crawl like flies between. The threat to Tess has consistently been expressed in terms of looking—both figuratively (as in the penetrating rays of the sun, to which Tess is symbolically sacrificed at Stonehenge) and literally, so that Tess has become obsessed with repelling the male gaze. Apparently, however, while to look at Tess is to violate her, not to look is worse still. The grotesque vision of the human face as featureless—as "only an expanse of skin"—suggests the worst threat of all: the utter extinction of the subject. It is into this context that Hardy introduces the paragraph about the Arctic birds, the most glaring and unqualified example of pathetic fallacy on the narrator's part in the novel. The attribution of human consciousness to the birds, their inexpressible "memory" of Arctic wastelands never otherwise to be perceived, foregrounds the question of the relationship between being and perception, and suggests the anxieties of a subject dependent for sustenance on an Other which will not look, and thus vulnerable to dissolution and fragmentation. The vision is that of a defaced or deformed or scattered body. The land around Flintcomb-Ash is imaged as an immense recumbent female, "bosomed with semi-globular tumuli—as if Cybele the Many-breasted were supinely extended there." Upon this gigantic but sterile mother lie scattered and relatively tiny fragments of the male body, the phallic stones which are mentioned in two different contexts by the narrator, and which Tess, characteristically, does not recognize. At Flintcomb-Ash the anxiety evoked by the idea of looking is revealed as having less to do with a female object than with a male subject.

The character who really has become invisible—who really is not being looked at in this section of the novel—is not Tess, whom we are still watching, but Angel. His departure for Brazil means his extinction as well as Tess's, for when he returns it is as an emasculated figure, prematurely aged and withered. Indeed, Angel after his illness is described in much the same terms as Clym Yeobright, another world-weary intellectual who seems to embody certain aspects of Hardy's own self-image. Angel's punishment, though less absolute and melodramatic than Alec's, is also a kind of death, a state of emotional and even physical attenuation and emasculation.

The pairing-off of Angel and Liza-Lu is interesting in this connection. As retribution for essentializing Tess, the text leaves Angel with an essentialized Tess, a girl who embodies, as Tess says, "the best of me without the bad of me." The very fact that Tess wishes this sterile pairing to be an actual marriage underscores its antierotic character and makes the compensatory pattern ironic, Tess's dying wish into a kind of curse.

Indeed, both Alec and Angel pay a heavy price for their misreading of the heroine. Alec is treated as a cardboard villain at the end even more than at the beginning of the novel. In one curious incident, however, the text does at least raise the question of whether Alec is not Tess's victim as surely as she is his. When Alec forces Tess to swear on Cross-in-Hand that she will never again tempt him, Hardy seems to be using the encounter primarily for some rather heavy-handed foreboding ("'Tis a thing of ill-omen"). But his language imbues the image with more specific associations.

Cross-in-Hand is not really a cross, but "the stump" of what the narrator says may once have been a more "complete erection." To anyone who has seen the not very impressive marker—which still stands—this seems unlikely, for the top is gently cupped rather than broken off. (The outline of the hand incised upon it is now completely obscured by lichen.) The "rude monolith" is more phallic in shape than the text, with its emphasis on a broken cross, makes it sound; yet at the same time Hardy's loaded language subliminally suggests castration. Alec, who fears surrender to Tess, makes her reassure him with an ambiguous gesture— "put your hand upon that stone hand, and swear that you will never tempt me"—which seems to invite the very involvement he apparently wishes to avoid. The incident may seem odd to the reader as well as to Tess; but while it suggests Alec's complicity in his own destruction, it also reminds us what the exclusive emphasis on Tess's victimization at the end of the novel may make us forget—that fascination with Tess kills Alec.

In her discussion of the figure of the fallen woman in Victorian literature and painting, [literary critic] Nina Auerbach points out that the stature and power the fallen woman acquires—even though she suffers for it—involves a certain triumph over the men who seduced her, renders them invisible and irrelevant. By including Tess in her discussion of this mythic pattern, Auerbach restores a meaning of the text from which we are conventionally distracted. Tess emerges a victimizer as well as a victim, and Hardy's fable turns reflexively against itself, revealing even as it attempts to unify Tess her genesis in dissolution and fragmentation.

My theme, then, is Hardy's necessary failure to construct an aesthetic whole not subject to such dissolution. The figures of Tess and of nature, set up to supplement one another, instead subvert one another, and mirror back, to the subject attempting to constitute itself through their reflection, a fragmented body. Hardy's desire, aimed with disconcerting directness at an unresponsive "nature," opens up the fissures in the Romantic project, and deconstructs a subject tenuously constituted in words.

Tess Is a Tragic Heroine

Bert G. Hornback

In the following selection, Bert G. Hornback argues that *Tess of the d'Urbervilles* is written as a classic tragedy. Tess's tragic fault is her submission to Alec, and this mistake is one that she cannot rise above to pursue any sort of happiness or full life. In her ritualized death, Hornback contends, Tess, not unlike other tragic heroines, somehow expiates the guilt of the other characters in the novel and the reader. Hornback is the author of *The Metaphor of Chance: Vision and Technique in the Works of Thomas Hardy*, from which this excerpt is taken.

Hardy seems to be trying to do two things: present the representative tragedy of *Tess of the d'Urbervilles* on the one hand, and argue the case of "A Pure Woman Faithfully Represented" on the other. The two, however, do not easily come together in a complementary way. The argument about society and its rules is not proved or demonstrated by Tess's fate; rather, she seems almost to work and act against Hardy's tentative assertion about the nature of morality. She has a mind of her own: a conscience and consciousness. And despite Hardy's seeming attempt to make her the victim of a ruthless, relentless society, or societal code, she becomes a tragic heroine. She develops a vision of herself and the world which is separate from Hardy's anticonvention propaganda and social criticism.

The significant hero cannot live or act in isolation from the world, nor can he be a hero if his situation is solely within society. Hardy places Tess very much in the local world of Wessex in space and in time. She acts within this world and, in one sense, according to its rules. Her consciousness, however, grows larger than that of the society in which she lives. As she is a descendent of the ancient d'Urbervilles, her heroic consciousness—and the point is

Excerpted from *The Metaphor of Chance: Vision and Technique in the Works of Thomas Hardy*, by Bert G. Hornback (Athens: Ohio University Press). Copyright © 1971 by Bert G. Hornback. Reprinted with the permission of the author. (Footnotes and references in the original have been omitted from this reprint.)

that heroism is so much a matter of consciousness—fulfills not only the now in which she lives but the history which she represents as well.

The significant hero has to make his own fate in the world, and then by the exercise of his consciousness he has to meet that fate. Neither public opinion nor the law of God will suffice to judge the hero. His experience must be personally conceived and comprehended, and its consequences absolutely associated with it in his understanding. The tragic denouement is inevitable, thus, not because of the intervention of some external force, but because the hero, in his consciousness of justice and the nature of things, insists that it be so. The hero then becomes larger than his world, larger than the normal world in which he performs his actions. Not only is the hero responsible for his fate; he defines the terms of his fate as well. . . . Tess's death at Wintoncester is much more, of course, than the hanging of a murderer, and more too than the death of a girl victimized by an oppressive social morality. Tess knows what her death means. When she says almost mystically at Stonehenge, "I am ready," she is speaking her comprehension of what must come. In order for us to understand what this is and why it is so impressive we must go back to the beginning. If we are to know this novel, we must read it all as a preparation for that statement, and we must determine how each element of the fiction fits the precise and specific focus of the statement. . . .

If we read *Tess of the d'Urbervilles* as a novel of social criticism or, even more simply, as but a story, this is probably quite true. What does the d'Urberville business have to do with Tess's seduction? What is the essential link between Tess's story and the description of the passing of an age in English history? Which is primary, the story or the history? If we read the novel carefully as Tess's tragedy these questions are answerable. Everything fits—except for the editorial criticism of the way we live now. And everything fits in the way it usually fits in Hardy's fiction—through the translation of the d'Urberville material into supportive metaphor, through the mythic correlation of details suggesting the single but representative act in the microcosm of time and space. The descriptive elements and Hardy's choice of details not only support and emphasize Tess's tragedy, they also carry the burden of that minor social and historical theme of the changing of an age. . . . The theme of the passing of an age is represented in the fall of Tess's family from landed gentry d'Urbervilles to peasant Durbeyfields; the interrelation of the generations of man is indicated partly by this and partly by the creation of a new d'Urberville in Alec, who acts irrevocably in Tess's present as well as from her past to bring about her tragedy. It is ironically the agony of Tess Durbeyfield—not d'Urberville—that makes her the figure she is and allows her to stand, for us and for Hardy, as representative of the heroic fate of man.

Tess's novel is written with a strong purpose, it seems: one which can only be called didactic. . . .

TESS'S TRAGIC FAULT

Tess's tragic fault is her seduction by Alec d'Urberville. This mistake intrudes throughout the novel to insist upon her destruction. As she leaves her seducer to return home, she meets the mad religious sign painter who warns her of the unforgetful and essentially unforgiving nature of man and the world, and exposes to us the intensity of her guilty self consciousness. In his manuscript Hardy first had the painter write "THE, WAGES, OF, SIN, IS, DEATH"; the fulfillment of this red prophecy comes, dramatically, in the death of Sorrow, in the murder of Alec, and in Tess's hanging. But then Hardy changed the legend to read, as it now does, in "staring vermillion": "THY, DAMNATION, SLUMBERETH, NOT." These words are to Tess much more immediately and personally "accusatory." The significance of the first sign is one of future thematic fulfillment, the kind of adumbration we find so easily, for example, in [the novels of writer] George Eliot. The second rendering, however, describes the whole philosophical and argumentative thesis of the novel––that the past is never dead—and at the same time creates a significant dramatic moment out of this oracular confrontation between Tess and the voice of her fate. Editorially, Hardy criticizes society for holding Tess responsible for her one sin, and for making her feel guilty for her submission to Alec; yet at the same time he creates in Tess a character whose substance is the very convincing honesty with which she feels that guilt. As she acts out the novel, and as Hardy forms the whole more and more about her, Tess moves constantly in relation to those red words: "THY, DAMNATION, SLUMBERETH, NOT." Tess's self-consciousness makes it seem to her "as if this man had known her recent history; yet he was a total stranger." The next sign he paints—"One," he says, "that it will be good for dangerous young females like yer- self to heed"—reads, "THOU, SHALT, NOT, COMMIT—" It is as though the commandment were written especially for her.

Her seduction haunts Tess both physically and psychi- cally. She is ritualistically conscious of it, keeping track of it and reminding herself of it . . . :

> She philosophically noted dates as they came past in the rev- olution of the year; the disastrous night of her undoing at Trantridge with its dark background of The Chase; also the dates of the baby's birth and death; also her own birthday; and every other day individualized by incidents in which she had taken some share.

This reflective consciousness is broken by a sudden impul- sive determination to try for a future, to free herself: "To es- cape the past and all that appertained thereto was to annihi- late it, and to do that she would have to get away." The place she chooses is Talbothays, in the valley of the Great Dairies and their luxuriant sensuousness. As she sets out "now in a direction almost opposite to that of her first adventuring," she thinks that "she might be happy in some nook that had no memories." She walks out across Egdon Heath to begin life anew, going, she supposes, to a new world. The narrator seems to agree with her conception, commenting that "To persons of limited spheres, miles are as geographical de- grees, parishes as counties, counties as provinces and king- doms." The world condenses, thus, in its physical size, and Tess becomes a larger member of it as a consequence.

One of the reasons for Tess's choice of Talbothays is that it stands "not remotely from some of the former estates of the d'Urbervilles, near the great family vaults of her grand- dames and their powerful husbands." The fall of the d'Urbervilles is completed, in one sense, in Tess's life; and their fall through the time of history serves as a metaphoric reminder for Tess of her own fall: "She would be able to look at them, and think not only that d'Urberville, like Babylon, had fallen, but that the individual innocence of a humble de- scendent could lapse as silently." At the same time, however, Tess participates in the past of the d'Urbervilles, repeats a legendary part of their history, and is destroyed by her asso- ciation with them. Her family, she senses, was so unusually old as almost to have gone round the circle and become a new one"; and in the repetition which Tess's life describes the "Fulfillment"—Phase the Seventh is so entitled—is both, ironic and redemptive.

TESS CANNOT ESCAPE THE PAST

Tess's migration from Blackmore Vale to "her ancestral land" suggests to the reader that she cannot escape her past, as she has hoped, that she cannot "annihilate" it, that she can never find, in this small, tight world, a nook that [has] no memories." This suggestion is underlined, and perhaps proved by a parallel example, almost immediately upon her arrival at Talbothays. In the opening words of Chapter 18, "Angel Clare rises up out of the past." He sees Tess: "then he seemed to discern something that was familiar, something which carried him back into a joyous and unforeseeing past, before the necessity of taking thought had made the heavens gray. He concluded that he had beheld her before; where, he could not tell." Their past together is from the time of innocence, from the time of the May-walk at Marlott on the day that John Durbeyfield discovered that his family indeed had a history. Tess's historic relation with Alec is the crime of her past which could have been prohibited, she thinks, if only Angel had danced with her on that day. His return into her life is too late, as it will be again at the end of the novel.

Angel's love for Tess reminds her in the legitimacy of its request of the illegitimacy of her affair with Alec. When Angel proposes to her, Tess rejects him "with grave hopelessness, as one who had heard anew the turmoil of her own past." Tess's mother "did not see life as Tess saw it," however; "That haunting episode of bygone days was to her mother but a passing accident." For Tess, her liaison with Alec is the primary fact and fault of her life. Part of her agony is that she is not given, until the end of the novel, the chance or the circumstances for confronting it, for living up to it and perhaps conquering it.

But at Talbothays, in a seemingly new and different world, Tess hopes to find another and simpler resolution to the problem. There she "appeared to feel that she had really laid a new foundation for her future." Under the mood of the place—and Talbothays, as it is described, is the embodied symbol of the sensuousness of innocent physical love—Tess determines to be free of Alec: "She dismissed her past—trod upon it and put it out, as one treads on a coal that is smouldering and dangerous." Eden thus recovered, as it were, Tess agrees to marry Angel. Seven days before their wedding, they drive off together into town. It is Christmas eve, and on such an auspicious occasion, in Hardy's time symbology, the smouldering past bursts into flame. Tess is confronted with the tale of her fall and is saved from its destructive impact only by Angel's refusal to believe the story. In her naiveté then, Tess assures herself: "We shall go away, a very long distance, hundreds of miles from these parts, and such as this can never happen again, and no ghost of the past reach there." Escape, as Tess sees it, is a matter of space; but in Hardy's world it is time—the undying moments of an oppressive and retributively demanding past—that must be reckoned with.

Finally, on New Year's eve, Tess tells Angel of her past, and she pays for her honesty. After Angel has left her, she meets the man who identified her before her wedding and runs from him as he presents her again with her fault. She flees to Flintcomb-Ash and there meets one of the other dairy maids from Talbothays. Marian suggests to her that they talk of the past in order to revive it, that they "talk of he, and of what nice times we had there, and o' the old things we used to know, and make it all come back again a'most, in seeming." Through Marian and what she says, and through the general progress of events in the novel, the past is consciously and intentionally carried forward alive in and existent with the present. Izzy, another Talbothays maid, two of the women from the d'Urberville estate at Trantridge, and the man Tess has run from all come to Flintcomb-Ash, trapping Tess amid suggestions of her past. Then, as though the occurrence of so many coincidental meetings justifies another and greater coincidental meeting, Alec d'Urberville himself intrudes upon Tess's present, at the end of Phase the Sixth. The metaphoric justification for these accidental meetings—through setting and the allusions to larger repetitions, history, and the condensation of time—will be discussed later. The point now is to conclude quickly the long catalog of the various intrusions of Tess's past into her present until, at the climax of the novel, the past is resolved and the present destroyed. Alec returns to Tess at Marlott, and later finds her at Kingsbere, amid her d'Urberville ancestors, at "the spot of all spots in the world which could be considered the d'Urberville home." Then Angel comes back, by way of the cross where Alec and Tess have met, and through the place of Tess's birth where he first saw her at the dance. He goes to Sandbourne, and creates at his arrival the thematic climax of the novel. Both lines of Tess's past meet her at once; she is living with Alec when Angel finally comes to claim her as his wife. The dramatic climax of the novel comes at Stonehenge, after Tess has made her heroic choice and has killed Alec. Her first fault catches her here. She has freed herself, cleansed herself—she is confident that Angel will "forgive" her now she has "done that"—but still she must pay for this "annihilation" of her past. The dilemma is the dilemma of tragedy; and in her almost trancelike state, Tess rises to heroism in accepting her fate. Her waking response to the presence of the deputies is almost mystical in its comprehension: "It is as it should be," she says; "I have had enough. . . . I am ready." What we understand here is the complementary meeting of Tess's story with the greater history of man. And in this symbolic place, to which it seems that Tess responds almost as much as we do, something of man's noble, heroic and paradoxical guilt is expiated by her sacrifice on the ancient altar stone. . . .

TESS'S FALL

The repetition of an ancient past in the present and the continuing existence of that past as a generally and mythically relevant force serve as supportive metaphors for the relentless pursuit of Tess by her own particular dramatic past, the tragic fault of her submission to Alec, which finally destroys her. Hardy paraphrases the line he used in *A Pair of Blue Eyes* and *The Return of the Native* to express the significance of all of this: "experience is as to intensity, and not as to duration." Intensity is central even to the way Tess looks at her own life. She sees herself as

> a woman living her precious life—a life which, to herself who endured or enjoyed it, possessed as great a dimension as the life of the mightiest to himself. Upon her sensations the whole world depended to Tess; through her existence all her fellow-creatures existed, to her. The universe itself only came into being for Tess on the particular day in the particular year in which she was born.

The universe which Tess creates out of her existence is tragic, and as it unfolds it becomes more and more evident that the seed of the tragedy is planted in the very beginning. The actual place of her temptation and submission, The

Chase, is a sort of ominously preserved Eden. It is "the old-est wood in England," "a truly venerable tract of forest land, one of the few remaining woodlands in England of un-doubted primaeval date." Her expulsion from this Eden sends Tess out upon the earth, to the small and withering ex-istence of her home at Marlott, and then, for escape, to the rich and seemingly second Eden of Talbothays, "the Valley of the Great Dairies . . . in which milk and butter grew to rank-ness . . . the verdant plain so well washed by the river Var or Froom." At Talbothays the "waters were clear as the pure River of Life shown to the Evangelist," and Tess's "hopes mingled with the sunshine in an ideal photosphere." When Tess is with Angel here in the mornings "they seemed to themselves the first person up of all the world," and it "im-pressed them with a feeling of isolation, as if they were Adam and Eve."

From Talbothays Tess flees to the hellishly postlapsarian world of Flintcomb-Ash, where with Marian she remembers "that happy green tract of land where summer had been lib-eral in her gifts . . . . green, sunny, romantic Talbothays." They try together to recall that Eden for their peace of mind, "to make it all come back again a'most, in seeming." But Tess cannot remain even at Flintcomb-Ash. She is hounded there, too, by Alec, who greets her saying: "A jester might say this is just like Paradise. You are Eve, and I am the old Other One come to tempt you in the disguise of an inferior ani-mal." Tess retreats, once more, eventually to Kingsbere, where Alec follows her again; and when he appears this time "the old Other One" is in the guise of one of Tess's an-cestors, "the oldest of them all." Finally, in flight after she has killed Alec, she comes to Stonehenge, the place of her sacrificial and salvific fulfillment.

STONEHENGE

The scene at Stonehenge is the most important in the novel. Hardy concentrates his whole effort here to insist on the size of his heroine and the greatness of her tragedy. At the same time this scene is the final and climactic representation of Hardy's own nondramatic point of view, and the voice of the critic speaks, proclaiming Tess the "victim."

There are two major sets of metaphors at work in this scene which finally come together as one in the murder of Alec. The first is the metaphor of blood, suggesting both

Tess's loss of her virginity and her final destruction. Tess wears a red ribbon at the traditional May-walk—and she is "the only one of the white company who could boast of such a pronounced adornment." She is splashed with the blood of the dying Prince, after he is speared by the shaft of the mail-cart. As a result of this misfortunate loss of the horse, Tess allows herself to be persuaded to visit her "relatives" at Trantridge. There she is fed the ripe, red strawberries from Alec's garden, and is decked in a spectacle of red roses, and pricks her chin on the thorns. After her seduction, she meets the sign painter who accuses her in "staring vermillion words." She returns to Marlott, and while working in the field her arm is bruised and abraided by the stubble, and bleeds. Then, life and convention having pursued her like fates or furies, and her crime having become so complex as to allow no easy retribution or resolution, Tess kills Alec, and his blood stains—crudely—through the ceiling as an ace of hearts. Though Tess's blood is not actually shed in the end, she is sacrificed symbolically at the place which supposedly would have required, in its own time, the spilling of blood.

The second pattern of symbolic reference used to prepare for the Stonehenge scene is a series of three white coffins or altars. The first is the "empty stone coffin" in the churchyard of the old d'Urberville mansion, in which Angel places Tess on the night of their marriage and mutual confession. Her past forces her, symbolically and in actuality, toward her future at Stonehenge, and disallows any free and satisfactory existence between those times. Tess has only three experiences in life: her seduction, and the twin acts of her revenge or expiation and her sacrifice. Her other experience, falling in love with Angel and marrying him, is denied to her in the meaning of his sleepwalk to the open coffin with her in his arms, and in her second burial on the altar at Stonehenge. The second of the stone symbols appears in Chapter 52, as the Durbeyfields arrive at Kingsbere and Tess enters the church of her ancestors. She passes "near an altar-tomb, the oldest of them all, on which was a recumbent figure." The figure is not an effigy, however; it is Alec. The stone slab on which he lies prefigures, ironically, the bed in which he is murdered. That bed, its white sheets stained with his blood, is the last of the stone symbols and the one in which the altar-coffin and blood metaphors are united. It is the altar of Tess's act of expiation for her fault. Although she finally does "annihilate" her past by destroying Alec, she does not really escape it, nor does she gain a future, except in her brief, wild honeymoon with Angel and in the lives of Angel and 'Liza-Lu beyond the end of the novel.

Tess's existence is governed by the law of tragedy relentlessly imposed and enforced. Hardy's insistence on his theme insures this. Though Tess is seduced, she is still—or finally—a pure woman. Her purity is redeemed throughout the novel in her heroism, and she is fulfilled in the end. The fulfillment is tragic, however, and thus in some sense it is sacrifice as well. It would be easy to say that Tess is sacrificed to the conventions of man's limitations, which is what Hardy wants to say, in part. More significant, however, is Tess's sacrifice of herself for the sake of her honesty and dignity; and in this Tess redeems man from his limitations, and achieves her freedom.

Though the scene at Stonehenge is not the best accomplishment of Hardy's art, it is his most ambitious attempt at rendering the world of the action in metaphoric and symbolic terms. With Stonehenge, he suddenly expands the dimensions and significance of Tess's tragedy to the extremes of suggestive reference. Tess is made to belong to Stonehenge, to its immensity in time and its incomprehensible towering aspect. The scene, however, may be too large for the rest of the novel, despite the preparation for it in the suggestions of sacrifice discussed above. Tess's tragic size is to be discovered primarily in the representative aspect of her life, as this is suggested by the history of the ancient line of d'Urbervilles, and the intensity of her existence is represented in the coincidental intrusions and recurrences of the past in the present. But nothing quite like Stonehenge can be anticipated from this. . . . In a novel not set physically on timeless, eternal Egdon Heath, or amid Roman and prehistoric ruins, Stonehenge seems perhaps too expansive and too much a symbolic place.

TESS'S DEATH AS METAPHOR

But these are aesthetic considerations. And though it may be argued that the Stonehenge scene is symbolically awkward or aesthetically outsized, this does not diminish its thematic and philosophic significance. Angel tells Tess that Stonehenge is "older than the centuries; older than the d'Urbervilles." And that it is so is just the point. Tess's tragedy has been suggested as the general tragedy of man, heightened and intensified by the conventional intrusion of the past—and its fault—into the present. This recurrence of the past has been supported, metaphorically, through the use of Tess's ancestry. Suddenly, now, the d'Urberville history is not enough; Tess's life and fate are greater and more significant than the d'Urberville history can indicate. As Tess becomes conscious of her relation to Stonehenge, we are asked to accept on the strength of this new metaphor of setting a greater symbolic dimension for the whole novel. Stonehenge is the old "heathen temple" where sacrifices were made to the sun in primal days, before the worship of any modern God. Tess is placed on the altar stone of that ancient worship, and Hardy remarks at the close that "the President of the Immortals, in Aeschylean phrase, had ended his sport with Tess." This would make it seem that Tess is sacrificed to the gods, to Fate, to the unsympathetic manipulator of man's destiny. Yet Tess's fault is her own volition, tragic fault, not an imposition of a necessary fate upon her from the beginning. Her fate is determined, in the tradition of tragedy, by her own act—by the act that initiates the action of the rest of the tragedy. And though her final destruction at Wintoncester is accomplished at the hands of men acting from the straight, cruel standards of society, it is done with Tess's full and understanding submission.

The Stonehenge scene is exemplary of Hardy's characteristic strength and weakness as an artist as well as of his dramatic vision. Hardy's art is best in its narrative, and his descriptive technique is usually superb. But for some reason he does not just describe Stonehenge, and the scene is flawed because of this. The narrator reports the arrival of Tess and Angel:

> He listened. The wind, playing upon the edifice, produced a booming tune, like the note of some gigantic one-stringed harp. No other sound came from it, and lifting his hand and advancing a step or two, Clare felt the vertical surface of the structure.

What is wrong here is not just the sentence structure, but more importantly the violation of the description by the intrusion of Angel. Hardy vitiates the force of the description with Angel's feeling the stone and, later in the same paragraph, "carrying his fingers forward" to discover "the collosal rectangular pillar," and "stretching out his left hand" to feel another. The presence of Angel denies Hardy the distance he needs for the representation of descriptive detail. Tess manages to speak her lines in the dialogue of the scene well enough, though Angel's remarks . . . are clumsy, crude, or inane. Together Tess and Angel identify the place as "Stonehenge," the "heathen temple." Then Clare says: "Yes. Older than the centuries; older, than the d'Urbervilles! Well, what shall we do, darling?" The same mistake appears again a few paragraphs later, as he says to Tess: "Sleepy are you, dear? I think you are lying on an altar." And he explains the object and timing of the ancient sacrificial rites at Stonehenge just as grotesquely:

> "Did they sacrifice to God here?" asked she.
>
> "No," said he.
>
> "Who to?"
>
> "I believe to the sun. That lofty stone set away by itself is in the direction of the sun, which will presently rise behind it."

Tess speaks her lines with simplicity and dignity. What she says brings up her association with the scene: "One of my mother's people was a shepherd hereabouts, now I think of it. And you used to say at Talbothays that I was a heathen. So now I am at home." And she humbly suggests the largeness of her existence in her symbolic isolation in the great, timeless temple of sacrifice:

> "I like very much to be here," she murmured. "It is so solemn and lonely—after my great happiness—with nothing but the sky above my face. It seems as if there were no folk in the world but we two; and I wish there were not—except "Liza-Lu."

Hardy's best method, however, is demonstrated a few paragraphs later, in strict narrative description:

> In a minute or two her breathing became more regular, her clasp on his hand relaxed, and she fell asleep. The band of silver paleness along the east horizon made even distant parts of the Great Plain appear dark and near; and the whole enormous landscape bore that impress of reserve, taciturnity, and hesitation which is usual just before day. The eastward pillars and their architraves stood up blackly against the light, and the great flame-shaped Sun-stone beyond them and the Stone of Sacrifice midway. Presently the night wind died out, and the quivering little pools in the cup-like hollows of the stones lay still.

The long descriptive paragraphs of the final chapter of the novel are equally effective. The distance of the narrator from the spot is such that no sound need be represented to the reader. Angel and 'Liza-Lu climb the hill out of Wintoncester "impelled by a force that seemed to overrule their will," and stand still "in paralyzed suspense" beside the first milestone. Tess's end is declared in the silent gesture of the raised black flag, and again the world returns to a more normal, more peaceful, less intense existence:

> And the d'Urberville knights and dames slept on in their tombs unknowing. The two speechless gazers, bent themselves down to the earth, as if in prayer, and remained thus a long time, absolutely motionless: the flag continued to wave silently. As soon as they had strength they arose, joined hands again, and went on. . . .

Tess of the d'Urbervilles is marred most by Hardy's frequent impatience and the resultant intrusiveness of his narrator. The novel is sometimes clumsy in its manner, mistaken in its diction, especially in dialogue, and insensitive or unsubtle in its choice and dramatization of scenes. Still, despite all of this, Hardy's great creative instinct substantiates the tragedy of a young country girl who becomes as large as the largest heroine through the intensity of her existence and her significant consciousness of that intensity, played in the metaphoric context of the descriptive and narrative references of the novel. The simple but impressive plot structure is based upon the coincidental recurrence of events and the characters involved in them. Coincidence is justified, as usual in Hardy's fiction, through the actual and dramatic relation of the past to the present and through large metaphors of association; and Hardy's convention, that "experience is as to intensity, and not as to duration," is described in the expansion of the time context of the story through the reference to history.

Thus, in the end, Hardy makes Tess Durbeyfield significantly one of the d'Urbervilles. Her being so places her in a more general and inclusive context than that in which country girls are usually found. It is our world, finally, in which she lives, and our fates which in some heightened sense she lives. Through her we know something more about the general, historical, and continuing plight of our race; and we know something more about the heroic acceptance of that plight. Though Hardy cries out in the end that "the President of the Immortals . . . had ended his sport with Tess"—and though we may want to agree with him—we know, surely, from our experience in the novel that it has been more real, more meaningful, and much more moving than that.

Tess Is Not a Victim

Rosemarie Morgan

In the following selection, excerpted from critic Rosemarie Morgan's book *Women and Sexuality in the Novels of Thomas Hardy*, Morgan argues that Tess is not a passive victim of her fate as so many critics claim. Morgan contends that Tess commands her world sexually, emotionally, and morally.

Much is made by critics of the passive Tess who yields to circumstance and fate. They were and are voicing the nineteenth-century liberal point of view that exonerated the fallen woman on the grounds that she was one of nature's unfortunates. Innately mute and trusting, passive and yielding, she suffered a weakness of will and reason and was not, therefore, responsible for her actions. These are the contours of the dominant cultural perspective and the language that shapes them: from [writer] Havelock Ellis to Roman Polanski it is the dumb, gentle, unthinking, passive Tess who too often survives in interpretation. This defeats Hardy's purposes entirely. There is no denunciation, in his entire *œuvre*, as unequivocal as his denunciation of the sexual double-standard in *Tess*. And I include under this heading the sexual double-standard that would not deny to the sexually active male the power of will and reason, the self-responsibility and moral integrity that is so often denied to the sexually active female. Hardy's Tess is a sexually vital consciousness and, without any shadow of doubt, to my mind, she owns each and every one of these qualities.

Victorian critics were in no doubt about her sexuality. She was, in their eyes, excessively voluptuous. They doubted, instead, her moral purity and, if they exonerated her at all it was on presuppositional grounds that voluptuousness went hand in hand with enfeebled powers of will and reason. Today, the reverse is the case. Tess has recovered her moral good sense but now has an enfeebled sexuality. Either way,

Excerpted from *Women and Sexuality in the Novels of Thomas Hardy*, by Rosemarie Morgan. Copyright © Rosemarie Morgan 1988. Reprinted with permission from Routledge and Kegan Paul. (References in the original have been omitted from this reprint.)

she is misrepresented. What Hardy denounces, in his creation of Tess, is the popular belief—handed down to us today in the form of the "dumb blonde"—that a voluptuous woman, a sexy woman, is intellectually vapid or morally "loose," or as many Victorians believed, diseased in body and mind. It is, in my opinion, the combination of sexual vigour and moral rigour that makes Tess not just one of the greatest but also one of the strongest women in the annals of English literature. My aim, then, . . . will be to resurrect Hardy's original strong Tess from the blurred stereotype of the sexually passive fallen woman, as critics and film-directors would have it. Indeed, from her first recognition of sexual overtures in Alec's fruit-thrusting gestures to her ecstasy in the "Garden" sequence, Tess expresses a fully developed sexual nature as sensitive to the needs of her impassioned lover as to her own auto-erotic powers and desires.

Here, as in *The Return of the Native*, Hardy's poetic sensibility comes into play to embed within seemingly innocuous figures of speech a language of sexuality which is neither fastidious nor fey but, rather, earthy and physical. For example, at a loss to explain to Angel how she would love him —and he is not the most perceptive of lovers—Tess instinctively draws close to the physical world of nature and sensuously rubs down the skins of the "Lords and Ladies"; which for some perverse reason rouses in Angel the desire to teach her *history*.

Even where such figurative evocations do approach the delicate violets-and-lace, virginal/funereal lilies category of description, they remain coherent and integrated. Alec's rose pressed into Tess's breast, for instance, with the collocation of pricking thorn, blood drawn, red petals, imagistically prefigures his violation of Tess and the loss of her virginity in "The Chase" episode.

But for Tess's own erotic energies Hardy reserves less overblown imagery. The resemblances or analogies he draws between the external world of natural phenomena and the internal world of feminine sensation evince and sustain vitality and vigour, and above all physicality and naturalness. The Tess sexually aroused by her passion for Angel is therefore centred in a world of lush fecundity, of vigorous regeneration:

> Rays from the sunrise drew forth the buds and stretched them into long stalks, lifted up sap in noiseless streams, opened petals, and sucked out scents in invisible jets and breathings. . . . Thus passed the leafy time when arborescence seems to be the one thing aimed at out of doors. Tess

and Clare . . . ever balanced on the edge of a passion . . . were converging, under an irresistible law, as surely as two streams in one vale.

In a manner not unlike the "mollusc" imagery in *The Return of the Native*, but with a sensual, pulsing emphasis upon the hidden springs of passion, Hardy evokes sexual readiness in both his young lovers. The warm, moist season, in which buds and stalks swell, stiffen, distend and dilate, is Tess's season as much as it is Angel's. The "sapling" which had "rooted down to a poisonous stratum on the spot of its sowing" is now "transplanted to a deeper soil": "physically and mentally" Tess burgeons into life, "never in her recent life . . . so happy as she was now, possibly never . . . so happy again."

Hardy extends use of the analogical metaphor further to render implicit what he may not render explicit. Tess's most important erotic scene is the widely discussed "Garden" scene. The suggestive imagery, symbolic setting and metaphorical action have all been variously interpreted as having their common referent in the Edenic myth, but it seems to me that Hardy has devised a deliberate parody. Tess never enters the garden; she remains on the outskirts from first to last, "behind the hedge" in an uncultivated tract of land where apple trees grow untended. There is no central tree set "amidst" (as there is in "Genesis"); rather, several trees are placed on the periphery and are patently "uncovenanted." Nor are they fruiting (knowledge); instead, they produce blossom (nescience). In keeping with the parody, the "Edenic" roles of the central characters are inverted. It is "Eve" who is lured "like a fascinated bird" and "Adam" who lures. Already "fallen" in that his "performance" is flawed, Angel sounds the seductive call-note that wanders "in the still air with a stark quality like that of nudity," while Tess is drawn close to the "Garden" yet remains withdrawn from it throughout. This emphasis suitably fulfils the promise of the subtitle, "A Pure Woman Faithfully Presented." There is no fall, for Tess, that renders her impure, just as there is nothing to render her impure by association. In Hardy's eyes (if not in Angel's), she remains beyond the boundary of sin-laden archetypes and man-made "Gardens" of diabolism and sexual shame.

Hardy's focus is upon untended, unfettered Nature. Angel's harp-playing lures Tess out, not into a covenanted or cultivated (man-made) garden but into the raw wilderness. Drawn by the call of his harp through a "profusion of growth" and into close proximity to the object of her passion, Tess listens "like a fascinated bird"—mesmerised but at the same time "winged" for flight:

> The outskirt of the garden in which Tess found herself had been left uncultivated for some years, and was now damp and rank with juicy grass which sent up mists of pollen at a touch; and with tall blooming weeds emitting offensive smells—weeds whose red and yellow and purple hues formed a polychrome as dazzling as that of cultivated flowers. She went stealthily as a cat through this profusion of growth, gathering cuckoo-spittle on her skirts, cracking snails that were underfoot, staining her hands with thistle-milk and slug-slime, and rubbing off upon her naked arms sticky blights which, though snow-white on the apple-tree trunks, made madder stains on her skin; thus she drew quite near to Clare, still unobserved of him.

The seductive moment for Tess, as she moves gradually closer to Angel, moves Hardy to hyphenate the world of nature that it might lean closer to her as she now assimilates her surroundings to her own consciousness, "-Milk," "-spittle," "-slime," "sticky blights"—the mucosa and emissions of biological sex—"rub off" upon Tess as much from the objects in nature which wet and stain her person, as from Hardy's linguistic hyphenations. With "damp and rank . . . juicy grass," bursting pollen at a touch, and upward thrusting "tall blooming weeds emitting offensive smells," there is no sense of a fastidious, antiseptic, deodorised, sexuality in Tess's world. Pungently scented (as surely it should be), burning to the senses, hot in hue—"red and yellow" and Virgilian "purple"—the physical world Tess assimilates to her erotic consciousness is as unadulterated as her own "pure" nature.

Psychologically realistic, too, is the vivid rendering of attraction/repulsion sensations as Tess passes from the intimately physical, elemental wilderness to draw closer and closer to transcendental ecstasy. In her abandonment to the world of sensation, voluptuously gathering nature's secretions and mucosa upon her person—the generative fluids of "sex"—so now she unleashes her passion:

> Tess was conscious of neither time nor space. The exaltation which she had described as being producible at will by gazing at a star, came now without any determination of hers; she undulated upon the thin notes of the second-hand harp, and their harmonies passed like breezes through her, bringing tears into her eyes. The floating pollen seemed to be his notes made visible, and the dampness of the garden the weeping of the gar-

den's sensibility. Though near nightfall, the rank-smelling weed-flowers glowed as if they would not close for intentness, and the waves of colour mixed with the waves of sound.

Reaching her plateau of sexual ecstasy Tess soars to such pitch of intensity that tears spring to her eyes as, at the same time, the world of sight, colour and sound fuse and dissolve in her consciousness. Fully in keeping with the intensity of her female sensation, her alternating "waves" of orgasmic dilation, so too the lush, vegetative "weed-flowers glowed as if they would not close for intentness," as Tess now glows, "her cheeks on fire" at Angel's approach. Suddenly feeling exposed, she draws off to a distance to utter herself in safe, circumlocutions. She speaks of the apple blossom falling and "everything so green"—in detumescence drawing only the "falling off" in nature to her consciousness. Fending off Angel's probings about her "indoor fears," which are at this moment fears of over-exposure, she cannot help but feel that the very trees themselves have "inquisitive eyes." Then, as she gathers that her sexual langour is not apparent to her lover, she waxes unselfconsciously philosophical and wanes to a wistfulness—to "sad imaginings" as if the melting ache that lingers on has phased to bittersweet, post-orgasmic *triste.*

Hardy's sensitive exposition of Tess in sexual ecstasy, the candour and poetic truthfulness of the evocation, gives forcible physical expression to a sexual consciousness refreshingly unvarnished, unprettified, and nowhere sanctified or trivialised to a delicate niceness. Ecstatic to the point of tears, Tess emerges as "pure" as the unbound wilderness, with which she is in complete accord. As its most vital centre of energy, she absorbs, indeed celebrates, all its exuding essences, forces, sensations with a joy that the original Eve, assimilated not to nature but to man's moral law, is denied.

Sexual passion actively informs Tess's consciousness, her wisdom, her moral sense, her emotional generosity. By the same token, her heightened sensibilities kindle in her the purity of feeling which sees fit, on the one hand, to abjure the father of her child because she does not love him, and on the other, to repudiate a heaven that has no place for a new-born infant's unbaptised soul. Far from being a passive victim, Tess embodies a fierce impulse to self-determination against daunting, and ultimately insurmountable, odds.

From her repudiation of an ethic which says she should play the hard-to-get Beauty in order to win her rich "cousin" into providing for his poor relations, to her final execution of that same violating, vulgarising "cousin," the mutinous Tess's least impulse is to suffer-and-be-still. Is it in fact a passive Tess who, as is frequently claimed, connives at her own fate by falling asleep at the wrong moment? Textual evidence does not support this claim. The drowsy Tess is, in every respect, a thoroughly *exhausted* Tess, and Hardy takes pains to elicit in detail the sheer expenditure of energy and unremitting fatigue she endures in her efforts to keep body and soul together—her family's as well as her own.

Hardy's emphasis is upon a physical, active Tess from the very outset. Affiliated to a "votive sisterhood," remarkable, we are told, for its survival—"either the natural shyness of the softer sex, or a sarcastic attitude on the part of male relatives, had denuded such women's clubs as remained . . . of . . . their glory and consummation"—Tess is first seen in procession with the "sisterhood" through the village of Marlott, whom she joins later "with a certain zest in the dancing" until dusk. Disturbed though, by "the incident of her father's odd appearance," she decides she should return home, whereupon she takes charge of her siblings, "six helpless creatures" in "the Durbeyfield ship." Eventually she retires to bed at eleven o'clock only to be awakened one-and-a-half hours later to undertake the family's marketing requirements. That the sixteen-year-old girl should then doze off on her journey is the most natural, the most inevitable consequence. It is not symptomatic of an innate passivity, or, as has also been claimed, a tendency to drift; nor does it demonstrate Hardy's idealisation of a somnambulistic, sexually inert female consciousness. If anything emerges from his treatment of this episode, it is not that Tess sleeps at an inappropriate moment but that she suffers an appropriation of her sleep!

The labour/woman exploitative, machine-grinding world in *Tess*, its exhausting demands closely linked at salient points throughout the text to Tess's beleaguered states of being, is quite clearly a causal factor in her tragedy: the taxing demands upon her energy and resilience have immediate, palpably felt repercussions upon her faculties. Hardy's most potent emblematic image in this context is, of course, the "red tyrant that the women had come to serve . . . which kept a despotic demand upon the endurance of their muscles and nerves."

The "buzzing red glutton," remorselessly grinding, bears a suggestive resemblance to the lusty Alec; man and machine alike reduce Tess to physical exhaustion and mental stupefaction:

A panting ache ran through the rick . . . (Tess) . . . still stood at her post, her flushed and perspiring face coated with the corn-dust, and her white bonnet embrowned by it. She was the only woman whose place was upon the machine so as to be shaken bodily by its spinning, and the decrease of the stack now separated her from Marian and Izz, and prevented their changing duties with her as they had done. The incessant quivering, in which every fibre of her frame participated, had thrown her into a stupefied reverie in which her arms worked on independently of her consciousness.

This condition of physical exhaustion inducing mental fatigue and stupefaction should not be confused with the transcendence Tess herself induces, in which she retains a sense of self, sensation and energy.

"I don't know about ghosts," she was saying; "but I do know that our souls can be made to go outside our bodies when we are alive."

"A very easy way to feel 'em go," continued Tess, "is to lie on the grass at night and look straight up at some big bright star; and, by fixing your mind upon it, you will soon find that you are hundreds and hundreds o' miles away from your body, which you don't want at all."

Tess's facility for transcendence, for summoning what is commonly known as an "out-of-body" experience, is an act of will, and not coextensive. . . . Tess in transcendence is not stupefied, not comatose. Quite the reverse. She remains in full possession of all her faculties. She assimilates to her consciousness the larger world of nature, its sounds, odours, its very essences, expanding, not contracting sensory experience, possessing not being possessed. In such a moment of great intensity, time too is suspended. Elsewhere aware of how little the individual is able to control her own existence, which is ever subject to the dictates of time and circumstance, Tess in transcendental ecstasy suspends both. Expanding time to fit her own "space," her private world of inner sensation intensified by mental transcendence to reach beyond corporeal bounds, Tess effortlessly shapes the spatial/temporal world to suit her own needs and desires. . . .

The Tess perceived by Hardy is a sentient, physical being inhabiting a palpably physical world. And her capitulation to

Alec, in "The Chase," is the uttermost expression of this physicality. She is quite simply exhausted. Hardy leads up to this episode describing, in detail, the hard material fact of life as it is lived, for Tess: the miles she walks, the meals she goes without, the hours she works, the sleep she lacks, the moments of repose she is denied.

We are told, for example, that upon this particular fateful day Tess's "occupations made her late" in setting out upon her three mile walk to Chaseborough. From this we infer that her employers, the d'Urbervilles, who have appointed her "supervisor, purveyor, nurse, surgeon and friend" to their "community of fowls," require her to labour on Saturdays. Firmly entrenched then, in an everyday world of work, Tess walks the three miles to Chaseborough. She makes her market purchases, and then sets out to find her companions for the night walk home. While she waits for their barn-dancing to conclude, Alec intervenes and Hardy takes this opportunity to focus upon her physical condition:

> She looked round, and saw the red coal of a cigar. Alec d'Urberville was standing there alone. He beckoned to her, and she reluctantly retreated towards him. "Well, my Beauty, what are you doing here?" She was so tired after her long day and her walk that she confided her trouble to him—that she had been waiting ever since he saw her to have their company home, because the road at night was strange to her.

Feeling, wearily, that her companions "will never leave off," Tess decides she can bear to wait no longer. Alec offers to hire a trap and drive her home but despite pangs of hunger and fatigue, and the lateness of the hour, she had "never quite got over her original mistrust of him"—so she turns down his offer. Frequently infuriated, but rarely cavalier with her feelings of pride and assertions of self-will, Alec departs with the half-approving retort: "Very well, Miss Independence. Please yourself. . . ." Shortly afterwards Tess sets off with her companions upon "a three-mile walk, along a dry white road," and if Hardy evokes a hazy consciousness here, it is quite appropriately on behalf of the inebriates: they follow the road, "with a sensation that they were soaring along in a supporting medium . . . as sublime as the moon and stars above them." For Tess, by contrast, there is only hard physical reality: "The discovery of their condition spoilt the pleasure she was beginning to feel in the moonlight journey." Then, following an imbroglio with the lusty Car Darch and her equally lusty compeers, Tess is provoked to a vituperative assault upon "whorage," which leaves her "almost ready to faint, so vivid was her sense of the crisis." At this point Alec reappears. Tess accepts his offer of escape and instantly gets "shot of the screaming cars in a jiffy!"—as he crudely puts it.

They engage briefly in a conversation that devolves not upon Tess's passive emotions but upon her feelings of anger; and from this focus upon her emotional "burning" to her "burnt-out" physical energies Hardy swiftly moves:

> She was inexpressibly weary. She had risen at five o'clock every morning that week, had been on foot the whole of each day, and on this evening had in addition walked the three miles to Chaseborough, waited three hours for her neighbours without eating or drinking, her impatience to start them preventing either; she had then walked a mile of the way home, and had undergone the excitement of the quarrel, till, with the slow progress of their steed, it was now nearly one o'clock. Only once, however, was she overcome by actual drowsiness. In that moment of oblivion her head sank gently against him.

Alec naturally takes advantage of this moment. Reining in he encloses "her waist with his arms to support her," whereupon, alert and defensive, Tess springs up and "with one of those sudden impulses to reprisal to which she was liable she [gives] him a little push," and almost precipitates him into the road.

This is not dumb, passive yielding but self-determined, volatile resistance. Nevertheless, Tess is unspeakably weary. Thus, when the couple find themselves lost, with Alec's connivance, she is bedded down upon the leaves he has prepared for her and, tenderly buttoned into his overcoat for warmth, instantly falls asleep. Sleeping, her body is appropriated:

> Why was it that upon this beautiful feminine tissue, sensitive as gossamer, and practically blank as snow as yet, there should have been traced a coarse pattern as it was doomed to receive; why so often the coarse appropriates the finer thus.

Hardy's word is "appropriates." The act is an act of theft, a dishonest appropriation of another's property with the intent to deprive her of it permanently. The term suffices to denote the moral nature of the act, which passes beyond sexual assault to take account of violation of rightful ownership. It is a fitting emphasis in a novel that stresses a sexual ethic that denies woman the right to control not only her own mode of existence but also her own body. . . .

Tess, then, is maid no more. Some weeks later, discovering that she is pregnant, she packs her belongings and leaves. And it is at this point that Hardy draws attention to her facility for uttering sexual feeling and meaning, quite lucidly, with little more than a gesture. Alec has followed, and caught up with her along the road, but fails to persuade her to return. Needled, he demands a kiss, whereupon Tess openly insults him by turning her head "in the same passive way, as one might turn at the request of a sketcher or hairdresser." Alec's frustration at her mockery of his needs turns swiftly to hurt and despondency:

> "You don't give me your mouth and kiss me back. You never willingly do that—you'll never love me, I fear."

As he knows only too well, Tess's mannered sufferance of his kiss tells of a strongly repressed antagonism, a refusal to yield to his desire. She had rested her eyes, we are told, "vaguely . . . upon the remotest trees in the land while the kiss was given, as though she were nearly unconscious of what he did." Repression is not submission. "The essence of repression, says [psychoanalyst Sigmund] Freud, "lies simply in turning something away . . . keeping it at a distance from the conscious." Tess's subtly expressive gestures and posture describe this psychological condition exactly! Distancing unwanted sexual advances she is simultaneously fully aware of how best she may repel them. There is, in passive resistance of this kind, deliberate, conscious rebellion and considerable self-control. Authentic passivity exerts no such controls. . . .

One of Tess's greatest psychological dilemmas, from her first encounters with Alec to her last enactment of the cashmere-wrapped, "embroidered" kept-woman, lies in resisting classification. To Alec she is Everywoman and Eve-temptress. To Angel, predictably, she is first stereotypal Goddess and later stereotypal fallen woman: "ill," "unformed," and "crude." To Hardy, though, she is complex, diverse, unique: fierce and gentle, regenerative and destructive, trusting and suspicious, philosophical, mystical and sexy. Accordingly, in her momentary drift into a frame of mind that passively accepts the dueness of Nemesis, Hardy discovers in her a complex interaction of passive and active impulses:

> Tess had drifted into a frame of mind which accepted passively the consideration that if she should have to burn for what she had done, burn she must, and there was an end of it.

Notice how Tess's passive frame of mind is countermanded here with a strong, active tonicity: the decisive, self-willed "and there was an end of it." Significantly, this phrase resounds with internal echoes of her own quickened articulations, whereas "drifted into a passive frame of mind" has no ring of Tess about it at all. Notice too, how her deliberations are imbued with raw elemental energy: "if she should have to burn then burn she must.". . .

The baptism sequence occurs in Tess's shortest Phase, "Maiden No More," and an important aspect of Hardy's presentation here is that her witnesses are a congregation of young children: Tess is described as she would appear through the eyes of a small child. This perspective is important to Hardy's emphasis here upon innocence. Tess's defiant act of baptising her illegitimate child, seen through the eyes of innocents, is the purest act of grace and loving-kindness. Whether or not Christian orthodoxy would deem her act sacrilegious, is to Hardy irrelevant. The relevance lies simply in innocence speaking to innocence, child-mother to child-son, before an audience of innocent children.

In the first instance, the focus is upon Tess's big words, big gestures (she "fervently drew an immense cross upon the baby with her forefinger"). This emphasis clearly indicates an open-eyed, open-mouthed audience. In keeping with this perspective, the minister of the sacrament/big sister Tess towers hugely, whitely, in her nightgown, an imposing figure in the eyes of her tiny, uncomprehending attendants. In addition, this sighting takes into account her actual physical condition: a work-worn girl-mother with tousled hair, weary eyes, and stubble-scratches on her wrists; Clearly, Hardy has not lost sight of the flesh-and-blood Tess even as child-like wonder infuses the scene with a sense of the marvellous—a half-ignorant, essentially open-eyed attempt to grasp the seemingly incomprehensible. Tess takes up her ministerial role:

> "SORROW, I baptize thee in the name of the Father, and of the Son, and of the Holy Ghost."
> She sprinkled the water, and there was silence.
> "Say 'Amen,' children."
> The tiny voices piped in obedient response "Amen!"
> Tess went on:
> "We receive this child"—and so forth—"and do sign him with the sign of the Cross."

Here she dipped her hand into the basin, and fervently drew an immense cross upon the baby with her forefinger, continuing with the customary sentences as to his manfully fighting against sin, the world, and the devil, and being a faithful soldier and servant unto his life's end. She duly went on with the Lord's Prayer, the children lisping it after her in a thin gnat-like wail, till, at the conclusion, raising their voices to clerk's pitch, they again piped into the silence, "Amen!"

As emblematic rite, baptism objectifies sin and guilt and enacts the release of the forces of darkness. Tess invokes this rite and utters the words of redemption over her child. Thus empowered to utter the spirit clean and new, the fallen woman/minister-of-the-sacrament is quite openly vindicated by her author. She cannot logically fulfil both roles. The one invalidates the other. Religious objections can scarcely be raised against the fittingness of her desire to mediate between Heaven and Hell, salvation and damnation, to anoint redemption upon the object of her "sin" (permissible, if "Romish" practice), for according to received doctrine no repentant believer is held to be irredeemable, and that has to include Tess in her "ecstasy of faith." In a sense, then, she utters her own redemption, for as surely as her "fall" stains (in Victorian eyes), so the blessings she invokes as consecrator of the sacrament effect a token cleansing of her soul.

(Tess) with much augmented confidence in the efficacy of this sacrament, poured forth from the bottom of her heart the thanksgiving that follows, uttering it boldly and triumphantly in the stopt-diapason note which her voice acquired when her heart was in her speech, and which will never be forgotten by those who knew her. The ecstasy of faith almost apotheosized her; it set upon her face a glowing irradiation, and brought a red spot into the middle of each cheek; while the miniature candle-flame inverted in her eye-pupils shone like a diamond.

Hardy does not, however, intend this scene merely to "carry" Tess into spirituality, into saintly transfiguration. Rather, she turns church ritual and dogma to her own advantage and subverts both. First, Hardy introduces the subversive element with the lightly mocking comment that,

Poor Sorrow's campaign against sin, the world, and the devil was doomed to be of limited brilliancy.

Then Tess, too, is sceptical:

In the daylight . . . she felt her terrors about his soul to have been somewhat exaggerated; whether well founded or not she had no uneasiness now, reasoning that if Providence would not ratify such an act of approximation she, for one, did not value the kind of heaven lost by the irregularity—either for herself or her child.

With Tess's defiant afterthought echoing the comment on the infant Sorrow's "campaign against sin, the world, and the devil," it becomes evident that Hardy is paying mere lip-service to an observance of Christian doctrine on the one hand, as do the lisping innocents, and making a mockery of it on the other. The concept of a sin-laden Tess and a sin-laden Sorrow is clearly risible in his eyes. Irony and scepticism point to his scorn of a cultural ideology that fosters, under the mantle of Christianity, both the myth of the fallen woman's guilt and the guilt of unbaptised innocents. . . .

Hardy's vindication of Tess is unequivocal. He does not "seem" to exempt her from the fallen woman's guilt but commits himself wholeheartedly to her exemption. She will and must triumph over a deterministic cultural prescription that would deny her ascendancy, both sexual and moral, after her fall. She has not earned but, rather, learned the guilt and sorrow, and Hardy (it not Angel Clare), is convinced, not only of her purity but also of her capacity for ascendancy.

In her sacramental cleansing of the infant Sorrow's guilt Tess enacts her own desire to liberate the innocent soul from damnation, to "bury" guilt and sorrow purged of all stain. Her mediating powers kindle, in turn, her own spiritual regeneration, which, following an interregnum, a time for changing from "simple girl to complex woman," urges her upon departure, upon a new phase, a new life.

The woman who usurps the male minister's role, who utters her own form of baptism, gives powerful voice to her longing to govern, to control her own existence. There are echoes of this will to self-determination and self-renewal in her repudiation of her dark ancestry. . . .

Hardy retains, then, for Tess, with her emotional generosity, sexual vitality and moral strength, the capacity to rise above her fall and, ultimately, to redeem the man who, bearing the values and sexual prejudices and double-standards of the society, fails to rise above them in the hour of need. Nor does Tess's last hour find her bereft of will, self-determination and courage. In knifing the heart of the man who so remorselessly hunts her down, she turns her own life around yet again; but this time with readiness, she says, to face her executioner.

Tess as a Pagan Goddess

Shirley A. Stave

Shirley A. Stave is an assistant professor of English at the University of Wisconsin Center–Waukesha County. In the following excerpt from her book *The Decline of the Goddess*, Stave gives an interesting interpretation of Tess's character. Stave claims that Tess's character and her fate imply that she has more in common with ancient pagan goddesses than with Victorian women. Hardy consciously associates Tess with these pagan images, Stave claims.

For many readers, Hardy's crowning achievement is his creation of Tess Durbeyfield, who has become one of the most memorable women characters in all of literature. Something about her haunts the imagination; she is at once child and woman, strong and fragile, masterful, and timid. In her, myth and history fuse. We are presented, on the one hand, with a very tangible English cottage girl and, on the other, with a goddess figure of immense stature. She exists in time while she remains timeless. . . .

Tess functions as one differentiated and marked, as one whose experience and consciousness are essentially different from those of her would-be peers, as one whose life is fated to enact a story already narrated and concluded. Read mythically, she becomes emblematic of the Great Goddess, the informing spirit of a Pagan consciousness.

Hardy emphasizes her mythic (i.e., nonhistorical, nonhuman) nature by endowing Tess with qualities that culture, particularly Victorian culture, claimed were alien to a woman's nature. One such quality is her queenly pride, which reveals itself first at the very beginning of the novel, when she attacks her friends who ridicule her drunken father. After the unfortunate incident involving Prince, when

Excerpted from *The Decline of the Goddess: Nature, Culture, and Women in Thomas Hardy's Fiction*, by Shirley A. Stave. Copyright © 1995 by Shirley A. Stave. Reprinted with permission of Greenwood Publishing Group, Inc., Westport, CT. (References in the original have been omitted from this reprint.)

Tess is coerced by her parents to "claim kin," it is her pride that causes her to hesitate. When, in her encounter with Alec, he insists she use the surname "Durbeyfield," rather than "d'Urberville," the name he has appropriated, Tess responds with dignity, "I wish for no better, sir." Pregnant with his baby, she not only refuses to marry him but will not even inform him of her condition, even though he has assured her that he will provide for her financially in such circumstances. "Any woman would have done it but you," says her mother, who apparently recognizes her daughter's extraordinary nature. Once Tess has borne the child, she goes to work in the fields "with dignity, and had looked people calmly in the face at times, even when holding the baby in her arms." It is this same pride that serves to sever her from Angel Clare once he learns of Tess' involvement with Alec. When her young husband rejects her, the text emphasizes that had Tess "been artful, had she made a scene, fainted, wept hysterically, in that lonely lane, notwithstanding the fury of fastidiousness with which he was possessed, he would probably not have withstood her." That Tess' pride—dignity, if we will—is often read as a flaw in her character, especially in this scene, reveals the double standard that characterizes a patriarchal culture. What is seen as unnatural, and therefore reprehensible, in Tess would be admired in a man; similarly, the behavior expected of Tess (fainting, weeping hysterically) would be considered irrational and weak in a man. The cultural construction of womanhood, which places limitations on women's behavior, is challenged by Hardy's characterization of this extraordinary woman.

In addition to her pride, Tess . . . possesses a strength—both physically and psychologically—that distinguishes her, especially in a culture that defined woman as essentially weak. Several times throughout the novel, Hardy portrays Tess' inner strength as compelling an otherwise uncaring person to respond to her strongly and sympathetically, even against his or her will. One such instance occurs after Tess has baptized her dying baby herself, taking onto herself the authority of the minister of God. Yet, when she informs the parson of what she has done, her strength of character impresses him so tremendously that he assures her *against his reason* that her action is acceptable. The narrative voice reveals satisfaction as it states, "The man and the ecclesiastic fought within him, and the victory fell to the man." Similarly, Tess' physical presence is so strong that one glance at her completely unravels Alec. Even as he is preaching a sermon, he is so shaken by seeing Tess that he is stricken dumb until she averts her gaze from him, and, even then, he lapses into confusion and becomes incoherent. . . .

A third quality denied women, specifically in Hardy's time, that Tess possesses, setting her apart from the historical, and therefore the human, is her sexuality. Repeatedly, Hardy describes Tess in sexual terms. . . . Hardy recognizes that sexuality is not a minor aspect of, nor a perversion within, human nature; rather, it is the life-force, that which is crucial to the existence of human nature. . . .

Tess' response to her own sexuality is important; she does not see herself as a victim of her sexuality. . . . Her sexual nature *is* her nature; it is not something that possesses her, some alien presence that determines her actions and denies her agency. Nor is it something she can, or would care to, relinquish. When, for example, Angel, distraught at her wedding night confession, begs her to tell him that her story about her past affair and the child she has borne is a lie, she refuses, even though Angel "would willingly have taken a lie from her lips, knowing it to be one, and have made of it, by some sort of sophistry, a valid denial." Similarly, in the bitter days after the confession, Tess' only advance toward reconciliation is a sexual one: she tilts her head to receive Angel's kiss, a gesture he declines to act upon. Words, the medium of culture, are not a viable alternative for Tess; she can act only according to her nature, and for that she is rebuffed. . . .

TESS AND PAGAN NATURE

The role nature plays in *Tess of the d'Urbervilles* transcends Romantic concepts of the natural. In speaking of the novel's "thematic concept of Nature as norm," [Hardy critic J.T.] Laird suggests Hardy is reminding his readers "that natural phenomena were once objects of veneration." Hardy does this by creating a world in which to some degree they still are. In this novel, he most clearly treats the worship of nature as a religion in its own right, claiming that "a saner religion had never prevailed under the sky." The sane religion he affirms is Paganism and Tess functions as its deity, its goddess. However, Paganism, rooted as it is in nature, celebrates deity as both female and male, as goddess and god. While in this text no nature god of the Gabriel Oak mode appears, the male deity appears as the sun, which consistently figures in significant ways in Tess' life, recalling the brother-sister deities who become consorts in many non-Christian religions. The sun cheers a disheartened Tess on her first morning at Tantridge, and she celebrates the sun's presence (albeit using the words of a Christian psalter) as she strikes out for a new life at Talbothays Dairy. When she sacrifices herself at Stonehenge, she is awakened by a rising sun, a consummation that results in her self-sacrifice. That Tess' actual death occurs on a July morning may not be accidental. The Pagan celebration of Lughnasa, a harvest festival in which the cutting of the grain is referred to metaphorically as the sacrifice of the Corn King, occurs in late July or early August. The cyclical nature of life is affirmed in the ritual through the seeds retained for next year's planting; it is understood that while the god has died (even as the sun begins waning, moving toward the dark of the year), the goddess (the earth) is pregnant with his son. Read in the context of this myth, Tess' death becomes terrifying, since she who is the bearer of life, the keeper of the seed, the goddess, herself is lost to the world and with her goes the possibility of renewal. . . . The sun does witness her death, but the consummation at Stonehenge that would have allowed for the birth of the new sun/son with the new crop is rendered ineffectual through the loss of Tess. With the death of the nature goddess, the sun is no longer a deity but simply a mass of burning gases.

The brilliance of Hardy's novel lies in the double articulation of Tess as both worshiper of nature and nature goddess. Her name, a form of Theresa, which . . . is Greek for "to glean" or "to reap," emphasizes her dual role within the novel. On the one hand, she is Tess the dairymaid, who through her tasks—milking the cows and harvesting the corn—functions as nature's loving worshiper. On the other hand, she is the goddess who sacrifices herself, the wheat which is gleaned. Angel becomes aware of her divine nature in their early mornings together at the dairy. In the time of transition from night to day, a liminal time that, as such, is mythically and mystically charged, Tess exhibits "a dignified largeness both of disposition and physique, an almost regnant power." Hardy goes on to add, "Then it would grow lighter, and her features would become simply feminine; they had changed from those of a divinity who could confer bliss to those of a being who craved it." It is her presence that makes the dairy a paradise for Angel and for the reader as well. Hardy keeps the narrative focus on Tess, making the other characters circle around her. It is her beauty that beautifies the dairy, her life that animates it, her spirit that infuses it. After the wedding, when Tess and Angel return to Talbothays, "the gold of the summer picture was . . . grey, the colours mean, the rich soil mud, and the river cold." When Tess despairs, the landscape echoes her despair; just as Ceres' grief for her daughter in the underworld turns the world cold and bleak, so Tess' grief at Angel's desertion unleashes a wild and terrible winter on the land. But for all her despair, Tess does not consider leaving the land, even though the narrative reveals that, with her "intelligence, energy, health, and willingness in any sphere of life," she would readily have found employment in a city. However, given the narrative fusion of Tess with the landscape, neither she nor the reader can conceive of such a move. The story of Tess takes place out of time and out of history—there are no cities to turn to within the mythic framework of the novel. When Tess finally does leave the land, mythic time and space are destroyed and the fall into history occurs.

Hardy is not subtle in his treatment of Tess' bond with a Pagan past. He might even be accused of excess in revealing her to be descended from Sir *Pagan* d'Urberville. Tess herself is introduced in the novel at a May Dance, a fertility ritual. . . . It is the women, the narrative stresses, who keep the Pagan customs such as the May-walking alive; all the men's clubs have abandoned the practice. The specific link between women and Paganism is established early in the text. As Tess sings a hymn to creation, Hardy points out that, although the words are Christian, the spirit behind them is far older, emphasizing that women, particularly those women who routinely work out-of-doors in nature, have not lapsed from the Pagan ways typical of humankind in an earlier period. Women, the text suggests, have more to gain in retaining their Pagan heritage since it empowers them and allows for the articulation of their sexuality, which Christianity adamantly strives to co-opt and repress. In its emphasis on virginity and chastity (certainly central themes of Hardy's novel) Christianity attempts to control the sexual behavior of women and to divide women against themselves. The narrative voice here consistently positions itself against the

Christian values, reading women's sexuality from a Pagan perspective. . . . Hence Joan Durbeyfield consistently advises her daughter to be circumspect in what details of her past she reveals to her intended husband. Joan, a wise woman of the folk, refuses to put men on any sort of pedestal; rather, she accepts a natural "conspiracy" among wise women, understanding that men have no right to make claims on women's sexual behavior. Joan understands that men accept the new patriarchal system because of the power they gain by it, but that women must subvert it if they are to claim their own empowerment. And for Joan, that empowerment involves the very natural act of sex. She sees Tess' affair with Alec as a natural, almost inevitable, act and never upbraids her daughter for bearing his child. Interestingly, some critics . . . consider her "amoral," presumably because her system of morality is grounded in an older, naturalistic, specifically Pagan world view, which threatens the patriarchy by refusing to give assent to it.

Throughout the novel, Hardy aligns Paganism with matriarchy by emphasizing Tess' bond with Joan. Jack Durbeyfield, like most fathers in Hardy, is not only ineffectual but never functions as any sort of an authority figure to Tess. Even in begetting Tess, his influence is limited. Although Tess bears the d'Urberville likeness, it is from Joan that she inherits her prettiness. It is also from Joan, her conjuring mother who keeps her copy of the *Compleat Fortune-Teller* in the outhouse because she so strongly believes in its power, that Tess inherits her link with Pagan ways. Significantly, Joan's family derived from the area near Stonehenge, where Tess returns to end her mythic journey. However, Hardy portrays Tess' earthly home in Marlott as sharing in Stonehenge's mythic time and space as well, particularly in that the people who live there cling to their beliefs in the witches and fairies that once haunted the locale.

Tess' matriarchal bond reveals itself most clearly when, anguishing over whether she should marry Angel, she seeks out her mother as "the only person in the world who had any shadow of right to control her action." From a patriarchal perspective, that right belongs first to her father and second to her affianced lover, but Tess allows neither man a claim over her actions. But Tess' mother is not the only mother figure in the text. When her own mother cannot physically be with her, Tess finds a spiritual mother in the old woman who serves her tea after her unsuccessful journey to find Angel's parents. Not accidentally, the old woman is the only villager Tess encounters; all the rest have gone to hear the now-Christian Alec preach. The woman's appearance in the deserted village at a time when Tess has just abandoned her search for Christian parents lends a fairytale quality to the incident; that a fairy godmother magically appear at the moment of Tess' need suggests the power of the matriarchal bond. . . .

TESS AND THE LIFE OF CHRIST

Tess' life and death can be read as a Pagan inversion of the life and death of Christ. Hardy has deliberately drawn parallels between the two, beginning with the cock's crowing on the day of her marriage. By joining herself with Angel, Tess is betraying her essence, is compromising herself to culture. Later that day, when Angel and Tess wash their hands in the same basin, Pontius Pilate's handwashing comes to mind. Tess, in response to Angel's query, "Which are my fingers and which are yours?" claims, "They are all yours," renouncing her right to self and to her own sexuality, making it easy for Angel to feel absolved of any guilt for the destruction he wreaks upon her. Later, Hardy interjects more echoes of Christ's life when Tess, Joan, and the Durbeyfield children can find no room in the inn when they travel to their spiritual homeland. Like Christ, Tess has her night of agony and her descent into the hell of life with Alec in a fashionable boarding house, completely removed from the natural world, which is her essence. Significantly, after this point, Tess no longer functions as the focalizer for the scenes, and the narrator voice no longer accesses her thoughts and emotions; as a result, the reader is distanced from Tess. The deity has withdrawn itself, and the human is no longer privy to her thoughts and feelings. The sacred has retreated, has become the stuff of legend, of the "word," but is no longer immediately available. Finally, like Christ, Tess endures a sacrificial death . . . at Stonehenge, a Pagan site which, significantly, feels familiar to her. She is sleeping on an altar when the authorities come for her. "It is as it should be," she says, . . . dying for the sins that have been committed against nature. But through the narrative distance, and through the diminishment revealed by the narrative after Tess' death, the reader understands that this ritual will not

be repeated. . . . With Tess' death the cycle of nature is rup-
tured and flattens into a linear telos. The old Pagan world
view has been defeated by a new Christian way of perceiving.

In Tess' life, that defeat results from the combination of
her relationships with two men belonging to the new order:
Alec the rake and Angel the saint. [One critic] speaks of Tess'
destruction as occurring first because of Alec's relentlessly
seeking his own pleasure but then also because of Angel's
"prudery." From a feminist perspective, what is significant is
Hardy's continual development of parallels which indicate
how, as [literary critic Anne Z.] Mickelson puts it, Angel and
Alec "are one and the same man. Their concept of woman
reflects society's view of her and the myths constructed
about women." That society, it is necessary to remember, is
informed by Christianity and characterized by patriarchy. . . .

TESS'S CORRUPTION BY CULTURE

However, Tess can be said to enable her own destruction in
the sense that she has been co-opted by culture. From early
in the novel, she gives her assent to the values of the patriarchy, of the culture alien to her Pagan Marlott. However,
she does not choose to be co-opted; the forces of the patriarchy bear down upon her with the speed and force of the
modern mail cart which impales Prince, her horse, pulling
his old-fashioned wagon. Although Tess has been reared in
Pagan Marlott, she has been educated to a degree in the National School, which has resulted in more than her simply
being able to speak two languages—folk dialect as well as
culturally sanctioned "proper" English—although the division in her speech metaphorically reflects the result of the
education overall. . . . Her contamination by [Victorian
morality] affects her perception, so that, for example, on her
return to Marlott after she has been Alec's lover, she sees her
beautiful village "now half-veiled in mist." Having accepted
to a degree culture's assessment of a seduced woman as
fallen, she can no longer see her home, the site of the old
values, clearly. [Hardy critic Jean R.] Brooks claims that Tess'
"consciousness isolates her" from the natural world. The
problem is one of perception. Hardy addresses this relativity, when, in discussing Tess' despair over her "fatherless"
child, he emphasizes that, removed from a societal context,
Tess would have delighted in her child's existence, adding,
"Most of [her] misery had been generated by her conven-

tional aspect, and not by her innate sensations." When her child grows ill, Tess moves even closer to embracing the values and the religion of the patriarchy. She becomes frantic to the point that she undertakes the baptism of her baby to prevent his damnation to the Christian hell that up until now she has not accepted as plausible, and even makes a cross for his grave. . . . While Hardy may be laughing bitterly, Tess is not; her anguish over the future of her dying baby is real and indicates the degree to which she has accepted Christianity's harsh doctrine. However, she remains capable of believing in the eventuality of her own renewal with the seasons and in the possibility of rediscovering joy. Only after she enters into a love relationship with Angel Clare, mythically her opposite, her enemy, and her destroyer, does she lose sense of who and what she is. Hardy's discourse makes it clear that Tess turns this Angel, this Christ, into her god. She, who is the essence of the natural and the physical, has "hardly a touch of earth in her love for Clare"; he becomes "the breath and life of [her] being." As she anguishes over whether or not to marry him, she wishes for a counsellor, even as she rejects her previous counsellor, her mother, having turned her back on the matriarchal bond. . . . She has accepted a moral system that is antithetical to everything she embodies, as well as violative of Hardy's perception of what permits the human to thrive. Tess' only true crime is abandoning her sense of self, allowing herself to become an object Angel can manipulate, but one cannot blame her for occupying the only space culture has permitted women to fill. She is so inculcated with patriarchal definitions of the status of women that "it pleased her to think [Angel] was regarding her as his absolute possession, to dispose of as he should choose." Her lack of her own self-worth leads her to the point where she even offers to be Angel's servant. Her identity is so determined by Angel that when he deserts her, she is virtually destroyed. She goes so far as to make herself ugly, dressing in old clothes and clipping off her eyebrows in a desperately self-destructive act. She begins to be ashamed of her sexuality, her essence, and wishes men would not look at her. The text reveals that she felt that "in inhabiting the fleshly tabernacle with which Nature had endowed her she was somehow doing wrong"; that she has arrived at such a perception indicates her complete inculcation with the teachings of the Christian patriarchy about physicality and sexuality, specifically insofar as those qualities bear upon women.

In her despair, Tess abandons even nature. . . . She poignantly writes to Angel, "The daylight has nothing to show me, since you are not here, and I don't like to see the rooks and starlings in the fields." If anything, nature terrifies her; she imagines witches and fairies behind hedges and trees. Her separation from nature—paralleled by Christ's descent into hell—takes her to the fashionable apartment where she wears elegantly embroidered dressing gowns. She is no longer Tess the dairymaid; she no longer functions as the embodiment of nature—she has lost her self, her identity. . . .

The novel's brilliance lies in its depiction of the fall into the historical, which is essentially Tess' story. The archetype dictates her fate. Just as the Great Goddess is now regarded by most of the Western world as a mythic figure, while Christ is considered real in some sense, so Tess' existence in the novel occurs in prehistory, in mythic time and space. But modern culture, science, religion, destroy the mythic, just as Tess and her world are destroyed by the many guises of the historical—the things that "actually exist": science, Christianity, the patriarchy. After her fall into the historical, living in a modern hotel in a modern city, where nature is not allowed to intrude except in very controlled ways, Tess temporarily returns to the mythic world (reminiscent of the short time Christ lives on earth after the resurrection) for her mysterious, dreamlike honeymoon with Angel Clare. But Angel is a part of history. Whether or not he loves Tess, she cannot exist for him. Mythic time and historical time can only overlap for brief moments. In the end, the historical invades the mythic, seizes it, carries it off, and kills it, while a waving black flag marks the execution of Tess the dairymaid.

Tess Is Admirable

Jean R. Brooks

Jean R. Brooks is the author of the book *Thomas Hardy: The Poetic Structure*, from which this article is excerpted. In this selection, Brooks argues that Tess engages in a fight to be recognized as an all-too-human individual in spite of the almost superhuman, mythic forces at work against her.

Tess of the d'Urbervilles is not about a pure woman betrayed by man, morality, and the President of the Immortals; her fight for re-acceptance and happiness; "the incessant penalty paid by the innocent for the guilty" . . . or the decay of the peasantry. All these aspects are there, but all are contributory to the major conflict suggested by the two parts of the title. "'Call me Tess,' she would say askance" when Angel Clare "called her Artemis, Demeter, and other fanciful names half teasingly," and it is as the dairymaid Tess, an individual human being, that she "had set herself to stand or fall by her qualities." But she is also Tess "of the d'Urbervilles," and the novel is shaped by the tension between the personal and impersonal parts of her being. The right to be human is not easy to assert against the laws of nature, heredity, society and economy which abstract from people "the differences which distinguished them as individuals.". . .

The plot is organized round the seven "phases" of Tess's personal story to give pointers to the direction in which her impersonal life is moving. Her first phase as "The Maiden" ends when Alec seduces her.

> An immeasurable social chasm was to divide our heroine's personality thereafter from that previous self of hers who stepped from her mother's door to try her fortune at Trantridge poultry farm.

The second phase follows Tess's return home with the consciousness of original sin on her—she looked upon herself as a figure of Guilt intruding into the haunts of Innocence"—to the birth and death of her baby, and her reinte-

Excerpted from *Thomas Hardy: The Poetic Structure*, by Jean R. Brooks (Ithaca, NY: Cornell University Press). Copyright © 1971 by Jean R. Brooks.

gration into country ritual. "The past was past; whatever it had been was no more at hand."

On one point she was resolved: there should be no more d'Urberville air-castles in the dreams and deeds of her new life. She would be the dairymaid Tess, and nothing more.

In Phase the Third, "The Rally," the experience and personality of the dairymaid Tess are enlarged at Talbothays by Angel Clare. The unpremeditated kiss that ends this phase means that "something had occurred which changed the pivot of the universe for their two natures." That "something," in the next phase, is that Tess hands over part of her self to the impersonal force of love. This phase follows the maturing natural relationship of two lovers "converging, under an irresistible law, as surely as two streams in one vale," until Tess's fatal confession on her wedding night. In Phase the Fifth, "The Woman Pays," the personal Tess is gradually depersonalized, first of all by the abstract ideal of purity which Angel prefers to her real human self, and secondly, when he has abandoned her, by the increasingly automatic mode of her life.

There was something of the habitude of the wild animal in the unreflecting instinct with which she rambled on—disconnecting herself by littles from her eventful past at every step, obliterating her identity.

Now seeking not happiness, but mere survival, she has a second recovery through endurance of winter weather and roughwork at Flintcomb-Ash. This time it is halted on her return from Emminster, when a meeting with Alec gives her "an almost physical sense of an implacable past which still engirdled her."

The closing in of her implacable past to submerge her personal identity occupies the sixth phase. She makes her last helpless gesture as an independent woman in the d'Urberville vaults, where her homeless family have camped for the night. "Why am I on the wrong side of this door!" In the last phase, the "coarse pattern" that had been traced "upon this beautiful feminine tissue, sensitive as gossamer," is fulfilled at Stonehenge, a place of religious sacrifice, and Wintoncester, ancient social capital of Wessex. Alec's murder and Tess's execution identify the personal Tess with the d'Urberville family type, the scapegoat victim of fertility rites, and those innate and external pressures which level down the human being into something less than human—"breathing now was quick and small, like that of a lesser creature than a woman."

The pivotal points in Tess's fight to be herself show fundamental parallels that compel comparisons and contrasts. These draw the lines of the "coarse pattern" for us. Tess has three "deaths" and three rebirths: the first at Talbothays into the fullness of human and natural existence; the second at Flintcomb-Ash into a lower plane of animal survival; the third in a metaphysical sense, when she hands over the meaning of her life to 'Liza-Lu and Angel standing, significantly, in the position of [Florentine painter] Giotto's "Two Apostles." Her two violations, physical and spiritual, invite comparison as well as contrast between Alec d'Urberville and Angel Clare. Both deny Tess the right to be human, Alec in obedience to the subhuman impulse of sex, Angel to the superhuman power of the image that substitutes essence for existence. Both are incompletely characterized when compared with the rounded humanness of Tess, but this is surely stratagem rather than error. Alec's resemblance to the Victorian stage villain and the morality Vice, and Angel's to one of his own unreal (angelic) conceptions of human nature, indicate their role as complementary agents of dehumanization. Both betray Tess in a world of paradisal lushness, though the resemblance should not blind one to the essential differences between Trantridge and Talbothays. Both feed her with fruit. Both are associated in action and commentary with fire; Alec in its red, murky aspect and Angel with its radiance—the fire of hell and heaven. . . .

Such parallels suggest a rich layer of archetypal myth directing the course of Tess's life. Hardy's rich poetic and narrative resources combine to bring out the deeper meaning of the novel by imaginative description of the way characters move and speak and relate to their environment. The central events are described in Darwinian [relating to evolutionist Charles Darwin] terms of struggle and adaptation, extinction and renewal of the species. But the discovery of Tess's ancestry initiates all the myths about the meaning of being human; myths that are explored in the rest of the novel through an intricate network of poetic cross-references. . . .

Nature and Tess's Role

Descriptions of natural phenomena, used so variously in Hardy's work, combine with colour symbolism to define

Tess's role as ritual victim. The sun-god, who demanded blood to perpetuate his life-giving powers, is much in evidence. Hardy's accuracy in conveying the effect of sunlight at different times of the day and year make these effects a poetic correlative to Tess's acceptance of her role. At Wellbridge Manor, just before she confesses, the low afternoon winter sunlight "stretched across to her skirt, where it made a spot like a paint-mark set upon her." The stain sets up reverberations not only of Prince's blood, which splashed her "from face to skirt," but also of the text-painter, who embodied her conventional sense of guilt in red letters, "THY, DAMNATION, SLUMBERETH, NOT." At Flintcomb-Ash, where the red threshing machine drives Tess with the impersonality of immutable law, "a wrathful shine" from the March sunset dyes the tired faces of the enslaved threshers with "a coppery light," giving to the human features the look of ritual masks that marked the men who surrounded Tess on the Stone of Sacrifice at sunrise, "their faces and hands as if they were silvered, the remainder of their figures dark." Even the benevolent morning sun of the Marlott harvest, "a golden-haired, beaming, mild-eyed, God-like creature," throws "stripes like red-hot pokers" on cottage furniture and intensifies the ruddy hue of the "revolving Maltese cross" on the reaping machine, reminding us that sun worship had its sacrificial aspect. At all times Tess is linked intimately to the natural world from which her consciousness isolates her. Hardy's double vision presents her both as an extension of nature moved by forces beyond her control—most obviously in the Talbothays idyll, where her sexuality blossoms with the maturing season—and as a subjective being whose moral awareness pushes her beyond the world of fertility myth to the world of knowledge gained and Paradise lost.

One world can be seen modulating into the other in Chapter XIV. The Marlott harvest shows the highest achievement possible to a way of life still closely linked to fertility ritual. It is a good life. All the details contribute to a picture of natural harmony: the youthful sun-god, taking a personal interest in the ritual, the reaping machine which starts with a non-mechanical ticking "like the love-making of the grasshopper," and the horses who pull it, made as much a part of the sun-directed pattern by their glistening brasses as the men by their twinkling trouser buttons. The women too are "part and parcel of outdoor nature," timing their dance-like movements to the unhurried pace of machine and horses. Once again, as in Chapter II, Tess is seen first as an integral part of landscape and ritual; as one of the field-women, who has "somehow lost her own margin; imbibed the essence of her surrounding, and assimilated herself with it." As Hardy describes the "clock-like monotony" of Tess's work in great detail, the tense changes to the eternal present (a common feature of Hardy's style when describing the un-changing rhythms of country labour) and the rhythm of binding controls the rise and fall of the sentences. The quiet rhythms, soft consonants and subtle vowel progressions are halted abruptly by the hardness of the last word as Hardy draws attention to the girl's bare arm: ". . . and as the day wears on its feminine smoothness becomes scarified by the stubble, and bleeds." The abrupt halt serves to remind us of Tess's connection, by now well-established through colour imagery, with the motif of sacrifice. The undertones are strengthened by the red "Maltese cross" to which Hardy draws attention and the ritual encirclement of small ani mals, which tallies closely with [anthropologist Sir James] Frazer's description in *The Golden Bough* of the killing of the corn spirit/vegetation god/scapegoat at harvest. But even this does not destroy the harmony. It is distanced by time, ". . . the doom that awaited them later in the day," and by the ritual pattern of their death, that abstracts individuality from par-ticipants in the dance. The choreography is continued by the children carrying the baby, who "rose above the stubbly convexity of the hill" to repeat the earlier movement pattern of the reaper and horses. Feeding the baby adds another feminine rhythm to the eternal ritual. The baby, the friend-liness of the rustics, the unhurried rhythm of work and re-pose where nature, animal, man and machine work to-gether in unforced harmony, build up a vision of a world where primal rightness has not yet taken the tinct of wrong.

The good life, doing what it must, with no hope, no de-spair, no human awareness or choice of action, has its own dignity. But certain elements in the scene—the moonlight progress, the sense of oneness with nature—throw the mind back to the drunken revel at Chaseborough, and the two scenes held in balance with Hardy's comment on Tess's sub-jective sensations demonstrate the falseness of a philosophy of harmony for the modern thinking and feeling human be-ing, who has emerged from innocence to awareness of alienation. "The familiar surroundings had not darkened because of her grief, nor sickened because of her pain."

THE BABY

There is something in Tess at war with nature which she needs the qualities denoted by Angel's name to bring out. Communal fertility ritual cannot cope with a personal "misery which transcended that of the child's simple loss." Her concern for the baby's individual soul belongs to the kind of Christianity practised, if not preached, by Angel's parents. Her passage thus from "simple girl to complex woman" is embodied in a striking visual image in the second half of the chapter, the baptism of her baby, which carries overtones still sounding from the harvest ritual. . . .

The sign of the cross that marks the baby baptizes Tess as a suffering human being. Conception in sorrow, toil for daily bread, frailty, freedom of will and awareness of human alienation are to define the new-created woman in place of nobility human and divine and innocence lost. Her "desires are limited to man and his humble yet formidable love" . . . —the basic human rights to live, love, work and be happy. She also takes with her to Talbothays an inheritance of vital animal instincts with which human values must come to terms. These are constantly present in Hardy's minutely detailed evocations of the maturing summer in the fertile Valley of the Great Dairies, where growth is felt as an active sexual force that affects vegetation, animals, maids and men alike. The details that denote the observant naturalist are selected by the poet to evoke simultaneously the mystery of the "great passionate pulse of existence" that orders the movement of the natural world, and a solid sense of everyday reality. . . .

The sense of reality is vital to the novel. It is the reality of the physical world in which a human being without God finds meaning and definition. Tess's response to it takes the obvious form of response through a lover. Angel and Tess are constantly seen as an image of the highest fulfilment in the human pair not divorced from the natural setting that is their present meaning and past history.

The sun was so near the ground, and the sward so flat, that the shadows of Clare and Tess would stretch a quarter of a mile ahead of them, like two long fingers pointing afar to where the green alluvial reaches abutted against the sloping sides of the vale.

TALBOTHAYS AS EDEN

Talbothays stands fair to become Paradise regained. It is a fully human paradise, that does not exclude moral awareness and unmerited personal suffering. It provides constant reminders of the doom of death and the shortness of life: butterflies trapped in the milkmaids' gauze skirts, "another year's instalment of flowers, leaves, nightingales, thrushes, finches, and such ephemeral creatures,"

> wooden posts rubbed to a glossy smoothness by the flanks of infinite cows and calves of bygone years, now passed to an oblivion almost inconceivable in its profundity.

Work is transformed from God's curse to a harmony with country rhythms and one of the factors in the growth of love, for every emotional crisis happens during the course of the dairy chores. The three milkmaids, suffering as individuals from a gratuitous passion which reduces each to "portion of one organism called sex" accept their pain with dignity and generosity. Sex itself is not evil at Talbothays: only thinking makes it so. Tess's spiritual quality of purity is rooted in her vital sexual nature. Talbothays gives hope of reconciliation between the natural harmony of a pre-conscious state and a respect for the conscious human self.

Angel Clare is seen as the "god-like" Adam to Tess's Eve. With his modern consciousness, advanced views and vaunted respect for the variegated Hodge, he has qualities of spiritual delicacy that could benefit an untutored Paradise. But the poetic undercurrents flowing through his encounters with Tess suggest that his angelic qualities have some kinship with the snake that deceived her in the earlier unconscious Eden. The snake is still there, in the form of her sex. "She was yawning, and he saw the red interior of her mouth as if it had been a snake's." It was a moment "when the most spiritual" beauty bespeaks itself flesh." The unweeded garden where Tess "undulated upon the thin notes of the second-hand harp" looks back to the sinister lushness of Marlott. Her inability to leave the spot, "like a fascinated bird" looks forward to her bird-like submission to her sexual master Alec on the rick. The distortion of reality produced by Angel's music on her subjective consciousness—

> The floating pollen seemed to be his notes made visible, and the dampness of the garden the weeping of the garden's sensibility. Though near nightfall, the rank-smelling weed-flowers

glowed as if they would not close for intentness, and the waves of colour mixed with the waves of sound . . .

—the confusion of senses and distances, the pollen, the sense of exaltation—"Tess was conscious of neither time nor space"—even the rhythm of the sentences, echo the self-deception of the Trantridge revellers. Yearning for absolute harmony is the other side of the coin of sexual attraction.

Hardy's double stress on the objective reality of the garden full of attractive but foul-smelling weeds and sticky blights that stain Tess as she is drawn towards the angelic music (played, as Hardy is careful to point out on a *second-hand* harp and with poor execution) and its subjective beauty when filtered through Tess's unweeded emotions, point the dangers as well as the advantages of the angelic power to transform the physical world into the spiritual. Tess's comment, after confessing her fears of life, "But *you*, sir, can raise up dreams with your music, and drive all such horrid fancies away!" marks the kind of deceiver Angel will be in this new conscious garden of Eden. The sham d'Urberville raised hopes of definition by human pedigree; the sham angel appeals to the human yearning for the absolute, which leads likewise to death. But ideal dreams persist. Angel is introduced into the story by a typically idealistic remark on William Dewey's deception of the bull with the Nativity hymn, which caricatures Angel's attempts to impose his superhuman vision on the living physical world. In a godless world human beings depend on each other for definition. But Angel betrays the humanness of Tess by his distorted perception. To him she "was no longer the milkmaid, but a visionary essence of woman"—Artemis, Demeter, Eve, a goddess. His preference of essence to existence adds a modern Existentialist slant to Hardy's version of the Paradise myth.

ANGEL'S VIEW OF TESS

Angel's replacement of the living Tess by a lifeless image is realized in a closely-woven poetic texture. It links together the various manifestations of automatic impulsion which drive Tess to her death when she leaves Talbothays. This can be seen clearly in Chapter XX where the identification with Adam and Eve is explicit. The chapter is built on tension between physical reality and distorted perception of it which is central to the novel.

Whilst all the landscape was in neutral shade his companion's face, which was the focus of his eyes, rising above the mist stratum, seemed to have a sort of phosphorescence upon it. She looked ghostly, as if she were merely a soul at large. In reality her face, without appearing to do so, had caught the cold gleam of day from the north-east; his own face, though he did not think of it, wore the same aspect to her.

The strange poetic effects of light and mist are just as natural, and just as neutral, as the physical solidity of the cows. It is the self-deceiving mind of Angel that takes appearance for reality. Hardy stresses the "preternatural" "non-human" quality of those early morning hours, yet "it was then . . . that [Tess] impressed him most deeply," not as a human being who craved warmth but as "a visionary essence of woman." . . . The unreal essence of fine lady he has created, dramatically embodied in the debased d'Urberville portraits "builded into the wall" like his fixed definition of purity moves him to turn from the living woman. . . .

Careful attention to the details of such scenes where Angel is a chief actor reveals his archetypal role as human agent of the impersonal powers which, once released, will destroy Tess's life. In Chapter XX the poetic force comes from the accumulation of lyrical details: in the sleepwalking scene, from dramatic details which form a poetic image. This scene, like the Stonehenge episode, has been criticized for its theatricality. But they are theatrical for a purpose. The staginess reinforces Hardy's Aeschylean [relating to playwright Aeschylus] image of Tess as "sport" for the President of the Immortals. Tess at Stonehenge and Angel in the sleepwalking episode are playing roles assigned to them by their buried selves. Psychology bears witness to the theatrical nature of the subconscious. Movement, gesture, speech, positioning, and props of the scene grow rings of evocation. The rigid stone coffin of an abbot in which Tess's living body is placed suggests the logical end of absolute aspirations, and the destructive force of the ascetic image which will hound Tess to the Stone of Sacrifice. To Angel, the human Tess is "Dead! Dead! Dead!" and his unconscious actions are eloquent of the repressed sexual guilt and fear of the powers of life that demand a sacrifice to purity. The precariousness of their position on the plank, Tess's trust and impassivity, and her failure to follow up her chance to take control, are all dramatic correlatives of the poetic under-pattern which drives Tess from Paradise a second time.

Tess's expulsion from the human Paradise thrusts her into the modern myth of the lonely, rootless exile from meaning. Talbothays has given her human awareness, meaning through love, and roots in the natural rhythms of life and work in a simple traditional community. Hardy's poetic treatment of Tess's new relationship to her surroundings after Angel's betrayal—the betrayal of god-in-man—shows what [novelist Albert] Camus calls "this divorce between man and his life, the actor and his setting" which constitutes the feeling of absurdity. The divorce begins immediately after Tess's confession. "All material objects around announced their irresponsibility with terrible iteration." Angel's absolute mode of perceiving is revealed as inadequate. The physical world that took its meaning from human emotion now exists only as a lumpish, alien factor in the elemental struggle to survive and endure.

Flintcomb-Ash brings sharply to the senses the bleak sterility of life without illusions, without love, without God, without a future goal or anything that gives a reason for living to the human being, irrelevant and abandoned on the surface of the earth in a wintry death-marked universe that does not add up. A patient accumulation of the manifestations of rain, wind and snow and their physical effects on Tess and Marian builds up a feeling of the obliteration of human identity by the "achromatic chaos of things." Tess's mutilation of her distinctive beauty is reflected in the huge, high swede field, over which the two girls crawl like flies: "it was a complexion without features, as if a face, from chin to brow, should be only an expanse of skin." Once again she is part of the landscape. But the arrival of apocalyptic Northern birds, "gaunt spectral creatures with tragical eyes" but no memory of the cataclysmic horrors they had witnessed, gives the lie to the impression that she is "a thing scarcely percipient, almost inorganic." The human consciousness that has brought Tess pain and exile has also brought her knowledge and memories of the Talbothays paradise which define her as a human being against the levelling flintiness of trivial existence. . . .

The details that evoke a mechanistic universe include all the impersonal forces that abstract meaning from a human being unprotected by providential design, ritual pattern, or love. One of them is time. The accelerated motion of the machine that dominates Tess, reinforced by Alec's renewed attentions, warns that time will not stand still. Nothing but her submission to conventional judgements stands in the way of another visit to Emminster; yet still Tess fails to stamp a meaningful pattern on the flow of time by decisive action. The pathos of Tess practising Angel's favourite ballads against his return should not hide Hardy's comment: "Tess was so wrapt up in this *fanciful dream* [my italics] that she seemed not to know how the season was advancing." Time in the shape of heredity controls her actions in the prophetic blow she deals to Alec with a gauntlet. Time combines with another false god of the void, economic interest, to rob the human being of significance. Hardy's metaphysical meaning, as usual, comes out of a physical situation. The dominance of machinery in late nineteenth-century Wessex was one of the factors which exiled man from work rooted in nature, and defined him by the profit motive and the production schedule. The homelessness of Tess's family ties the metaphysical sense of exile from meaning to concrete economic pressures which drive man unresting over the earth with no place to go.

The logical end of all depersonalizing forces is the d'Urberville vaults where Tess, in terms of the hunt metaphor, is run to earth. The reproachful gleam of the unloaded furniture, and the spoliation of the d'Urberville tombs, build up a powerful picture of a world dead to human values. It is completed when the sham d'Urberville rises from the "mere stone reproduction" on the oldest altar tomb, to challenge the "hollow echo from below" with the false values that too often define the modern exile in a universe shaped by death—money and sex uncontrolled by meaningful ritual. The scene looks back to the stone coffin in which Angel places a Tess who is dead to him in her human aspect, and forward to the Stone of Sacrifice. . . .

After Alec's murder, Tess and Angel re-live with the poetic intensity of a drowning man a telescoped and accelerated version of Tess's life, which points her archetypal role by blending motifs from all three myths. Tess's lonely journeys over the surface of Wessex have defined her archetypal exile from harmony. Since leaving Talbothays all her journeying, with the significant exception of the abortive trip to Emminster, has pointed in the direction of Stonehenge. In a universe shaped by death, it is the only journey to end in fulfilment. . . . The lush woodland which recalls the richness of

Talbothays and the barren Salisbury plain which recalls the Flintcomb-Ash period flank the belated fulfilment of the wedding night in a mansion whose furnishings recall Wellbridge Manor. The fulfilment is as childlike, as "temporary and unforefending" as their plans of escape. Ironical echoes of the earlier innocence at Marlott—seclusion, the dreamlike atmosphere, the sense of suspended time—hint at the impossibility of Paradise for two responsible living human beings. "Within was affection, union, error forgiven: outside was the inexorable." Tess and Angel can only achieve absolute harmony by "ignoring that there was a corpse."

Tess's fate acknowledges the power of death, which allows no-one to remain unsoiled. . . . Tess, in spite of her vigilance, collaborates at times with the power of death—with her desire for oblivion, her submission to impersonal forces and concepts through her love for Angel, her relapses to waiting on Providence when her responsible consciousness tells her that there is no Providence to wait on. Stonehenge and Wintoncester, with their symbols of an order based on death defined blackly against the empty sky, provide a fitting end to this modern myth about the maintenance of human identity against the void. Hardy gives full weight to the impersonal agents of that order. Yet while his cosmos robs the human individual of meaning, his poetry puts it back again.

The poetic vision gives supreme importance to Tess's inner, unique experience of the world through her sensations and emotions; unusually detailed for Hardy. She is also defined by the poetry of her work. Even the harsh work at Flintcomb-Ash borrows poetic beauty from the transformations of frost and snow and the tragic evocations of the Northern birds who share and universalize Tess's will to live. The differing kinds of work take their special rhythm from the rhythms of her life, sensitively realized in narrative and speech structure. The rhythms of Talbothays, slow and contemplative or simple and passionate, reflecting her sweep to maturity with its hesitations, crises, reprieves and rallies, build up a very different emotional response from the monotonous, consonantal rhythm of mechanical work at Flintcomb-Ash, or the deadness of shocked existence, detail after dragging detail in flat bald sentences, at Wellbridge Manor. Hardy's dialogue is not always inspired: Perhaps even Angel would hardly have met the greatest crisis of his life with, "My God—how can forgiveness meet such a grotesque—prestidigitation as that!"—but Tess's stupefied simplicity in the quarrel, her bare statements of truth—"It is in your own mind what you are angry at, Angel; it is not in me"—catch the intimate cadences of a noble and passionate woman. Her qualities even infect the rougher speech of her companions. Izz Huett's "She would have laid down her life for 'ee. I could do no more," and "Her mind can no more be heaved from that one place where it do bide than a stooded wagon from the hole he's in" have the noble ballad simplicity of Tess's personal rhythms. This personal rhythm is set frequently against the dance-like rhythm of scenes where human beings become part of an automatic process—the harvest, the garlic picking, the threshing. Yet the personal rhythm prevails in an overwhelming sense of Tess's beauty of character.

Tess dies, but the meaning of her life, and of the whole book, lies in her vibrant humanity, her woman's power of suffering, renewal, and compassion, which has restored Angel to his rightful nature as Man, conscious of guilt and imperfection. One could not wish to be angel or animal while Tess exists in her human love, passion, beauty, trust, forgiveness, pity, sensitivity, responsibility, endurance, dignity, integrity, and spiritual light. To accept her mortality and the terrible beauty of the earth, to discover the absurdity of immutable law that makes of her fineness a death-trap, and yet to oppose her will against the universe as she found it and make moral choice that it is better to do this than that, is to answer the question of "The Blinded Bird," "Who is divine?"

Chronology

1840

Thomas Hardy is born in Dorset, England, on June 2, the eldest of four children born to Thomas and Jemima Hardy.

1848

Begins school at Stinsford National School; *Communist Manifesto* of Karl Marx published.

1849–1855

Attends Dorchester British school; studies Latin, French, and mathematics; Crimean War.

1856–1860

Is apprenticed to architect and church restorer John Hicks in Dorchester until 1860; continues to study Latin and Greek.

1860

Works as an architectural assistant to John Hicks; reads controversial theological and scientific writings, including *The Origin of Species;* begins to write poetry.

1862

Moves to London; works as an architectural draftsman under Arthur Blomfield.

1863

Wins an architectural prize from the Royal Institute of British Architects for an essay on bricks; is elected to the Architectural Association; reads English writers and poets.

1865

Story "How I Built Myself a House" is published; begins to write poetry seriously, though publishes none.

1867

Returns to Dorset and career as an architectural assistant; begins writing a novel, *The Poor Man and the Lady.*

1870

Begins second novel, *Desperate Remedies;* travels to Cornwall on business and there meets Emma Lavinia Gifford, his future wife.

1871

Desperate Remedies is published; begins work on *Under the Greenwood Tree* and *A Pair of Blue Eyes.*

1872

Becomes engaged to Emma Gifford; decides on a career in writing; friend Horace Moule commits suicide at Cambridge; *Under the Greenwood Tree* is published.

1873

A Pair of Blue Eyes is serialized in *Tinsley's Magazine.*

1874

Far from the Madding Crowd is serialized in *Cornhill* and subsequently published to great acclaim; Hardy marries Emma on September 17 and moves to London.

1875

Hardy and Emma move to Paddington, then to Swanage, Dorset; Hardy begins work on *The Hand of Ethelberta.*

1876

The Hand of Ethelberta is published; moves to Sturminster Newton in July; tours Germany.

1878

The Return of the Native is published; moves to London; *An Indiscretion in the Life of an Heiress* is serialized.

1879

Begins writing short stories for magazine publication.

1880

The Trumpet Major is published; is ill for several months, and, though bedridden, completes the serialization of *A Laodicean.*

1881

A Laodicean is published; returns to Dorset.

1882

The Woodlanders is published; begins *Two on a Tower.*

1883

Two on a Tower is published; begins building a house near Dorchester; publishes *Romantic Adventures of a Milkmaid.*

1884

Begins work on *The Mayor of Casterbridge.*

1885

Moves to Max Gate, the house he designs.

1886

The Mayor of Casterbridge is published.

1887

The Woodlanders is published; is offered a substantial advance for *Tess of the d'Urbervilles;* tours Continent.

1888

"The Profitable Reading of Fiction" is published; *Wessex Tales* is published.

1889

Publisher rejects first half of *Tess.*

1890

"Candour in English Fiction" is published.

1891

A Group of Noble Dames and *Tess of the d'Urbervilles* are published; Tess is criticized as immoral, but sells well.

1892

Our Exploits at West Poley and *The Pursuit of the Well-Beloved* are published.

1894

Publishes *Life's Little Ironies; Jude the Obscure* published to poor reviews; Hardy decides to devote career to poetry.

1896

Writes "In Tenebris" trilogy and "Wessex Heights."

1897

The Well-Beloved is published.

1898

Publishes *Wessex Poems,* his first book of verse.

1900

Sigmund Freud's *Interpretation of Dreams* is published.

1901

Publishes *Poems of the Past and the Present;* death of Queen Victoria.

1903–1909

Publishes the epic poem *The Dynasts* and *Time's Laughingstocks.*

1910

Receives the Order of Merit.

1912

Death of Emma; receives the gold medal of the Royal Society of Literature; *A Changed Man and Other Tales* is published.

1913

Magdalene College makes Hardy an honorary fellow.

1914

Marries Florence Dugdale; publishes *Satires of Circumstance;* World War I begins.

1917

Publishes *Moments of Vision;* begins work on an autobiography; Russian Revolution begins.

1920

Receives honorary doctor of letters from Oxford University.

1922

Late Lyrics and Earlier is published.

1923

The Famous Tragedy of the Queen of Cornwall is published.

1924

Hardy adapts *Tess* for the stage, it is performed in Dorchester and London.

1925

Human Shows Far Phantasies Songs and Trifles is published.

1928

Dies on January 11, is buried in Poets' Corner, Westminster Abbey, next to Charles Dickens; *Winter Words* appears after his death.

FOR FURTHER RESEARCH

BIOGRAPHY

Edmund Blunden, *Thomas Hardy*. London: Macmillan, 1951.

Ernest Brennecke Jr., *Thomas Hardy's Universe: A Study of a Poet's Mind*. London: Unwin, 1924.

Douglas Brown, *Thomas Hardy*. London: Longmans, 1954.

Kay-Robinson Denys, *The First Mrs. Thomas Hardy*. New York: St. Martin's, 1979.

Evelyn Hardy, *Thomas Hardy: A Critical Biography*. London: St. Martin's Press, 1954.

Florence Emily Hardy, *The Early Life of Thomas Hardy, 1840–1891; The Later Years of Thomas Hardy, 1892–1928*. New York: Macmillan, 1928, 1930.

Michael Millgate, *Thomas Hardy: A Biography*. Oxford, England: Clarendon Press, 1982.

Carl J. Weber, *Hardy in America*. Waterville, ME: Colby College, 1946.

CRITICAL WORKS

Joseph Warren Beach, *The Technique of Thomas Hardy*. New York: Russell & Russell, 1949.

Harold Bloom, ed., *Modern Critical Interpretations of Thomas Hardy*. New York: Chelsea House, 1987.

Thomas Braybrooke, *Thomas Hardy and His Philosophy*. New York: Russell & Russell, 1928.

Lance St. John Butler, *Alternative Hardy*. London: Macmillan, 1989.

Richard Carpenter, *Thomas Hardy*. New York: Twayne, 1964.

Peter J. Casagrande, Tess of the d'Urbervilles: *Unorthodox Beauty*. New York: Twayne, 1992.

R.G. Cox, ed., *Thomas Hardy: The Critical Heritage*. New York: Barnes & Noble, 1970.

R.P. Draper, ed., *Hardy: The Tragic Novels*. London: Macmillan, 1975.

John Goode, *Thomas Hardy: The Offensive Truth.* New York: Basil Blackwell, 1988.

Ian Gregor, *The Great Web: The Form of Hardy's Major Fiction.* Totowa, NJ: Rowman and Littlefield, 1974.

Dale Kramer, *Critical Essays on Thomas Hardy: The Novels.* Boston: G.K. Hall, 1990.

Juliet McLauchlan, *Tess of the d'Urbervilles,* Notes on English Literature Series. Oxford, England: Basil Blackwell, 1972.

Kevin Z. Moore, *The Descent of the Imagination: Postromantic Culture in the Later Novels of Thomas Hardy.* New York: New York University, 1990.

Michael H. Parkinson, *The Rural Novel.* New York: Peter Lang, 1984.

Penelope Vigar, *The Novels of Thomas Hardy: Illusion and Reality.* London: Athlone Press, 1974.

Peter Widdowson, ed., *Tess of the d'Urbervilles.* New York: St. Martin's, 1993.

Terence Wright, *Tess of the d'Urbervilles.* London: Macmillan, 1987.

HISTORICAL BACKGROUND

Francoise Basch, *Relative Creatures: Victorian Women in Society and the Novel.* New York: Schocken, 1974.

Margaret Fuller, *Women in the Nineteenth Century.* New York: Norton, 1971.

Katherine Moore, *Victorian Wives.* New York: St. Martin's 1974.

R.J. White, *Thomas Hardy and History.* New York: Barnes & Noble, 1974.

G.M. Young, *Victorian England: Portrait of an Age.* London: Oxford University Press, 1953.

WORKS BY THE AUTHOR

Collected Poems of Thomas Hardy. New York: Macmillan, 1928.

The Collected Letters of Thomas Hardy. 7 vols. Eds. Richard L. Purdy and Michael Millgate. Oxford, England: Oxford University Press, 1978–1990.

Tess of the d'Urbervilles. Eds. Juliet Grindle and Simon Gatrell. Oxford, England: Clarendon Press, 1983.

Tess of the d'Urbervilles, Norton Critical Edition. Ed. Scott Elledge. New York: W.W. Norton, 1965.

1The Works of Thomas Hardy in Prose and Verse. 24 vols. London: Macmillan, 1912–1931.

INDEX